# SOCIAL WORK & MENTAL HEALTH

# SOCIAL WORK &

*A guide for the approved social worker*

# MENTAL HEALTH

*edited by M. Rolf Olsen*

TAVISTOCK · LONDON AND NEW YORK

First published in 1984 by
Tavistock Publications Ltd
11 New Fetter Lane,
London EC4P 4EE

Published in the USA by
Tavistock Publications
in association with Methuen, Inc.
733 Third Avenue, New York,
NY 10017

Typeset by Keyset Composition,
Colchester, Essex
and printed in Great Britain
at the University Press, Cambridge

*British Library Cataloguing in*
*Publication Data*

Social work and mental health. – (Social
science paperback ; 269)
1. Psychiatric social work – Great Britain
2. Mentally ill – Care and treatment –
Great Britain
I. Olsen, M. Rolf   II. Series
362.2'0425'0941      HV689

ISBN 0-422-79000-1
ISBN 0-422-79010-9 Pbk

# Contents

*List of contributors*                                                    vii
*Preface*                                                                  ix

Part One   LEGISLATION AND POLICY                                           1

1   Contemporary social policy towards the                                  3
    mentally disordered
    *Ann Davis*
2   Historical analysis: the key factors which                             13
    led to the amendment of the Mental Health Act 1959
    *Rolf Olsen*
3   The Mental Health Act 1983                                             20
    *Rolf Olsen*
4   The roles and duties of social services                               41
    departments and the approved social worker
    *Rolf Olsen*

    Specimen examination paper 1                                          50

Part Two   PERSPECTIVES OF MENTAL DISORDER                                 59
           AND MENTAL HANDICAP

5   Clinical perspectives of mental disorder                              61
    *Derek Anton-Stephens*
6   Social perspectives of mental disorder                                77
    *Rolf Olsen*
7   A critical appraisal of the medical                                   84
    model in psychiatry
    *Brian Sheldon*
8   Perspectives of mental handicap                                      101
    *Derek Thomas*

Part Three   ALTERNATIVES TO HOSPITAL CARE                                117

9   Residential care                                                     119
    *Ann Davis*

10 Day care 129
Ann Davis
11 Boarding-out and substitute family care 138
Rolf Olsen

Part Four ISSUES RELATING TO THE DELIVERY OF SERVICES 147

12 Developing comprehensive local services 149
Ann Davis
13 Working with volunteers and self-help groups 158
Ann Davis and Lynne Muir
14 Teamwork 168
Lynne Muir
15 Working with other professions 177
Ann Davis

Part Five SOCIAL WORK METHOD AND PROCESSES 185

Introduction 187
Rolf Olsen
16 Interviewing 189
Lynne Muir
17 Groupwork practice 198
Lynne Muir
18 Behavioural approaches with psychiatric patients 209
Brian Sheldon
19 The management of crisis in the psychiatric emergency 219
Rolf Olsen
20 Evaluation of outcome to intervention 228
Brian Sheldon

Specimen examination paper 2 241

Specimen examination paper 3 244

Appendix 1 Drugs acting on central nervous system 247
Appendix 2 Checklist of key mental health statutory 249
and voluntary agencies
Appendix 3 Model answers and notes to specimen examination 254
papers 1–3

References 261
Name index 273
Subject index 277

# List of contributors

Derek Anton-Stephens, B.A., M.B., B.Ch., D.P.M., M.R.C.Psych.

Ann Davis, B.A., M.Sc.

Lynne Muir, B.A., B.S.W., M.S.W.

Rolf Olsen, Dip.Soc.Sc., M.Sc., Ph.D., Dip.Ment.Health

Brian Sheldon, M.Phil., Dip.Soc.Studies, Dip.S.W.

Derek Thomas, B.A., D.C.P., A.B.Ps.S.

# Preface

The Mental Health Act 1983 amends and consolidates the law relating to mentally disordered persons contained in the Mental Health Act 1959 and the Mental Health (Amendment) Act 1982. The main provisions came into force on 30 September, 1983. The central purposes of the Act are with the rights and legal position of those mentally disturbed people who need special protection and control – just under 10 per cent of those who require admission to psychiatric hospital. To this end the Act made far-reaching changes in the procedures for the compulsory admission and management of the mentally disturbed person, and improved the rights of appeal. It also laid new duties on local authority social services departments, created the 'approved social worker' (ASW), and made explicit the duties and authority of the ASW in relation to compulsorily detained persons. To qualify for 'approval' by the employing authority the social worker must first successfully complete an examination approved by the Central Council for Education and Training in Social Work (CCETSW).

This book is intended, first, for those social workers in statutory and voluntary departments who carry responsibility for, and are involved in, the provision of services for the mentally disordered and those with whom they live; and second, for those practising or studying to become ASWs. To this end it undertakes a broad analysis of social work and mental health, and provides the knowledge and information that is needed to qualify and continue practising as an ASW. The book is divided into five interrelated parts, which together:

— summarize and interpret the law and discuss the major provisions of the 1983 Act
— examine contemporary social policy towards the mentally disordered
— evaluate competing perspectives of mental disorder and mental handicap
— consider alternatives to hospital care
— describe the ideal service design and extend the understanding of the organization, structure, and policy contexts in which mental health services are provided and developed
— consider the distinctive contribution of the social sciences to the understanding and management of mental disorder
— promote skills in the planning and delivery of emergency and follow-up services
— describe social work processes in the care of the mentally disordered
— describe techniques for the evaluation of the outcome of social work intervention and services
— summarize the British National Formulary of drugs which act on the central nervous system
— provide a check list of key mental health statutory and voluntary services

As well as serving as a manual for social work with the mentally disordered, it is also a primer for those social workers preparing for the examination for ASWs, and specimen examination and answer papers are included.

Since the Mental Health Act 1983 refers to 'he' throughout, for reasons of both consistency and style, this book follows the same convention.

The whole is partly based upon the experience gained by the contributors during their participation in the training of ASWs and in development of services in a number of local authorities; in particular the counties of Cheshire, Kent, and Warwickshire. We record our thanks to these authorities and their staffs, together with our gratitude for the abundance of experience, goodwill, and enthusiasm which they brought to the partnership.

M. Rolf Olsen
Birmingham University
January 1984

# PART ONE
# LEGISLATION AND POLICY

# 1

# Contemporary social policy towards the mentally disordered

## Ann Davis

There are two main reasons why social workers should look at current government policy towards people with mental disorders. First, policy statements from government and their interpretation and implementation at local level, shape the services and situations in which clients and social workers find themselves. Government policies affect the quantity and quality of the resources available to mentally disordered people and consequently the choices that can be made in response to individual and family difficulties. Therefore, in a field where resources are scarce and choices limited, it is vital that ASWs are aware of the wider policy context in which they are working.

Second, and equally important, it is inevitable that the implementation of the Mental Health Act 1983 places fresh demands on existing local services. Questions will have been and will continue to be asked about the capacity of staff and specialist provision to meet these demands and develop initiatives in response to them. Managers of social services departments and local politicians are being pressured to review the scope and balance of their policies and provision. ASWs, as specialist practitioners, have a key role in local services. However, if they are to play an informed part in departmental reviews they will need to be familiar with the options that have emerged with current policies. To engage in this process creatively they must have a sound grasp of the shape and direction of policies at both national and local levels.

It is impossible to outline current policy towards people suffering from mental disorder as if it were a clear, coherent strategy. It is not. It is a patchwork of legislation, white papers, inquiries, working party reports, Ministers' statements, etc. which focus on a spectrum of specialist services. Mentally disordered and mentally handicapped people are also affected by changes in wider social policy. Central and local government policies with regard to health, housing, employment, education, social security, transport, and the personal social services are also relevant to any consideration of the way in which current policies are shaping the lives of mentally disordered people.

This chapter identifies some of the main elements in policy towards the mentally disordered. It moves on to consider likely future directions and finally suggests ways in which ASWs might begin to relate policy issues to their local situations.

## Policy and people with mental disorder

It is impossible to understand current policies towards people who are mentally disordered without looking at the past. Just as it is impossible to work in this area without drawing on specialist resources which are still housed in buildings, the majority of which were constructed over a century ago, designed for pauper lunatics.

The foundations of our current policies were laid in professional and government pronouncements in the 1950s and early 1960s. The Royal Commission on the Law relating to Mental Illness and Mental Deficiency (1954–57), found that their witnesses were 'generally in favour of a shift of emphasis from hospital care to community care' and in the light of this the Commission recommended 'a general reorientation away from institutional care in its present form and towards community care' (HMSO 1957).

This statement was made at a time when a few hospitals were beginning to move some of their longer-term patients back into the community. But these local reorientations were the exception rather than the rule and some 150,000 people remained resident in hospitals for the mentally ill and mentally handicapped.

It was Enoch Powell, then Minister of Health, who placed full government support behind reorientation from institutional to community care. In his speech delivered to the Annual Conference of the National Association of Mental Health (MIND) held in 1961, he conjured up a vision of specialist hospitals 'isolated, majestic, imperious . . . rising unmistakable and daunting out of the countryside' (MIND 1974) casting a blight over local communities in which people were suffering from mental disorder. Powell pledged the government to remove this blight within fifteen years, replacing the large hospitals with small specialist units, part of local district general hospitals, which would cater for those in need of psychiatric treatment.

This blueprint for the future was given more detailed form the following year with the publication of A Hospital Plan for England and Wales (Ministry of Health 1962). The plan outlined not only the growth of district general hospital units but also the expansion of a range of local authority community services which would ensure that individuals suffering from mental illness could remain in their own communities and still receive specialist help. For the mentally handicapped the plan regarded specialist hospital care as the most appropriate option.

The experience of the 1960s was that only part of this blueprint started to become reality. The large mental illness hospitals began to contract, but those individuals leaving them, and the relatives and others with whom they went to live, rarely found support from alternative community services. Local authority expenditure in this area was derisory and there were few attempts jointly to plan the contraction of large hospitals across health and local authority structures. As a result patients and their relatives were left to manage the consequences of policy change alone. Many individuals found themselves living in the worst accommodation that the private rented sector of the housing market had to offer, isolated from life in the surrounding community.

Yet the focus of government and media concern in the late 1960s and 1970s was rarely on the grim realities of 'community care'. The conditions found in the large institutions still held the centre of the arena. The creation of the Hospital Advisory Service (1969) to report to the Secretary of State on the hospitals caring for the mentally disordered and elderly, and the public enquiries at Ely (DHSS 1969), Farleigh (DHSS 1971b), and Whittingham (DHSS 1972) reflect this. From the professional and academic press the work of Barton (1976), Goffman (1961), Morris (1969), and Wing and Brown (1970), pointed up the dehumanizing and disabling effects of institutional life.

There was therefore little questioning by government that their policies of 'community care' had been misconceived. Indeed, by 1975 two White Papers had been published which gave more detailed guidance to local authorities and health authorities on the future development of the re-orientated services for the mentally disordered.

## Towards better services

Better Services for the Mentally Handicapped (DHSS 1971a) and Better Services for the Mentally Ill (DHSS 1975) are still the cornerstones of current government policy towards the mentally disordered. They contain some account of the failures of the past. In particular the slow growth of

community-based services compared with the contraction of large institutions. But both documents avoid addressing in depth the reasons for
this disappointing progress. In contrast both give detailed attention to the
services of tomorrow – the level of resources required to provide each
individual in need with a local service based on co-ordinated, multi-
disciplinary input from the health and local authority services and their
personnel. They acknowledge the important role of the voluntary organizations in this pattern of services and the need to ensure that mentally
disordered people and their families have access to general as well as to
specialist welfare provision.

There is no time-scale attached to the change proposed in these documents, just an acknowledgment that the programme is a 'long term' one.
In Better Services for the Mentally Ill a much more pessimistic note is
sounded, reflecting Britain's entry into a period of economic recession and
public expenditure cuts.

'It is clear that the scope for making progress during the next few years
will be limited. Without increased community resources the numbers in
mental hospitals cannot be expected to fall at the rate they might otherwise have done. . . . But . . . we believe, that in a period of severe
financial restraint it is even more important that there should be a clear
statement of policy objectives against which priorities can be assessed.'

(DHSS 1975: iii)

However, the problems faced in realizing 'Better Services' in local
situations were not just financial ones, they were also organizational. By
the time Better Services for the Mentally Ill was published there had been
other changes in the services which had a duty to develop community
care. Both local authority mental welfare departments and the National
Health Service (NHS) had experienced major reorganizations.

As far as the local authority departments were concerned the tripartite
divisions created in 1946 and 1948 between children, welfare, and mental
welfare departments had been swept away by the Local Authority Act
1970. This enacted the necessary legislation for local authorities in
England and Wales to create single social services departments and
provide the community-based family-orientated services outlined in the
Seebohm Report (DHSS 1968).

The 1974 NHS reorganization had also dismantled a tripartite system of
administration, in which hospital, community, and general practitioner
services were separated. In its place a structure was erected which
integrated hospital and community health provision at regional, area, and
district levels. The service also lost its option to employ social work staff.

These reorganizations, together with changes in local authority boundaries in 1974, led to some considerable administrative headaches for those
involved in implementing and working towards the visions outlined in

the 'Better Services' documents. Mechanisms to ensure the co-operation, collaboration, and joint planning required had to be devised. Two different bureaucratic structures with distinct responsibilities and priorities had to create them and make them work. Only at area health authority level were the health service boundaries conterminous with local authority social services departments, yet the changes that were needed to move towards 'Better Services' had to take place at district level and 'a district' often meant different populations to health and social services departments.

Local authority social services departments had considerable scope, after 1974, to determine the ways in which they would make social work provision to the health service. They also chose different ways of liaising at management and planning levels with district and area health author-ities. Health authority staff were often perplexed by these variations.

The difficulties that health and social services staff faced in making reorganization work for mentally disordered people were compounded by the fact that over 80 per cent of the mentally ill people receiving specialist hospital care were still in large, isolated institutions. These hospitals were being asked to carry out a number of tasks. They were being pressured to contract, improve the quality of care provided, *and* integrate with the mental health services in the districts they served. These pressures were not only considerable but conflicting and remain so today. A useful review of this topic is contained in the Nodder report on Organisational and Management Problems of Mental Illness Hospitals (DHSS 1978). This shows clearly the dilemmas that current policy has brought the specialist hospitals.

While commentators, like Kathleen Jones, have argued that the health and social services reorganizations of the 1970s 'meant the destruction of the unity in the mental health field' (Jones 1977: 9) by removing specialist services from both the health and local authority departments, others have pointed to some gains, at least in social services reorganization. White and Holden (1979) point to the real increase in resources which the new local authority social services departments devoted to both mentally ill and mentally handicapped clients after reorganization. But this was an increase from an extremely low base and has not been substantial enough to shift the balance of services between health and local authorities. It is this shift that is crucial to the realization of the 'Better Services' pattern and government policies have not addressed themselves sufficiently to this issue.

The introduction in 1976 of 'Joint Finance Arrangements' was designed to promote greater collaboration in the planning of services between health and social services departments in order to develop community-based mental health services. Support from joint finance was available for capital and revenue schemes in such a way as to ease local authorities into taking on the whole cost of new community-based projects. Support for capital projects was limited to a 60 per cent funding. As for revenue projects a maximum of five years was set for the local authority gradually to take on the whole cost of the scheme. With increasing uncertainties in local authority budgets, social services departments and area health authorities did not take full advantage of joint financing.

In 1981 the *Care in the Community* (DHSS 1981b) consultative document noted that the most consistent problem experienced in joint working between health and social services departments had been lack of local authority finance to carry forward joint financed schemes. The period of take-up has now been extended to thirteen years in order to encourage and increase local authority participation. In addition, central government is encouraging voluntary organizations, housing associations, and local education authorities to become involved in joint funding applications. So while this measure has promoted collaboration and change it has not been sufficiently resourced to play a leading role in effecting the shift required to put mental health provision on the 'Better Services' path.

**Policy in the 1980s**

There has been no let up in the government's push towards community care for mentally disordered people in the 1980s. The 1980 government review (DHSS 1980) of progress since Better Services for the Mentally Handicapped noted the gap between required and actual provision but still exhorted those concerned to push towards the 'Better Services' blueprint. The 1981 consultative document *Care in the Community* heralded its discussion of the ways in which 'appropriate community services' might be developed with the statement that 'Most people who need long-term care can and should be looked after in the community. This is what most of them want for themselves and what those responsible for their care believe to be best' (DHSS 1981b).

At the same time there has been no let up in the difficulties being faced by those attempting to develop community-based services. The continuing restraint on public expenditure has affected both the health service and local authority departments and there is no evidence that the mentally disordered are being protected from the repercussions. The reorganization of the NHS in 1982 removed the area health authorities and therefore the only tier of the health service conterminous with local authority social services departments. Local health and local authority personnel are still working to re-establish mechanisms which promote collaboration despite the new structure. Evidence is growing of the effects on both the mental disordered and their families of community care which does not ensure adequate housing, daytime occupation, or outside professional support. The disproportionate burden of caring that falls on women as the result of community care policies is also a matter of growing concern (Equal Opportunities Commission 1982).

The chasm that exists between government policy statements and the provision available to those suffering from mental disorder is all too apparent to those working in the mental health services. Evidence submitted for the Review (DHSS 1976) which culminated in the Mental Health Act 1983, amply documents the failures since the 1950s to shift resources firmly behind community care. Indeed, the Act itself is principally concerned with compulsory admission and detention in hospital. It does little to promote community care developments: it does nothing to change the fact that services for mentally disordered people are chronically under-resourced and administratively complex; and it does not contain any measures to re-direct budgets from the maintenance of crumbling and unpopular hospitals to alternative local facilities.

In response to criticisms of its current policies, the government is pointing to the untapped potential of voluntary organizations, relatives, and the private sector to help in closing the gap between policy blueprints and reality. There is little evidence as yet to support government optimism that these sources have what it will take to shift the pattern of services in the 1980s, but social workers will find themselves directed to consider the voluntary, informal, and private systems alongside the statutory systems in which they are employed.

## Conclusions

This brief review of the major elements of contemporary social policy towards mentally disordered people has highlighted the complex and contradictory framework within which ASWs are working. For almost thirty years governments have maintained that the future of the mental health services lies in developing community-based provision and dismantling large institutions. Yet the changes made in the administration, organization, and financing of these services have placed barriers in the path of steady progress towards this vision. As a consequence practitioners and clients in the mental health field are in a world of scarce and often fragmented resources and there seems little reason to expect this to change in the near future.

# Social policy and local priorities: worksheet

This review should provide you with a basis from which to begin to look at the ways in which policies are being implemented in your own local area. To test and increase your knowledge of the policy context in which you are working a worksheet of basic questions follows. These can be answered individually or in groups drawn from the same local authority area or district. When you have answered all these questions you should find that you have:

1 Increased your awareness of the priority that is being given to the mentally disordered by your department and the related health authorities.
2 Increased your knowledge of the local planning processes which affect mentally disordered people.
3 Identified the key actors in local authority, health, and voluntary organizations who are influencing resources and future plans.
4 Increased your awareness of the local parameters in which change has, and is, taking place.

Having answered the worksheet questions you may like to consider the part you can play in influencing local change and developments for the mentally disordered.

1  What district/area do you work in?

2  What is (are) the related health district(s)?

3  What percentage of your social services department budget was spent on the mentally ill in the last financial year?

4  What percentage of your social services department budget was spent on the mentally handicapped in the last financial year?

5  What percentage of the district health authority's budget was spent on the mentally ill in the last financial year?

6  What percentage of the district health authority's budget was spent on the mentally handicapped in the last financial year?

7 Does your department have a written policy on the development of services for mentally ill people?

    If *yes*:   When was it written?

               Who was it written by?

               What are its implications for your area/district?

    If *no*:    Why?

8 Does your department have a written policy on the development of services for mentally handicapped people?

    If *yes*:   When was it written?

               Who was it written by?

               What are its implications for your area/district?

    If *no*:    Why?

9 Does your district health authority have a written policy for the development of services for mentally ill people in your district?

    If *yes*:   When was it written?

               Who was it written by?

               What are its implications for your district/area?

    If *no*:    Why?

10 Does your district health authority have a written policy for the development of services for mentally handicapped people in your district?

    If *yes*:   When was it written?

               Who was it written by?

               What are its implications for your district/area?

    If *no*:    Why?

11 Who is responsible in your district/area for health and social services liaison?

    Where are they based?

    What are their responsibilities? (Include a list of the regular committees they attend.)

12 Is there a group/committee/working party that is currently meeting to develop and monitor services to mentally ill people in your district?

    If *yes*:   Who is on it?

               What are its terms of reference?

    If *no*:    Why?

13 Is there a group/committee/working party that is currently meeting to develop and monitor services to mentally handicapped people in your district?

   If *yes*:   Who is on it?
              What are its terms of reference?

   If *no*:    Why?

14 Which are the voluntary organizations making most contribution to services for mentally ill people in your district?

15 Which are the voluntary organizations making most contribution to services for mentally handicapped people in your district?

16 What have been the *three* most significant developments in services for mentally ill people in your district/area over the last five years?

17 What have been the *three* most significant developments in services for mentally handicapped people in your district/area over the last five years?

# 2

# Historical analysis:
# the key factors which led
# to the amendment of the
# Mental Health Act 1959

*M. Rolf Olsen*

In 1976 the DHSS issued a consultative document which contained the conclusions of an inter-departmental committee (IDC) which had been set the task of considering whether amendment was required to the Mental Health Act 1959. The IDC thought that the 'considerable changes in mental health services and practices' that had taken place since 1959 suggested that the time was ripe for change. However, in reaching this conclusion the committee 'did not suggest that very fundamental change is required, but that some amendment to the present Act might be beneficial to all concerned' (DHSS 1976: 1, 2). With the document came the invitation to all those with an interest to contribute their views.

The passing of the Mental Health Act 1959 was generally heralded as a significant advance in the management and care of the mentally ill because it was thought to give the necessary legal framework in which to provide and develop an enlightened mental health service. It is probably the most important and radical legislation yet devised for the management of mental disorder. However, it did contain imperfections which became increasingly apparent in the ensuing eighteen years. These imperfections were not highlighted by advances in the remedies available to the mentally ill, as some would claim, but stemmed from the continuing public sympathy towards the mentally ill, and the considerable shift in

the locus of care from hospital-based treatment towards what we euphem-
istically call 'community care'.

None the less, two of the three major tenets of the Act – that as much
treatment as possible should be given on a voluntary basis, and that it
should where possible be provided within the community – remain at the
forefront of professional and political thinking. It is the third principle –
the proper provision for those who present a danger to themselves or
others, and for whom compulsory management appears necessary – that
caused concern, particularly with social workers, many of whom are not at
ease in the compulsory admission and care of the mentally ill, nor certain
of their role and contribution to the management of the psychiatric
emergency.

In my view the source of this unease lay in a number of unresolved
issues.

## The dichotomy between principles and practice

Davis in Chapter 1 has shown that the most fundamental concern relates,
and remains central, to the visible contradiction between the stated political philosophy and beliefs guiding our thinking and attitudes towards
the care of the mentally ill, and the actual resources made available. This
contradiction is most apparent in the much heralded White Paper, Better
Services for the Mentally Ill (DHSS 1975). On the one hand, this sleight-of-
mouth paper declared the privations of the mentally disordered and the
resources required to remedy them; yet on the other, made plain that very
little material progress could be expected in the foreseeable future.

A thread that runs throughout the evaluations of the transition of our
mental health services from a separate specialized care based upon large
isolated institutions, to care within the community, is the concern about
the effects of dispersal on patients, their living groups, and the wider
community. In spite of proven need the evidence confirms that we continue to discharge patients to the community without adequate services
and support. It is a sad fact that a quarter of a century after the Report of the
Royal Commission on the Law Relating to Mental Illness and Mental
Deficiency (HMSO 1957), there is no comprehensive system of community
care for the mentally disturbed. Instead, it is a principle which remains in
our imagination to inspire future ideals, to support our fancy that what we
are currently doing is in the best interests of all, to deaden our anxieties
about the hurt that this policy may cause patients and their families, and to
help us to bear the fact that in spite of the political acceptance of the
necessity for the provision of comprehensive community care services,
the need will in the foreseeable future remain, in the words of Barbara
Castle when Secretary of State for Social Services, 'simply a statement of
objectives' (DHSS 1975: iv).

## Lack of resources

Davis also argues that this public and political ambivalence results in the maintenance of adverse discrimination in the allocation of scarce public funds. Potentially, mentally disordered and emotionally disturbed people form the largest consumer group in our health and social services. In spite of this, Bill Utting, Chief Social Work Services Officer of the DHSS, is reported to have expressed his concern to the 1979 annual meeting of the Association of Directors of Social Services (ADSS) that forecasts of local authority personal social services expenditure for 1979/80 showed that only 1.2 per cent was to be allocated to mentally ill people, and 7 per cent to mentally handicapped people, compared with nearly 23 per cent for children and 37 per cent for elderly and younger physically handicapped people (Utting 1979). Capital expenditure forecasts show similar adverse discrimination.

Within the overall short-changed mental health budget the allocation is skewed in favour of the health services in spite of policies which propose the development of community care. It is estimated that 95 per cent of all mentally disordered people live in the community, yet only 5 per cent of the overall mental health budget is devoted to them; in contrast the remaining 95 per cent is allocated to that 5 per cent of psychiatric patients who are in hospital.

Similarly, there remains a lack of resources in the shape of professional commitment. The field of mental disorder remains unattractive to most professional groups, and along with the mentally handicapped carries little prestige and suffers a high level of professional neglect. It is regrettable that in many departments the care of this group remains the least glamorous of the social work tasks, and it is often handed over to social work aides and untrained workers. The uninterest contrasts sharply with the esteem of children, reflected in policies and practice that divert a disproportionate amount of scarce time and resources to their care.

## Management of the psychiatric emergency

The third issue that prompted the social work campaign for legislative reform lay in its concern about the mismanagement of the psychiatric emergency. The scant and now outdated available evidence (Clarke 1971; Jackson 1967), shows that social workers mismanaged the psychiatric emergency and did not consider their casework skills to be of much value in the crisis situation. The result was that they approached the psychiatric crisis in a state of reluctance, confusion, and apprehension. It has been shown that, with one or two notable exceptions, our solution to the emergency situation that cannot be contained within the living group is to remove the person defined as the patient to hospital, no matter whether the cause is thought to lie within the person himself, the nature of his relationships, the social environment, or in disease processes. Teamwork between doctors and social workers is often absent, there is limited understanding of respective roles and obligations, and the admission process is often poorly co-ordinated. This cannot be regarded as satisfactory, and we must ask ourselves whether it is possible to intervene more thoughtfully and with greater efficacy. From several points of view, the personal, social, and economic gains to be made by interventive strategies which do not rely solely on hospitalization appear to be considerable.

In spite of this understanding social work has paid scant regard to its own role and contribution to the successful management of the psychiatric emergency. This neglect gives cause for concern, particularly as the utilization of the crisis in the mental health emergency as the optimum moment for social work intervention is a concept, if not a technique, that has been known to social workers for more than twenty years. However, in spite of its long pedigree, the notion has received little attention in social work literature and there has been little systematic evaluation of its application or its effectiveness in practice.

### Inadequate recruitment policies and training

In large part the explanation for the unsatisfactory situation lay in the inadequacy of the local authority, Mental Welfare Officer (MWO) recruitment policies, and in the almost total absence of adequate basic and advanced training in mental health. In 1977, shortly after BASW's (1977) campaign for reform began, David Dunne reported findings that led him to conclude that only one third of London boroughs and 43 per cent of all other authorities in England and Wales required their MWOs to hold a professional social work qualification. Nearly half of the authorities automatically authorized social workers to act as MWOs on appointment, irrespective of whether the worker had an interest in mental disorder or had studied the subject (Dunne 1977). This evidence demonstrates that employing local authorities, the DHSS, and the CCETSW have paid little regard to the social worker's role and contribution to care of the mentally disordered in general, or to the successful management of the psychiatric emergency.

The reported unsatisfactory outcome to social work intervention in the mental health crisis also suggests poor initial education and training for social work. The limited time for training, together with the size of the syllabus and fieldwork requirements, prohibits attempts to provide a comprehensive training, and at present it is quite possible for a 'trained' social worker not to have studied mental disorder or to have worked with a mentally disordered person during training.

Of course it was never intended that a Certificate of Qualification in Social Work (CQSW) course should provide other than a basic training, and it was expected that the majority, if not all, of social workers would undertake post-qualifying training within two to five years of the CQSW, and thereafter at regular intervals. However, neither the government, professional organizations, nor social workers themselves press for such a scheme. In addition, whilst it is well known that the ADSS reports its favour of post-qualifying training, directors consistently fail to support such initiatives or to underwrite CCETSW's efforts in this direction. The result is that we have no vigorous programme of specialist or advanced training in social work in Britain.

Similarly, with one or two exceptions (notably the Skillmill in the North East, and the Mental Health Training Programme in Cheshire) in-service training prior to the 1983 Act was generally poor and non-effective.

## Uncertainty of the social worker's professional duties

The fifth set of issues that prompted social workers to advocate for reform related to the uncertainty about their professional duties and roles in effecting an application for compulsory admission. Prior to the Mental Health Act 1959, except in instances where a person was wandering at large, a Duly Authorized Officer was required to make a statement before a Justice before effecting a compulsory admission to hospital. This require-ment had the benefit of providing some defence of the patient's rights, ensuring the propriety of the admission, and guarding against wrongful certification. The Mental Health Act 1959 reflected the optimism generated by new drugs, new skills, changing attitudes, and the developing social services, and abolished the Justice's involvement in the procedure. However, in so doing it did not clearly prescribe who should take over the Justice's specific responsibilities, and many thought that the MWO would assume this role. This was not to be. The ambiguity of the 1959 Act, the weakness of the social worker's position relative to the power of the alliance between GP and psychiatrist, the level of social workers' ignor-ance about mental disorder and its management, and the right of relatives to make the application ensured that this role would not be assumed by the social worker *or* anyone else party to the procedure. The result was that the safeguards previously offered to the patient were lost.

Further, the 1959 Act did not ascribe particular functions to the MWO which were applied independent of the doctor or relative. The result was that the social workers' role was often defined administratively rather than therapeutically, and little attention was paid to their role in preventing or averting admission to hospital.

## The rejection of compulsory psychiatric intervention

The question of whether social workers should carry responsibility for enforcing compulsory care/treatment is one that causes concern for a number of social workers. It is a question that persuaded a number against active lobbying in favour of greater involvement in the process.

In 1978, at the height of the campaign for legislative reform, Thomas Szasz opened his condemnation of compulsory psychiatric intervention with these words, uttered by Alexander Solzhenitsyn in protest against the 'mental hospitalization' of Zhores Medvedev in 1970: 'The incarceration of freethinking, healthy people in madhouses is spiritual murder . . . a variant of the gas chamber, and even more cruel' (Szasz 1978). Szasz goes on to ask the important question, 'If the compulsory admission to psychiatric hospitals of "healthy people" is so abhorrent, what then makes it medically and morally justifiable when it is imposed on "sick people"? What is there about mental illness that makes a mental patient a fit subject for a psychiatric procedure which, were he not insane, would, according to Solzhenitsyn, constitute "spiritual murder"?' In Szasz's view there is no justification, and he claims that we are being increasingly constrained in our daily behaviour by treatment and procedures imposed by psychiatric and other authorities (including social workers) which has no parallel in the administration of criminal law. He believes that the legitimacy of this coercion rests not on the medical model of illness but on the paediatric model of care, in which the patient is treated like a child by the psychiatrist who acts *in loco parentis*. The results are that individuals are no longer held to be morally responsible for their behaviour, those who control them are regarded as their therapists rather than gaolers, and their prison is relabelled 'hospital'.

In answer to the question should the individual be allowed to harm himself or others, Szasz unequivocally says yes, if to intervene results in a threat to individual freedom or loss of liberty. 'Granted, some of the increase in liberty so gained might be at the cost of the impaired health or even death of some persons who make themselves ill or who want to kill themselves. That is because freedom entails the right to make the "wrong" choice.' On the question of how to control individuals who injure others, he is equally adamant: 'All such behaviour is a matter of crime, and should be controlled by means of the criminal law.'

It is tempting to ignore or dismiss these views as extravagant, dogmatic, inconsistent, prejudiced, and anti-scientific. However, to do so would result in our failure to reply to two fundamental questions. First, should the mentally ill be subject to special legislative provision? And if so, should social workers be involved in enacting such provision?

The answer to the first question is best sought by considering the outcome if Szasz's solution, which fails to discriminate between the delinquent and the mentally ill, were adopted. Up to the middle of the eighteenth century the mad were treated brutally and were outside the protection of the law. To argue for a return to solutions that are based upon the belief that all behaviour is criminal in intent or self-determined inevitably leads to a system of blame and punishment rather than understanding and treatment.

Similarly, if it is believed that social and environmental factors contribute to the development of stress, behavioural and psychiatric disorders, sometimes to extreme degrees of disturbance, then social workers must try to establish the truth of that belief. Further, they have an obligation to bring knowledge and expertise to situations in which it is thought that an individual requires care and/or treatment to which he will not agree. This obligation assumes a responsibility to defend the rights of the individual to deviate or dissent, to insist that the needs of the patient and his living group are stated, to ensure that the contribution of significant familial and social factors to the disorder is acknowledged and understood, to commit the social work agency to the care and support that are required, as well as being a duty to contribute to the decision whether to enforce compulsory care.

## Conclusion

This summary of the major factors that prompted social work to campaign for legislative amendment leaves no doubt of the need for reform. However, most would argue that because our mental health services are the most neglected and under-financed of all NHS/social services provision, the concentration on legal rights was myopic and mistaken. Of course the real issues are concerned with the need for a substantial increase in resources; standards of care; effective support for the living group; social, educational, and employment opportunities, etc. However, in the light of government economic policies, legislative amendment is the best that could be achieved. It is to be hoped that highlighting individual rights, clarifying professional duties, and increasing the rights of appeal will make good the injustices borne by the mentally disordered.

# 3
## The Mental Health Act 1983

## M. Rolf Olsen

The Mental Health Act 1983 consolidates the law relating to mentally disordered persons contained in the Mental Health Act 1959, and the Mental Health (Amendment) Act 1982. The main provisions came into force on 30 September, 1983, but the ASW will be introduced on 28 October, 1984. Until then the powers and duties placed upon the ASW will be enacted by those designated MWO on 30 September, 1982.

The granting of the Royal Assent to the Mental Health (Amendment) Bill on 28 October, 1982 marked the successful conclusion to the labour of Larry Gostin and to the campaign mounted by a number of organizations, notably MIND and BASW, concerned to restore to the disturbed psychiatric patient involuntarily detained in mental hospital some of the rights expected and enjoyed by those of us not so detained. Also, there is no doubt that in large part the substantial and fundamental improvements are due to a sympathetic Parliament and a tribute to the House of Commons Special Standing Committee, which sat on twenty-two occasions. The Committee displayed an exceptional level of commitment and comprehension of the issues at stake. The official reports of their proceedings show that numerous amendments and additional clauses were the outcome of members reaching conclusions which owed more to the evidence and debate than to party and political divisions. The overall result is that in future the safeguards afforded to the mentally disordered are considerably greater than might have been expected.

The five main principles that prompted the campaign were:

1 Every mentally disordered person may legitimately expect that their rights will be safeguarded.
2 The procedures for effecting a compulsory admission will be carried out in pursuance of the Act and accompanying regulations.
3 Compulsory care should be in the least restrictive conditions possible.
4 The professionals concerned with treatment and care are adequately trained and their competence assessed.
5 The quality of care and treatment does not fall below the accepted minimum.

The aims of this chapter are to summarize and interpret the major provisions of the Mental Health Act 1983. It is not intended to provide an exhaustive account of the detailed legislation. For this readers are referred to *The Mental Health Act 1983: A Guide for Social Workers* (BASW 1983) and to the suggested reading-list on pp. 38–40. Reference will be made to the duties placed upon social services departments and the ASW, but a more detailed discussion of the duties is undertaken in Chapter 4.

*Table 3.1*  Admission by legal status 1966, 1970, 1974–79.[1] Mental illness and mental handicap hospitals and units in England and Wales[2]

| | Sections of the Mental Health Act 1959 | | | | | | | | | other compul- sory powers[3] | total |
|---|---|---|---|---|---|---|---|---|---|---|---|
| year | 25 | 26 | 29 | 30 | 60 (+65) | 72 | 73 | 135 | 136 | | |
| 1966 | 11,912 | 1,938 | 17,916 | 45 | 1,517 | 159 | 17 | 13 | 1,159 | 447 | 35,123 |
| 1970 | 11,143 | 1,214 | 17,260 | 79 | 1,472 | 117 | 14 | 11 | 1,485 | 350 | 33,145 |
| 1974 | 7,452 | 800 | 13,559 | 179 | 1,237 | 60 | 10 | 4 | 1,561 | 219 | 25,081 |
| 1975 | 7,196 | 780 | 12,835 | 206 | 1,278 | 47 | 13 | 9 | 1,600 | 217 | 24,181 |
| 1976 | 6,868 | 791 | 12,057 | 218 | 1,177 | 46 | 11 | 13 | 1,588 | 188 | 22,957 |
| 1977 | 6,889 | 836 | 10,257 | 253 | 1,067 | 60 | 13 | 9 | 1,516 | 148 | 21,051 |
| 1978 | 6,356 | 1,003 | 8,938 | 244 | 1,042 | 59 | 11 | 9 | 1,624 | 123 | 19,407 |
| 1979 | 6,042 | 1,172 | 8,398 | 299 | 975 | 89 | 14 | 10 | 1,623 | 99 | 18,721 |

*Source:* Table 1.1 in *Reform of Mental Health Legislation*, Cmnd 8405.
*Notes:*
[1] *Source:* Mental Health Enquiry.
[2] Figures include Special Hospitals.
[3] Other sections of the Mental Health Act 1959 or other Acts, for instance, an admission may be recorded under Section 47 of the National Assistance Act, 1948.

# Part I   Application of Act

The provisions of the Act affect the 'reception, care and treatment of mentally disordered patients and the management of their property and other related matters' (Section 1(1)).

### The definition of mental disorder (Section 1(2))

The definition of mental disorder is unchanged from the 1959 Act. It means 'mental illness, arrested or incomplete development of mind, psychopathic disorder and any other disorder or disability of mind'. However, for most purposes of applying the Act it is not enough for the patient to be suffering from any of the four categories specified above, but must be suffering from one of the four categories of mental disorder which are specified – mental illness, severe mental impairment, mental impairment, or psychopathic disorder. What do these terms mean?

*Mental illness*  This term remains undefined; therefore its operational definition and usage is a matter for clinical judgement.

*Severe mental impairment*  Means 'a state of arrested or incomplete development of mind which includes severe impairment of intelligence and social functioning and is associated with abnormally aggressive or seriously irresponsible conduct'.

*Mental impairment*  Those with a lesser degree of mental handicap 'which includes significant impairment of intelligence and social functioning and is associated with abnormally aggressive or seriously irresponsible conduct'.

It should be noted that these terms replace the terms 'subnormality' and 'severe subnormality' in the 1959 Act, and result in a more restricted definition to distinguish the small minority of such patients who need to be detained from the majority who do not.

The difference between 'severe' and 'not severe' is not clear, and rests upon distinction between 'severe' and 'significant', which is a matter for clinical judgement. However, the distinction between the two is important because, as will be seen, there are differences in the grounds on which patients can be detained or received into guardianship.

*Psychopathic disorder*  Means 'a persistent disorder of mind (whether or not including significant impairment of intelligence) which results in abnormally aggressive or seriously irresponsible conduct'.

As in the 1959 Act, the disorder must be *persistent* before the patient can be classified as psychopathic. It must also result in abnormally aggressive or seriously irresponsible conduct.

As with mental impairment 'treatability' is no longer mentioned in the definition. However, the effect of Sections 3, 37, and 47 are that those patients with psychopathic disorder or mental impairment cannot be compulsorily admitted for *treatment* unless it can be stated that such treatment is likely to alleviate or prevent deterioration.

### EXCLUSIONS FROM THE DEFINITIONS OF MENTAL DISORDER

Section 1(3) of the Act states that a person may not be dealt with under the Act as suffering from mental disorder purely by reason of promiscuity, other immoral conduct, sexual deviance, or dependence on alcohol or drugs. But it is recognized that these conditions might be associated with mental disorder.

# Part II   Compulsory admission to hospital and guardianship

Part II of the Act details the grounds for recommending and applying for compulsory admission or guardianship other than through the courts by persons qualified to make the recommendation and application, and the length of detention under the various orders.

### Admission for assessment (Section 2)

Section 2 authorizes admission *for assessment* or for *assessment followed by treatment* for up to 28 days on the grounds that the patient:

(a)  is suffering from mental disorder 'which warrants the detention of the patient in hospital for assessment (or for assessment followed by medical treatment) for at least a limited period'; *and*

(b)  'Ought to be so detained in the interests of his own health or safety or with a view to the protection of others'.

This section replaces Section 25 of the 1959 Act. The word 'observation' has been replaced by the word 'assessment'. This is a worthy distinction in that the word 'assessment' prescribes an active evaluation which 'observation' does not. Note that patients admitted for assessment come under Part IV of the Act which allows treatment to be given, under certain circumstances, without consent.

MEDICAL RECOMMENDATIONS

An application for admission for assessment should be founded on the written recommendations, in the prescribed form, of two registered medical practitioners, both of whom must have examined the patient personally, and state that the person is suffering from mental disorder and ought to be detained. The recommendations must be signed on or before the application date. If the patient was examined by the doctors at separate times, not more than 5 days must have elapsed between the examinations.

One of the practitioners must be 'approved' (under Section 12(2) of the Act), and at least one of the two practitioners must, if practicable, have previous acquaintance with the patient. One of the recommendations may be given by a doctor on the staff of the hospital to which the patient is to be admitted. The conditions under which both medical practitioners may work in the hospital where the patient is to be admitted are listed in Section 12(3)(4).

Hospital and other staffs should make certain that procedures are established to ensure that full and appropriate clinical, social, and psychological assessment takes place.

## Admission for treatment (Section 3)

Section 3, which replaces Section 26 of the 1959 Act, authorizes admission for treatment for up to 6 months on the grounds that the person:

(a)  is suffering from mental disorder of a nature or degree which makes it appropriate for him to receive medical treatment in hospital; and
(b)  in the case of psychopathic disorder or mental impairment, such treatment is likely to *alleviate or prevent a deterioration of the condition* (note the introduction of a 'treatability test'); *and*
(c)  it is necessary for the health or safety of the patient or for the protection of others, and it cannot be provided unless he is detained under this section.

It should be noted that first, a person suffering from 'any other disorder or disability of mind' cannot be detained under this Section. Second, the mental disorder must be of a nature or degree that makes it appropriate for the patient to receive medical treatment in hospital. A person may meet the criteria of mental disorder but not be in need of medical treatment in a hospital because he can be treated in the community or under guardianship. Third, a patient suffering from psychopathic disorder or mental impairment may not be detained under this section unless it is likely to alleviate or prevent a deterioration in the condition. Fourth, it must be necessary for the health or safety of the patient, or for the protection of others, and this cannot be provided unless he is detained.

There are no longer any age limits for the admission of patients suffering from mental impairment or psychopathic disorder.

MEDICAL RECOMMENDATIONS

The application shall be founded on two written recommendations, on the prescribed form, of two registered medical practitioners, one of whom should be approved for the purposes of Section 12(2). Both must give grounds for their opinion that compulsory admission is necessary, the reasons why medical treatment in hospital is necessary, and why the patient cannot be suitably cared for outside of hospital, be treated as an out-patient, or admitted as an informal patient. One of the practitioners should, if practicable, have had previous acquaintance with the patient.

Other than in exceptional circumstances, only one medical recommendation may come from a practitioner on the staff of the hospital to which the patient is to be admitted – for private patients neither doctor may be on the staff. If the medical practitioners examined the patient separately, not more than 5 days must have elapsed between examinations.

## Admission in an emergency (Section 4)

In exceptional cases of urgent necessity 'an emergency application' for assessment may be made, provided that compliance with the Section 2 admission procedure 'would involve undesirable delay'. This section replaces Section 29 of the 1959 Act. It should be noted that the use of this section may deprive a patient of his primary safeguards, the opinion of an approved psychiatrist and/or an ASW. Therefore it should be used only in strict emergencies in which compliance with the requirements for Section 2 would, in the words of the Act, 'involve undesirable delay' (4(2)).

MEDICAL RECOMMENDATIONS

Only one medical recommendation is required, but the practitioner must have seen the patient within the previous 24 hours. If practicable, this should be a practitioner who has had previous acquaintance with the patient.

EXPIRY OF EMERGENCY DETENTION

The detention will end after 72 hours from the time of admission, unless (a) the second medical examination required for a Section 2 admission is received by the hospital managers within that period; and (b) the two medical recommendations comply with the requirements in Section 12 governing a Section 2 Admission for Assessment.

## Applications in respect of informal patients already in hospital (Section 5)

An application for compulsory admission under Section 2 or 3 may be made for a patient already in hospital as an informal patient, if it appears to the registered medical practitioner responsible for the patient's treatment (or to one other registered medical practitioner who may be nominated by him) 'that an application ought to be made'.

The detention period lasts for up to 72 hours. This allows time to obtain a second recommendation.

A trained nurse of the prescribed class may also detain an informal patient who is already being treated for mental disorder if it appears:

(a) 'that the patient is suffering from mental disorder to such a degree that it is necessary for his health or safety or for the protection of others for him to be immediately restrained from leaving the hospital'; and

(b) that it is not practicable to secure the immediate attendance of a medical practitioner for the purpose of furnishing a report under Section 5(2).

The holding power lasts for 6 hours from the nurse recording the reasons for the action, or until earlier arrival of the responsible medical practitioner or nominated practitioner.

## Guardianship (Section 7)

A person who has attained the age of 16 years may be received into guardianship. A guardianship application may be made on the grounds that:

(a) he is suffering from mental disorder, being mental illness, severe mental impairment, psychopathic disorder, or mental impairment of a sufficiently serious nature as to warrant a guardianship order; and

(b) it is necessary in the interests of the welfare of the patient or for the protection of others.

The application may be made by the nearest relative or by an ASW. The applicant may name as guardian either the local social services authority or any other person including the applicant himself. But if an individual is named as guardian it will have no effect unless the local social services authority for the area where the guardian resides accepts the application on his behalf; and the person must state in writing that he is willing to act as guardian.

A guardian should be able to appreciate the disabilities and needs of the mentally disordered, and be able to provide sympathetic and appropriate care.

Every guardianship application shall be forwarded to the local social services authority named in the application as guardian, or, as the case may be, the social services authority for the area in which the guardian resides. An application for guardianship by an ASW must not be made if the nearest relative objects to it. The ASW must consult the nearest relative of the patient before making such an application, unless it would not be reasonably practicable to do so, or would involve unreasonable delay.

A guardianship application should be founded on the written recommendations of two registered medical practitioners, both of whom must give the grounds for their opinion that the patient needs to be received into guardianship.

The powers of the guardian conferred by the guardianship application are:

(a) the power to require a patient to reside at a place specified by the authority or person named as guardian;
(b) the power to require the patient to attend at places and times so specified for the purpose of medical treatment, occupation, education, or training;
(c) the power to require access to the patient to be given at any place where the patient is residing, to any registered medical practitioner, ASW, or other person so specified.

The duration of a guardianship is up to 6 months. This period can be extended by a renewal order for a further 6 months, and then for a further period of one year, and so on for periods of one year at a time.

A written order discharging the patient may be made by the responsible medical officer, the responsible local social services authority, or by the nearest relative of the patient, who may seek an independent opinion before exercising that right.

# Part III  Patients concerned in criminal proceedings or under sentence

Part III of the Act embodies three proposals originally advocated by the Butler Committee (HMSO 1975): remand to hospital for a medical report; remand to hospital for treatment; an interim hospital order to determine whether a hospital order would be suitable.

The purpose of these proposals is to provide the courts with opportunity to require a person to attend hospital for assessment and/or treatment and to receive psychiatric recommendations before final decisions about management are taken.

However, these new powers *did not* come into force on 30 September, 1983, but will be introduced, if necessary by stages 'as resources allow', by an order made by the Secretary of State.

### Remand to hospital for report on mental condition (Section 35)

This section empowers Crown Courts or Magistrates Courts to remand an accused person to a hospital specified by the court for a report on his mental condition. The power applies to the following categories of person:

(a) accused people awaiting trial before Crown Court or people charged by a Crown Court but not yet sentenced, *for an offence punishable with imprisonment; or* who have been arraigned before the court but have not yet been sentenced or otherwise dealt with;
(b) people convicted by a Magistrates Court of an offence punishable with imprisonment; people charged with such an offence if the court is satisfied that they committed the offence; or a person consenting to the exercise of the powers under this section.

A person may be remanded to hospital for report on the written or oral evidence of one medical practitioner approved for Section 12 of the Act, if the court is satisfied that the person may suffer from one of the four disorders *and* if the court is satisfied that it would be impracticable for a report on his mental condition to be made if he were remanded on bail. Remand to hospital *does not* apply if the person has been convicted for the offence and where the sentence for the offence is fixed by law.

Remand to hospital will only be ordered if arrangements have been made for admission within 7 days. Meanwhile the court will direct the person to be kept in a place of safety. Further remands can be made for completing the assessment without bringing the accused before the court, if the person is represented by counsel or a solicitor and if written or oral evidence from the medical practitioner shows that further remand is necessary in order to complete the report. Further remands may be for 28 days at a time with a maximum of 12 weeks. The court may at any time terminate the remand. If the person absconds while on remand to hospital he may be arrested and taken back to court and the court may terminate the remand and deal with him as if no remand had been given.

### Remand to hospital for treatment (Section 36)

A Crown Court may, instead of remanding an accused person in custody, remand him to a specified hospital, if satisfied on the written or oral evidence of two registered medical practitioners that he is mentally ill or severely mentally impaired 'of nature or degree which makes it appropriate for him to be detained in hospital for medical treatment'.

An accused person is: anyone in custody awaiting trial before the Crown Court for an offence punishable with imprisonment (other than murder) or who at any time before sentence is in custody in the course of a trial before a court for such an offence.

Remand for treatment can be made only if the person can be admitted to hospital within 7 days of the remand. Meanwhile the court will give directions for the accused to be detained in a place of safety.

Further remands may be made on the basis of written or oral evidence of the responsible medical officer, and without the patient attending the court if he is represented by counsel or a solicitor, and one or other is given an opportunity of being heard. The maximum time for further remand is 28 days. In all 12 weeks, and remand may be terminated if it appears to the court appropriate to do so.

### Interim hospital orders (Section 38)

These are designed to assist the courts and the hospitals in determining whether it is appropriate to make a hospital order. The offender's response to hospital can be evaluated without irrevocable commitment should it prove unsuitable.

If a person is convicted before Crown Court of an offence punishable with imprisonment, or is convicted by a Magistrates Court of an offence punishable on summary conviction with imprisonment, and the court is satisfied on the written or oral evidence of two medical practitioners that:

(a)  an offender is suffering from one of the four disorders; *and*
(b)  a hospital order may be appropriate;

then the court can make an interim hospital order. This can be done in the absence of the offender if he is represented by counsel or a solicitor and the representative is given an opportunity to be heard. This court must first be sure that admission can be effected within 28 days of the order.

The duration of the initial order is up to 12 weeks to be specified by the court, renewable for up to 28 days at a time; maximum total 6 months. If the offender absconds he may be arrested without warrant and be brought back to court where the hospital order may be terminated. The court will terminate an interim hospital order once a decision is made about a hospital order or some alternative way of dealing with the offender.

## Hospital and guardianship orders (Section 37)

Where a person is convicted before the *Crown Court* of an offence *punishable with* imprisonment (except where the sentence is fixed by law), or is convicted by a Magistrates Court of an offence punishable on summary conviction with imprisonment, and if the mental health grounds (summarized below) are satisfied, then the court may authorize his detention in a specified hospital or place him under guardianship of a specified local social services authority or other persons approved by the social services authority.

The grounds for making a hospital order are:

(a) that the court is satisfied, on the written or oral evidence of two registered medical practitioners, that the offender is suffering from mental illness, psychopathic disorder, severe mental impairment, or mental impairment, and that either:

    (i) the mental disorder is of a nature or degree which makes it appropriate for him to be detained in a hospital for medical treatment and, in the case of psychopathic disorder or mental impairment, the treatment is likely to alleviate or prevent a deterioration in his condition;

*or*   (ii) if the offender is at least 16 years old, the mental disorder is of a nature or degree which warrants reception into guardianship;

*and*

(b) that the court, having regard to all the circumstances, is satisfied that an order under this Section is the most suitable method of dealing with the case.

If a person is charged before a *Magistrates Court* with an offence, and the court *would* have the power under 37(1) to make an order if it convicted the accused, then if the court is satisfied that the accused committed the offence the court may 'if it thinks fit' make an order without convicting him.

A hospital order will be made under this Section only if the court is satisfied that the patient can be admitted to a specified hospital within 28 days beginning with the date of the order. (The 28-day period would exclude any period when the patient was at large having escaped.) In the meantime the court will direct that the patient is conveyed to be detained in a place of safety. A guardianship order can be made only if the local authority or nominated guardian is willing to receive the person into guardianship.

### Restriction order (Section 41)

If the Crown Court makes a hospital order and it appears to the court necessary for the *protection of the public from serious harm*, then the court may order the offender to be subject to special restrictions either without limit of time or for a specified period. Such an order is a 'restriction order'. A patient subject to a restriction order or restriction direction will be referred to as a 'restricted patient'.

A restricted patient can be discharged, absolutely or with conditions, by the Home Secretary or a mental health review tribunal (MHRT). If the discharge is conditional the patient may be directed to live in a specific place or to attend for treatment, or be recalled to hospital at any time while the restriction order is still in force.

# Part IV   Consent to treatment

The issue of consent to treatment taxed the Parliamentary Select Committee perhaps more than any other. In spite of returning to the problem on more than one occasion the end result is a complex compromise which is not entirely satisfactory. Part IV (Sections 56–64) of the Act is largely concerned with consent to treatment of long-term detained patients, but certain safeguards for the most serious treatments also apply to informal patients. With this exception Part IV does not apply to informal patients, nor does it apply to those detained under short-term orders.

### Treatment requiring consent AND second opinion (Section 57)

Section 57 refers to those groups of treatments which can be given only in non-emergencies *with* the consent of the patient *and* if an approved doctor and two approved persons who are not medical practitioners have certified in writing that the patient is capable of understanding the nature and likely effects of the treatment, and has consented to it; *and* that the approved doctor has certified in writing that, having regard to the likelihood of the treatment alleviating or preventing a deterioration of the patient's condition, the treatment should be given.

Before giving such a certificate the approved doctor *must* consult two other professionals concerned with the patient's medical treatment. Of these one must be a nurse and one must be neither a nurse nor a medical practitioner – e.g. a social worker, psychologist, occupational therapist. The only such treatment listed in the Act is 'any surgical operation for destroying brain tissue or for destroying the functioning of the brain tissue'. The regulations (Regulation 16) also include *hormone transplants* for the purpose of reducing male sexual drive.

### Treatment requiring consent OR second opinion (Section 58)

Section 58 refers to those treatments which in non-emergencies can be given only *with* the patient's consent *or*, if an approved doctor sent by the Commission has certified in writing that the patient is not capable of understanding the nature, purpose, and likely effects of that treatment, or has withheld his consent to it, but that having regard to the likelihood of its alleviating or preventing a deterioration of his condition, the treatment should be given.

Before giving a certificate the approved doctor must consult two other persons who have been professionally concerned with the patient's medical treatment, and of those persons one must be a nurse and the other must be neither a nurse nor a medical practitioner.

So far the only treatment specified in the regulations is electroconvulsive therapy (ECT).

### Medication (Section 58)

Medication and any treatment not specified in Sections 57 or 58 may be administered without consent by any means for up to 3 months, provided 3 months has elapsed since the medicine was first administered. To continue beyond 3 months without consent, the Commission must be approached to provide a second opinion as outlined under Section 58.

### Urgent treatment (Section 62)

The safeguards will not apply to urgent treatment which:

(a)  is immediately necessary to save a patient's life; or

(b) which (not being irreversible) is immediately necessary to prevent a serious deterioration of his condition; or

(c) which (not being irreversible or hazardous) is immediately necessary to alleviate suffering by the patient; or

(d) which (not being irreversible or hazardous) is immediately necessary and represents the minimum interference necessary to prevent the patient from behaving violently or being a danger to himself or others.

# Part V   Mental health review tribunals

Part V of the Act describes the roles and responsibilities of the Mental Health Review Tribunals (MHRTs), independent bodies established under the 1959 Act to hear appeals by or on behalf of detained patients. There will continue to be a tribunal within the area of each Regional Health Authority in England and Wales. The functions of a tribunal may be exercised by any three or more of its members. In practice, tribunals consist of a legal member (president), a medical member, and a lay member. These are appointed from tribunal offices which provide the administrative support.

The opportunities to appeal to a tribunal have been considerably increased, and it is anticipated that the number of tribunal reviews will grow from just under 1,000 per annum in 1982/83 to about 5,000 per annum. The most important periods of eligibility for appeals to a tribunal are as follows: patients admitted for assessment may apply within the first 14 days of admission; those patients detained for treatment or received into guardianship order may apply once within the first 6 months, once during the next 6 months, and once during each subsequent period of 12 months. If a patient detained in hospital for treatment does not apply to a tribunal and no referral to a tribunal is made on his behalf within the 6-month period of the compulsory admission, then the hospital managers must refer the case. And subsequently, after any 3-year period without a tribunal review (or one year in the case of patients under 16 years old) the managers must refer the case to a tribunal.

An application to be heard by a tribunal must be made in writing. Significantly, the Act provides for legal aid to enable the patient to have legal representation. For non-restricted patients the tribunal may also authorize payment of travel expenses, subsistence, and loss of earnings to applicants, witnesses, and patients.

### Discharge by tribunals (Sections 72–4)

A tribunal has the power to direct the discharge of patients admitted for assessment if it is satisfied that the patient is:

(i) not suffering from mental disorder of a nature or degree which warrants hospitalization for assessment; or

(ii) if his detention is not justified in the interests of his own health or safety or to protect others.

A tribunal *must* direct the discharge of any other detained patient, except restricted patients, if it is satisfied that the patient is:

(i) not suffering from one of the four disorders to a degree which makes it appropriate for him to be detained for treatment; or

(ii) if it is not necessary for the health or safety of the patient or for the protection of others.

A tribunal can direct discharge on a *future* date, and in the meantime recommend that the patient be granted leave of absence, or transferred to another hospital or into guardianship. If these recommendations are not complied with, the tribunal may then reconsider the case. These new powers were introduced so that a period of time would be made available to be used to prepare after-care arrangements.

Restricted patients may apply to a tribunal:

(a) in the period between the expiry of 6 months and the expiry of 12 months beginning with the date of the relevant hospital order or transfer direction; and

(b) in any subsequent period of 12 months.

An MHRT shall order the *absolute* discharge of a restricted patient:

(a) if satisfied that the patient is not suffering from a mental disorder at all, or not of a nature or degree which warrants his detention in hospital for treatment; or

(b) that his treatment is not necessary for his own health or safety or for the protection of other persons; and

(c) that it is not appropriate for the patient to remain liable to be recalled to hospital for further treatment.

If a patient is absolutely discharged under this Section, then both the hospital order and restriction order will cease to have effect. If satisfied on points (a) and (b) above, but not satisfied as to (c), an MHRT may direct a conditional discharge. Where a patient is conditionally discharged under this Section, he may be recalled to hospital by the Secretary of State, and the patient must comply with any conditions imposed at the time of discharge by the tribunal or at any subsequent time by the Secretary of State.

Where a patient is subject to a restriction *direction*, and applies or is referred to an MHRT, the tribunal shall notify the Secretary of State whether, in their opinion, the patient would, if subject to a restriction *order*, be entitled to be absolutely or conditionally discharged under Section 73, and in the event of his not being discharged whether he should continue to be detained in hospital.

If the tribunal recommends an absolute or conditional discharge and has not recommended continued detention in hospital, then the Secretary of State will be obliged to issue a warrant directing the transfer of the patient to a prison or other institution where he might have been detained had he not been detained in hospital. If the Secretary of State fails to issue such a warrant within 90 days, then the managers of the hospital will transfer the patient to prison or other suitable place.

# Part VI   Removal and return of patients within United Kingdom

Part VI of the Act provides the Home Secretary with powers under which certain categories of detained patients and patients under guardianship may be moved between England and Wales and other parts of the UK, the Channel Islands, and the Isle of Man, while remaining under detention or guardianship; or may be retaken in those places when absent without leave. It also provides powers for moving mentally ill patients who are neither British nor Commonwealth citizens with the right of abode, from hospitals to countries abroad.

# Part VII   Management of property and affairs of patients

Part VII makes no changes to the powers and functions of the Court of Protection as set out in Section 101 of the 1959 Act. Overall the function is to manage the property and affairs of *any* person, whether in hospital or not, when it is satisfied on the basis of medical evidence that the person is incapable of doing so by reason of mental disorder. (For a detailed account and policy analysis of the Court of Protection see Gostin 1983b.)

# Part VIII   Miscellaneous functions of local authorities and the Secretary of State

The functions of local authorities will be considered in Chapter 4. There are a number of miscellaneous functions of the Secretary of State for Health and Social Services which demand particular consideration.

### The Mental Health Act Commission (Section 121)

A Mental Health Act Commission has been set up as a special health authority by the Secretary of State, and like other health authorities it will have to comply with directions from him; otherwise it is independent in functions and in the advice it offers.

The membership of about ninety includes lawyers, nurses, psychologists, social workers, and laymen in equal numbers of about 12, and about 25 doctors. The larger number of doctors is because medical members have more duties, for example with regard to providing second opinions and consent-to-treatment issues.

The Commission is divided into regional groups based on three centres in London, Liverpool, and Nottingham (see Appendix 2 for addresses). It also has a Central Policy Committee which takes the lead in preparing proposals and in preparing a bi-annual report of the Commission's activities.

The main functions of the Commission are:

(a) appointing approved medical practitioners and other professionals for consent to treatment duties (these may include Commission members);
(b) visiting and interviewing patients detained under this Act;
(c) investigating complaints by a detained patient or ex-patient which he feels were not satisfactorily dealt with by the hospital managers;
(d) investigating complaints made by persons who are not patients as to the exercise of powers or duties under this Act;

(e) where a complaint is made by an MP, reporting the results of the investigation to him;
(f) receiving reports from responsible medical officers on the treatment of patients where Section 57 or 58 safeguards have been necessary;
(g) the Secretary of State may, after consulting the Commission and other interested bodies, extend the scope of the Commission to include informal patients;
(h) reviewing any decision to withhold a postal package if
  (i) a patient applies to the Commission, and if he is in a special hospital and a package was withheld which he wished to send out; or
  (ii) the patient or sender of a package applies to the Commission where a package was withheld having been addressed to a patient in a special hospital.
  The application must be made within six months of a notice informing the patient that the package was being withheld.
(i) visiting patients – persons authorized by the Commission may visit and interview patients (and if a registered medical practitioner, may examine in private any patient). They may also inspect any records of the detention or treatment of the patient.
(j) the Commission must in its second year and every subsequent second year, publish a report on its activities. These will be laid before both Houses of Parliament.

The Commission will, on behalf of the Secretary of State, prepare and from time to time propose amendment to a Code of Practice for the guidance of registered medical practitioners and other professionals concerned with the admission and treatment of patients suffering from mental disorder.
The Code must have two parts:

(i) guidance in relation to the compulsory admission of patients;
(ii) guidance in relation to the medical treatment of patients.

The Code does not have the force of law, but everyone involved should pay close regard to it. Failure to do so could be taken as evidence of bad practice. Copies of the Code will be laid before Parliament.

## Duties of hospital managers (Sections 132–33)

Hospital managers have a duty to provide certain information to detained patients and their nearest relatives. In particular hospital managers must take the necessary steps as soon as practicable after the start of the detention to ensure that a patient understands the following:

(a) under what Section and provisions he is being detained, and the implications of the provisions;

(b) what rights he has to apply to an MHRT;
(c) the possibilities and restrictions for discharge from hospital;
(d) the giving and withholding of consent;
(e) the role of the Mental Health Act Commission;
(f) his right to send or receive correspondence, and the constraints upon this right.

The information must be given orally and in writing; and a copy should, if practicable, be given or sent to the nearest relative.

Section 133 requires that at least seven days before a patient is discharged the hospital managers must, where practicable, inform the nearest relative of the proposed discharge (unless the nearest relative has asked not to be informed of discharge).

## Correspondence (Section 134)

Hospital managers have particular responsibilities in relation to correspondence sent by or to detained patients. The provisions vary according to whether the patient is informal, detained in an NHS hospital, or detained in a special hospital such as Broadmoor. There are no restrictions placed on voluntary patients' correspondence. A postal packet sent by a detained patient in an NHS hospital may be withheld if the addressee requests it in writing. Post sent *to* a detained patient may not be withheld. Correspondence sent *by* a detained patient in a special hospital may be withheld if it is likely to cause distress to the addressee or any other person not on the staff of the hospital, or cause danger to any person. These powers are modified if the postal packet is sent by or to the patient by privileged persons or bodies, such as MPs, MHRT, etc.

## Listening and suggested reading

AUDIO TAPES

Olsen, M. R. *The Mental Health Act 1983*, Tapes 1 and 2. Produced by N. Tutt and G. Giller from Information Systems (Lancaster), Caton House, High Casterton, Kirkby Lonsdale, Cumbria.

ESSENTIAL READING

Mental Health Act 1983. London: HMSO.
BASW (1983) *The Mental Health Act 1983: A Guide for Social Workers*. Birmingham: BASW.
DHSS (1983) Mental Health (Hospital, Guardianship and Consent to Treatment) Regulations 1983. London: HMSO.

DHSS (1983) Mental Health Act Commission Regulations 1983. London: HMSO.
DHSS (1983) Mental Health Review Tribunal Rules 1983. London: HMSO.
DHSS (1983) Mental Health Act 1983 – Patients' Leaflets. London: HMSO.
Code of Practice (to be prepared by the Mental Health Act Commission).
CCETSW (1983) Regulations for Training and Assessing the Approved Social Worker. London: CCETSW.


BACKGROUND READING TO LEGISLATION

Mental Health Act 1959. London: HMSO.
DHSS (1976) A Review of the Mental Health Act 1959. London: HMSO.
Mental Health (Amendment) Act 1982. London: HMSO.
*Hansard* Reports (1982), House of Commons Special Standing Committee, Mental Health (Amendment) Bill 1982.
BASW (1977) *Mental Health Crisis Services – A New Philosophy.* Birmingham: BASW Publications.
Gostin, L. (1975/77) *A Human Condition*, Vols 1 and 2. London: MIND Publications.
Gostin, L. (1983) *A Practical Guide to Mental Health Law.* London: MIND Publications.
Gostin, L. (in press) *Contemporary Historical Perspectives on Mental Health Reform.*
Gostin, L., Rassaby, E., and Buccan, A. (in press) *Representing the Mentally Ill and Handicapped: A Guide to Mental Health Review Tribunals.* London: Oyez Press.
Bluglass, R. (1983) *A Guide to the Mental Health Act.* Edinburgh: Churchill Livingstone.
Gostin, L. (in press) *Mental Health Services*, 5th edn. London: Shaw & Sons.


SOME SUGGESTED READING ON SOCIAL WORK WITH
THE MENTALLY DISORDERED

Hudson, B. (1982) *Social Work with Psychiatric Patients.* London: Macmillan.
Meacher, M. (ed.) (1979) *New Methods of Mental Health Care.* Oxford: Pergamon Press.
Olsen, M. R. (ed.) (1976) *Differential Approaches in Social Work with the Mentally Disordered.* Birmingham: BASW Publications.
Olsen, M. R. (ed.) (1979) *The Care of the Mentally Disordered: An Examination of Some Alternatives to Hospital Care.* Birmingham: BASW Publications.

Sheldon, B. (1982) *Behaviour Modification: Theory, Practice, and Philosophy*. London: Tavistock Publications.

Wing, J. K. and Olsen, M. R. (1979) *Community Care of the Mentally Disabled*. Oxford: Oxford University Press.

Fisher, M., Newton, C., and Sainsbury, E. (1984) *Mental Health Social Work Observed*. London: Allen & Unwin.

Butler, A. and Pritchard, C. (1983) *Social Work and Mental Illness*. London: Macmillan.

# 4

## The roles and duties of social services departments and the approved social worker

*M. Rolf Olsen*

It was argued in Chapter 2 that in part the campaign for the reform of the role of social work in the management of the psychiatric emergency is explained by anxiety about the mismanagement of the psychiatric emergency, the inadequate recruitment policies, unsatisfactory basic social work training, the lack of post-qualifying training, and the uncertainties about the social worker's professional duties. To remedy the belief that in the field of mental health social workers were untrained and unsafe, BASW (1977) and others (e.g. see Dunne 1977; Olsen 1979b/c, 1981, 1982, 1983) argued that, in the absence of judicial oversight it is essential that social workers involved in the implementation of mental health legislation, which results in the loss of individual rights, should possess the appropriate professional values and have undertaken the level of training that this complex task demands.

To achieve this BASW, in its published response (BASW 1977) to the consultative document issued by the IDC (DHSS 1976), proposed sixty amendments to the 1959 Act. In relation to the training and duties of the social worker these may be summarized as follows:

1 To investigate the patient's social situation and to identify, in consultation with others involved, the extent to which social and environmental pressures have contributed to the patient's behaviour.

2 To use his professional skills to help resolve any social, relationship, or environmental difficulties which have contributed to the crisis, and to mobilize community resources appropriately.
3 To know the legal requirements and to ensure that they are complied with.
4 To form his own opinions, following an interview with the patient, with those closest to him, and with others involved, as to whether compulsory admission is necessary having regard to any alternative methods of resolving the crisis, and of securing necessary care or treatment.
5 To ensure that care and treatment is offered in the least restrictive conditions possible.

These duties place immense responsibility on the individual worker to exercise considerable expertise and judgment. This demands good preparation and comprehensive education and training. BASW did not consider that any person employed as a social worker, trained or not, should be empowered to exercise these powers, and proposed that in the long run they should be enacted only by 'ASWs', trained and experienced in social work with the mentally disordered. These persons would, in addition to being qualified social workers, be required to have undertaken post-qualifying training in social work with the mentally disordered on programmes approved by CCETSW, with successful candidates to be entered on a register.

The report went on to argue that every mentally disordered person has the right to expect that the professionals concerned with his care are adequately trained and competent, and that his rights will be safeguarded. Those who operate the Act are not always sufficiently conscious of the extraordinary powers that it gives them: powers that have no parallel in law, and that deprive the mentally disordered person of virtually all safeguards available to those who are not disordered. As there is no judicial oversight, the presence of a social worker in committal proceedings is essential. If he is to be effective, however, it is vital that he possesses the appropriate level of training and skill.

THE DUTIES LAID UPON SOCIAL SERVICES
DEPARTMENTS AND THE ASW

It is gratifying that to a greater or lesser extent the 1983 Act embraces all five of BASW's proposals.

## Functions of local authorities

APPOINTMENT OF ASWs (SECTION 114(1))

Section 114 provides for MWOs to be replaced by ASWs from 28 October, 1984. Until that date MWOs will carry out the functions given to the ASW under the 1983 Act. The changeover date on 28 October, 1984 will not affect anything carried out by an MWO before that, whether or not he then becomes an ASW. Anything in the process of being done on that date may be continued by an ASW.

This section also provides that each local social services authority shall appoint a *sufficient number* of ASWs to carry out the functions given to them by the Act. The 'sufficient number' will be a matter for each authority. No doubt each will wish to consult with representatives of unions and professional bodies, and will take account of such factors as population size and spread, geographical size, previous admission rates, whether to provide a 'fire brigade service' or widespread training, whether to maintain an out-of-hours emergency duty team, etc.

APPROPRIATE COMPETENCE (SECTION 114(2))

Nobody can be appointed as an ASW unless the local social services authority has approved him as having appropriate competence in dealing with people who are suffering from mental disorder.

TRAINING REQUIREMENTS (SECTION 114(3))

In approving a person the local authority will have regard to the requirements as directed by the Secretary of State for Social Services. In drawing up the regulations the Secretary of State will be guided by the CCETSW.

The effect of Sections 114(2) and (3) is that whilst the training and approval of ASWs is solely a matter for the local authorities, they cannot approve a social worker unless he has first passed an examination prescribed by the Secretary of State on the advice of CCETSW under regulations presented in July 1983.

WELFARE OF HOSPITAL PATIENTS TO WHICH THE LOCAL AUTHORITY HAS SPECIAL RESPONSIBILITIES (SECTION 116(1)(2))

Where a local authority has special responsibilities for a patient admitted to a hospital or nursing home, it shall arrange visits to the patient and shall undertake other functions which would be expected of a parent. This section applies to

(a)  a child admitted to hospital in respect of whom the rights and powers of a parent are vested in a local authority;
(b)  a person admitted to hospital who is subject to the guardianship of a local social services authority;
(c)  a person in hospital where the functions of his nearest relative under this Act or under the Mental Health (Scotland) Act 1960 are for the time being transferred to a local social services authority.

## DUTY TO PROVIDE AFTER-CARE (SECTION 117(1–3))

The Act imposes *a duty* on the district health authority and the social services department to provide, in co-operation with relevant voluntary agencies, after-care services for patients who have been detained for treatment (Section 3), under a hospital order (Section 37), or in hospital following a transfer direction (Sections 47 or 48).

The duty continues until the two authorities are satisfied that the person no longer needs such a service.

## GUARDIANSHIP APPLICATIONS (SECTION 11(2))

Every guardianship application shall be forwarded to the local social services authority named in the application as guardian, or, as the case may be, the social services authority for the area in which the guardian resides. The application, and the guardian if a private individual, must be accepted by the authority. The application does not take effect until it has been accepted by the local authority.

## PROVISION OF SOCIAL REPORTS (SECTION 14)

Where a patient is admitted to hospital under Section 2 (assessment) or 3 (treatment) following an application by the nearest relative, the hospital managers must notify the social services department for the area where the patient lived, and a social worker (not necessarily an ASW) must as soon as practicable interview the patient and provide the managers with a report on his social circumstances. The report should consider all the circumstances of the case: these will include the past history of the patient's mental disorder, his present condition, and the social, familial, and personal factors bearing on it, the wishes of the patient and his relatives, and medical opinion. The opportunity to direct any social worker to interview the patient provides scope, where appropriate, to request the investigation by a social worker who knows the patient and his living group.

A nearest relative may ask a social services authority to direct an ASW to investigate whether a patient should be compulsorily admitted or admitted to guardianship. If in any such case an ASW decides not to make an application, he must as soon as practicable inform the nearest relative of his reasons in writing. This request will usually but not always be confined to 'Admission for Assessment' Section 2(2) and 'Guardianship' 7(2). The duty is placed on the authority, but the judgement as to whether an application ought to be made rests with the ASW.

## The duties of the ASW

DUTY TO MAKE APPLICATION FOR ADMISSION (SECTION 13(1))

When relatives are unable or unwilling to make application it is the duty of an ASW to make an application for hospital admission of a patient or for guardianship within his local authority area if, having taken into account the wishes expressed by his relatives or any other relevant circumstances, the ASW thinks it necessary or proper to make the application. The duty is placed upon the ASW, not the local social services authority. The ASW must exercise independent professional judgement. He must take into account medical opinion, but must ultimately decide for himself solely on the basis of the statutory criteria and without undue influence either from the doctor or local authority.

The ASW should help relatives making the application by providing and explaining the forms.

The person making the application must have seen the patient within the previous 14 days or 24 hours in the case of emergency application.

Gostin in his guide to the Act argues

'The statutory functions of the ASW relate primarily (but not exclusively) to matters which affect the liberty of the individual. Parliament expressly decided that there should be an application based upon particular statutory criteria (Section 13(2)) which would be separate from the supporting medical recommendations. The ASW's powers and duties under Section 13 would not have been enacted if it had been intended that medical opinion alone should authorise compulsory admission. Each professional should be expected to contribute to the final decision only what is appropriate to his own knowledge and experience. Mental health legislation has for some time recognised that mental disorder alone does not render a person liable to be detained; the person's social situation and community-based alternatives to hospital care must also be taken into account. Assessment of these latter factors is the ASW's primary claim to a professional as distinct from a purely procedural role. The ASW therefore has a responsibility to maintain complete independence and impartiality when assessing a patient's needs in the context of his family and social situation, and the care and support which can, and *should*, be provided in the community.

In each case of compulsory admission, whether it be for benevolent reasons or for the prevention of physical harm to others, a person is deprived of liberty. The statutory procedure for admission must be followed strictly and accurately, and it is the responsibility of the ASW to see that this is so, both in his capacity as a statutory officer with duties conferred by the Act and as a professional seeking to ensure that care and treatment are provided in the least restrictive setting possible. The protection of a patient's "liberty interest" is particularly important because compulsory admission under Part II of the Act does not require prior judicial review.'

(Gostin 1983a: 22–3)

There is nothing in the Act which bars hospital-based social workers from making application; however, to ensure independence of opinion it is preferred that the ASW is not a colleague of the doctors making the recommendation, nor a member of the hospital team which will receive the patient.

## DUTY TO INTERVIEW THE PATIENT (SECTION 13(2))

Section 13(2) lays two important duties upon the ASW. First, the ASW, before making an application, must interview the patient in a suitable manner; and second, must satisfy himself that detention in hospital is, in all the circumstances of the case, the most appropriate way of providing the care and medical treatment that the patient needs. Note the 'duty' to interview the patient. There is also a requirement to consider 'all the circumstances' of the case; this will include past history and present personal, family, and social circumstances. The ASW must satisfy himself on the availability and suitability of alternative arrangements. If detention in hospital is not necessary, but alternative community-based methods of management are not available, this should be recorded on the application.

The duty to 'interview in a suitable manner' requires the ASW to speak with the patient in person. This requirement will present difficulties of interpretation when the patient does not understand English, refuses to communicate, prevents the interview from taking place, or has hearing or speech difficulties.

## APPLICATION OUTSIDE OWN AUTHORITY'S AREA (SECTION 13(3))

An ASW may make an application in respect of a patient outside his own local social services area. This is permissive, not a mandatory duty. This may be necessary, for example, if authorities share an out-of-hours service, or if it is necessary to detain an informal patient in a hospital outside his geographical residence.

## OBLIGATION TO INFORM NEAREST RELATIVE (SECTION 11(3–4))

The ASW making the application must take all practicable steps to inform the nearest relative (if any) that the application is about to be or has been made, and of the relative's powers to effect the discharge of the patient. In the case of admission for treatment or for guardianship the ASW should consult nearest relatives before making application. If the relative objects the ASW cannot proceed. An unreasonable objection is one of the grounds, Section 29(3), for a court to transfer powers of nearest relative to another person.

## AUTHORITY TO CONVEY TO HOSPITAL (SECTION 6(1))

The applicant or any person authorized by the applicant will take the patient to hospital. The authority expires 14 days after the medical examination, or in the case of an emergency application within 24 hours of the time when the application was made, whichever is earlier.

The ASW has a responsibility to ensure that the patient, as far as possible, understands the situation and knows his rights; and also to make certain that the admission is carried out in the best possible manner. If the ASW judges that they are unable to transport the patient, or if the patient is unwilling to be moved, it is the duty of the health authority to provide an ambulance. The applicant should provide written authority to escorts to move a patient.

## CORRECTING APPLICATIONS (SECTION 15(1–4))

Those who sign recommendations and applications should make sure that they comply with the requirements of the Act. Those who act on the authority of documents should make sure that they are in a proper form and correctly completed. Documents should be carefully examined when the patient arrives at the hospital. The managers should nominate an officer to undertake this task. It is particularly important to ensure that the time limits have been complied with. Except in 'emergency' applications:

(a)  the applicant must have seen the patient within 14 days;
(b)  the dates of medical examinations are not more than 5 days apart;
(c)  the dates of signatures of both medical recommendations must not be later than date of application;
(d)  admission must take place within 14 days of the date of the later medical recommendation.

If within 14 days of admission for assessment or treatment, it is found that the application is incorrectly completed, or if a medical recommendation is incorrect or defective, it may, with the manager's consent, be amended by the person who signed it, or if necessary a fresh medical recommendation must be obtained.

## WARRANT TO SEARCH AND REMOVE PATIENTS (SECTION 135(1–3))

If an ASW is satisfied that a person believed to be suffering from mental disorder:

(a)  has been, or is being ill-treated, neglected, or not kept under proper control; or
(b)  is unable to care for himself and is living alone,

he may give information to this effect on oath to a Justice of the Peace (JP) who may then issue a warrant enabling a named constable to enter the premises and, if necessary, remove the person to a safe place for assessment. The patient may be detained for up to seventy-two hours under this section. The constable must be accompanied by an ASW and a doctor. In the case of a patient who is liable to be detained in hospital and who is thought to be in a particular premises where admission to authorized persons has been refused, the JP may issue a warrant authorizing a constable to enter the premises and remove the patient. The patient may then be detained for seventy-two hours under this section. The constable must be accompanied by a doctor and by any other person authorized to take or retake the patient to hospital.

A place of safety refers to residential accommodation provided by local social services authorities, a hospital, police station, mental nursing home, or residential care home for mentally disordered persons, or any other suitable place where the occupier is temporarily willing to have the patient.

These duties, placed upon social services authorities and ASWs, have important implications for both the organization and practice of social work with the mental health emergency. At best they will do much to remedy the unsatisfactory situation reported in Chapter 2, and will improve the level and quality of social work with the mentally disordered and those with whom they live. However, a great deal rests upon the quality of training and the resources to be made available. Elsewhere (Olsen 1983) I have expressed my doubts that the current CCETSW's training proposals – which place great value on academic assessment to the neglect of education and training – will be universally achieved. Similarly, current expenditure forecasts provide little hope that the present level of neglect will be much improved.

The main responsibility for enacting both the requirements and the spirit of the Act now rests with the Chairmen and Directors of Social Services, training officers, educators, and the ASWs themselves. If they unite to promote adequate training programmes, an acceleration of the transfer of resources, and in a refusal to accept the *status quo*, then a better professional service will emerge.

## SPECIMEN EXAMINATION PAPER 1

*M. Rolf Olsen*

Mental health legislation and its implications
for the task of the approved social worker

## PAPER 1 SHOULD BE ATTEMPTED WITHOUT REFERENCE TO LEGISLATION OR ANY OTHER MATERIAL

### TIME – 1 HOUR MAXIMUM

*(Answers – Appendix 3)*

1   From the following list indicate the four definitions of mental disorder identified in Section 1(2) of the Mental Health Act 1983.

Tick appropriate
boxes

a) mental disorder
b) mental impairment
c) mental handicap
d) mental illness
e) arrested or incomplete development of the mind
f) psychosis
g) psychopathic disorder
h) any other disorder or disability of the mind

2   Tick the persons qualified to make applications for compulsory admission.

a) any relative
b) ASW
c) any social worker
d) approved psychiatrist
e) GP
f) nearest relative

3   Tick the duties of the ASW stated in the Mental Health Act
    1983.

    a)  to make application for admission
    b)  to interview doctor
    c)  to interview the patient
    d)  to inform the nearest relative of admission
    e)  to satisfy himself that detention in hospital is
        most appropriate way of providing care
    f)  to obtain patient's consent to treatment
    g)  to arrange transport of patient to hospital

4   What are the grounds for the admission or guardianship of a
    patient under the following sections of the 1983 Act?

Tick appropriate boxes in all
4 columns

|   | Section 2(2) | Section 3(2) | Section 4(1 2) | Section 7(1 2) |
|---|---|---|---|---|
| a) Is suffering from mental disorder as set out in Section 1 | | | | |
| b) Is suffering from mental disorder as set out in Section 1, which warrants detention in hospital for assessment or for assessment followed by medical treatment | | | | |
| c) Ought to be so detained in the interests of own health or safety *and* with a view to the protection of others | | | | |
| d) Ought to be so detained in the interests of own health or safety *or* with a view to the protection of others | | | | |
| e) Is suffering from mental illness, severe mental impairment, psychopathic disorder, or mental impairment which is of a nature or degree which makes it appropriate for him to receive medical treatment in hospital | | | | |

*(continued)*

|  | | | |
|---|---|---|---|
| f) In the case of psychopathic disorder or mental impairment, treatment is likely to alleviate or prevent deterioration | | | |
| g) Compliance with requirements of other sections would involve undesirable delay | | | |
| h) It is necessary for health or safety of the patient or for the protection of others that he should receive such treatment, and it cannot be provided unless he is detained under this section | | | |
| i) Is suffering from mental disorder, being mental illness, severe mental impairment, psychopathic disorder, or mental impairment, and his mental disorder is of a nature or degree which warrants reception into guardianship | | | |
| j) It is necessary in the interests of the welfare of the patient or for the protection of other persons | | | |
| k) Patient is at least 16 years old | | | |

5   The 1983 Act states that the ASW shall:

Tick appropriate boxes

a) Interview the patient to the best of his ability

b) Interview the patient in a suitable manner

c) Consider whether detention in hospital is desirable

d) Satisfy himself that detention in hospital is in all the circumstances of the case the most appropriate way of providing the care and medical treatment of which the patient stands in need

e) Before or within a reasonable time after an application of admission for assessment the ASW shall take such steps as are practicable to inform the person (if any) appearing to be the nearest relative that the application is to be or has been made

f) Before or within a reasonable time after any application the ASW must inform the relative caring for the patient that the application has been or will be made

6   For how long may a trained nurse of the prescribed class detain an informal patient under Section 5(4)?

Tick appropriate box

   a)   3 hrs
   b)   6 hrs
   c)  12 hrs
   d) 24 hrs
   e) 72 hrs

7   For how long may the RMO detain an informal patient under Section 5(2)?

Tick appropriate box

   a)   3 hrs
   b)   6 hrs
   c)  12 hrs
   d) 24 hrs
   e) 72 hrs

8   What is the maximum duration of detention under the following sections:

   Section 2(2) ...................................
   Section 3(2) ...................................     Insert correct
   Section 4(1–2) ...............................     period of time
   Section 7(1–2) ...............................

9    The applicant must have seen the patient personally within so
     many hours/days ending with the application. Insert correct
     number of hours/days for:

     Section 2(2)  .....................................
     Section 3(2)  .....................................
     Section 4(1–2)  ...............................
     Section 7(1–2)  ...............................

10   Where a patient is admitted to hospital on the application by the
     nearest relative (except Section 4(1–2)), the local social services
     authority shall arrange for a social worker to interview the
     patient:

                                                          Tick appropriate
                                                               box

     a)  within 24 hrs
     b)  within 3 days
     c)  within a reasonable time
     d)  as soon as is practicable
     e)  as soon as possible

11   Under Section 135(1) which of the following persons can
     provide information on oath so that a JP may issue a warrant
     to search for and remove patients?

                                                          Tick appropriate
                                                               box

     a)  a constable
     b)  any relative
     c)  nearest relative
     d)  the GP
     e)  an approved psychiatrist
     f)  an ASW
     g)  a nurse

12   To whom must an application for admission be addressed?

     ........................................................................................
     ........................................................................................

13  Which of the following persons may make a written order discharging the patient?

Tick appropriate boxes

a) any relative
b) the GP
c) the RMO
d) an approved doctor
e) an appointed doctor
f) the hospital managers
g) the nearest relative

14  Can the nearest relative discharge a patient if the RMO bars the discharge?

Tick appropriate box

Yes

No

15  How much notice must the nearest relative give if he or she wishes to discharge the patient?

..................................................................................

16  A patient liable to detention under Section 18(4) of the Act who goes absent without leave may not be taken into custody after the expiration of how many days? (Insert correct number) ........

17  Can an ASW make application for admission or guardianship outside the geographical area of the authority by which he was appointed:

Yes

No

18  Which is the correct sequence of continued detention for a patient detained under guardianship?

Tick appropriate box

a) 6 months
   1 year
   2 years
   2 years . . . at a time

*(continued)*

b) 1 year
   1 year
   2 years
   2 years . . . at a time     ☐

c) 1 month
   6 months
   1 year
   2 years . . . at a time     ☐

d) 6 months
   6 months
   1 year
   1 year . . . at a time     ☐

19   Rank the following persons in order of importance for the purposes of defining the nearest relative. (Place the numbers 1–8 on right according to seniority.)

    a) father or mother    ..............
    b) husband or wife    ..............
    c) brother or sister    ..............
    d) son or daughter    ..............
    e) grandchild    ..............
    f) grandparent    ..............
    g) nephew or niece    ..............
    h) uncle or aunt    ..............

20   How long must a co-habitee have been living with the patient to be regarded as spouse for the purposes of the Act? ................

21   How long must a non-relative have lived with the patient in order to be treated as the nearest relative for the purposes of the Act? .................................................................

22   May a Crown Court authorize the detention in a specified hospital or under guardianship of a person convicted of an offence punishable with imprisonment?

Tick appropriate box

    a) Yes if person agrees
    b) Yes if nearest relative agrees
    c) Yes
    d) No

23  Group 1 treatment (destructions of brain tissue, certain hormone transplants) can be given only if:

   a) Two doctors agree
   b) Two doctors and two other professionals agree
   c) Nearest relative and two doctors agree
   d) Patient consents and two doctors agree
   e) Patient consents, and if an approved doctor and two other approved persons who are not medical practitioners agree, and the approved doctor certifies that the treatment should be given
   f) Two relatives and two doctors agree

24  Group 2 treatment (e.g. ECT) can be given only if:

   a) Two approved doctors, sent by the Mental Health Act Commission, agree
   b) Two approved doctors, sent by the Mental Health Act Commission, agree and the patient consents
   c) Nearest relative, patient, and independent doctors agree
   d) None of these propositions (a–c) is true

25  May a detained patient withdraw his consent before completion of treatment?
   a) Yes
   b) Yes, except in an emergency
   c) No

26  Under Section 62(1) what are the four requirements governing the administering of 'urgent' treatment?

   a) ................................................................................
   b) ................................................................................
   c) ................................................................................
   d) ................................................................................

27  When are detained patients eligible to make applications to an MHRT?

| Category of admission | Period of eligibility to make application to MHRT |
|---|---|
| a) Detained for assessment | .................................... |
| b) Detained for treatment | .................................... |
| c) Detained for guardianship | .................................... |

28  The membership of the Mental Health Act Commission includes representatives of:

a) ...........................................
b) ...........................................
c) ...........................................
d) ...........................................
e) ...........................................
f) ...........................................

29  Name the main functions of the Mental Health Act Commission:

30  Who has the *duty* to inform patients of their rights?

Tick appropriate
box

a) the ASW
b) the RMO
c) the hospital managers
d) the nearest relative
e) the Mental Health Act Commission
f) the GP

31  Under Section 5(3) how many other registered medical practitioners may the doctor in charge of the patient's treatment nominate to act for him in his absence? ...........................

PART TWO

PERSPECTIVES OF
MENTAL DISORDER AND
MENTAL HANDICAP

# 5

# Clinical perspectives
of mental disorder

## *Derek Anton-Stephens*

It is not possible for the social worker to respond adequately to the greater involvement in the management of mental illness envisaged in current legislation without an awareness of psychiatric thinking and terminology. Whatever one's views on the 'medical model' of mental illness, it is useful to know what is likely to be passing through the minds of the medical people who will also be involved in implementing many of the provisions of the Mental Health Act 1983.

### Terminology and classification in psychiatry

There is no entirely satisfactory scheme of classification of mental illness; the one used here will serve its purpose for those who have no better. Without some such framework around which to organize our thoughts and observations the innumerable varieties of human aberration become overwhelming. Medical diagnosis is not a sterile exercise: used correctly, it gives those dealing with an individual patient access to the mass of information gathered over many years by investigation of similar patients. It would be foolish to ignore such help.

Some overall term is needed to denote the whole field, and *mental disorder* is as good as any and has the merit of being acceptable to medical and legislative minds – as do the concepts of *arrested development* and *mental illness.* The unsatisfactory term *psychopathy* will need to be clarified subsequently; its use arises from the importance of distinguishing the clinical concepts of *personality disorder* and *psychopathic personality* on the one hand from the legalistic concept of *psychopathic disorder* on the other. Mental illness has no specific definition within current legislation, but is held to exclude alcoholism, drug abuse, and sexual anomaly when these conditions occur in the absence of other recognizable illness.

The terms *psychosis* and *neurosis,* although theoretically suspect, are retained because of their common usage and their practical implications. If by psychosis we denote a mental illness which produces behaviour disturbing to others and into the true nature of which the sufferer has no 'insight' (that is, has no awareness that the disturbing behaviour arises from an illness in himself and, therefore, no motivation to seek help in respect of it) we have not only the basis of the many 'lunacy laws' of the past two hundred years but also the reason for the provision of the 'asylum' and 'mental hospital' buildings throughout the land, into which sufferers from psychotic illness have been (and still are) liable to find themselves segregated from the rest of society. Whereas, neurosis – being a condition which, however much suffering it causes, tends not to produce behaviour that actually frightens others – has not seemed to society to call for segregation. Nor does the sufferer from neurotic illness usually need any legal compulsion to seek help.

## The major psychiatric disorders

### PRIMARY AND SECONDARY PSYCHOSIS

The subdivision of psychosis into 'primary' and 'secondary' groupings is an essential process in the medical recognition of these conditions and in the determination of their treatment and prognosis. *Primary psychosis* means that the illness has, as it were, arisen in its own right; it is not the result of some preceding physical injury or disease. *Secondary psychosis* means the opposite, that the illness (or 'syndrome' to be less dogmatic) *is* the result, the symptom, of some preceding physical injury or disease. In everyday medical usage the term *organic psychosis* is the one most frequently applied to these secondary, symptomatic conditions; and it is worth bearing in mind that it does not necessarily follow that because organic psychoses are the result of physical disease, primary psychoses are psychological in origin.

## The organic syndromes

### MEDICAL CAUSATION

Degenerations of the brain due to old age or to disease of the cerebral arteries ('arteriopathic' is a better term for this than 'arteriosclerotic') account for most of the cases that occur in everyday practice. Nevertheless, toxic substances (with alcohol leading the field), brain injury due to trauma (road-traffic accidents are the peace-time counterpart of high-explosives in war), and neoplasms (the correct term for tumours, cancers, and growths) provide their quota: so, too, do various infections leading to inflammation of the brain and its coverings (encephalitis and meningitis). The distinction between these various physical causes, and the treatment of the underlying cause itself, is a medical matter: the role of the social worker lies in the recognition, at the earliest moment, of the possibility of such physical illness being the reason behind the disturbed behaviour or altered personality that has necessitated social work intervention. Do not let psychological theory blind you to the existence of purely physical pathology.

## Dementia and delirium

Both these terms apply to the psychiatric end result of the physical diseases underlying the organic psychoses. The difference is one of timing. *Dementia* is the chronic (or slowly developing) process which takes, as a general rule, months or years; *delirium* is the acute (or quickly developing) process which takes hours or days. The latter is far less of a problem for the social worker than the former, but delirious outbursts due to alcohol or minor infections afflicting those, especially the elderly, who are subsisting on an inadequate diet are not uncommon, and 'bad trips' induced by drug abuse are part of the current scene.

### THE CLINICAL PICTURE OF DEMENTIA

To say that in dementia there is a progressive loss of all acquired mental faculties, although true, is too general for practical use. It is more useful to think of this degeneration as affecting, within wide variations of time and intensity, the three major aspects of our existence – our intellect, our emotional feelings, and our behaviour. In each there is a characteristic loss or diminution of a previously existing function.

*The intellectual loss*  A failure to register new events, so that the past becomes easier to deal with than the present and memory shows typical 'organic' change: distant happenings are well remembered; recent ones far less so. The end result is complete disorientation: all effective touch is lost with the here and now – surroundings, people, time-relationships all become jumbled and disjointed. It is to this state of affairs that the term *confusion* is correctly applied.

*The emotional loss*  A failure to experience deeply or consistently the emotional responses of life, with quick changes from one mode to another (*emotional lability*), often with what, in a non-dementing person, would be less than appropriate cause. The end result is the inane apathy which supersedes the equally inane fatuity that is associated with extreme old age; an apathy interspersed with little outbursts of anger or fear, which often pass away as though they had never been.

*The behavioural loss*  A failure of inhibitory control, so that basic (and therefore primitive) drives and desires become progressively less controlled and the individual becomes less 'civilized', less socially conventional, less sensitive to the needs of others. The end result is that of *regression* to childish (and ultimately infantile) modes of conduct, with the loss of control over bowels and bladder heralding a degree of deterioration which society finds unacceptable.

The *change of personality* brought about by these interacting deficits is a slow process: it may take years for the full picture to emerge (during the passage of which many people die, often from unrelated illness, without ever reaching the state of advanced dementia) and it is often the story told by relatives that gives the clue, rather than the clinical presentation on any one day. It should be borne in mind that any such change of personality in someone over the (purely arbitrary) age of forty-five should always raise the suspicion of organic illness.

THE MANAGEMENT OF DEMENTIA

From the point of view of the social worker, the management of dementia is a matter of endeavouring to adapt the client's environment to his failing ability to deal with it, and to offering material and emotional support to his relatives (many of whom can be put under very great emotional stress by the changing habits and personality of a loved one). In the great majority of cases, advanced dementia will require nursing care in hospital, where any treatable underlying illness can be investigated and dealt with, and where attempts at rehabilitation and resocialization can be undertaken. This particularly applies to dementing patients leading isolated existences, often with inadequate food-intake, who are deprived of the therapeutic stimulus of human company. Attendance at hospital-based day centres usefully combines both the medical oversight and the social stimulation. But it will often fall to the lot of the social worker, in consultation with the GP, to take the decision that in the interests of all concerned the time has come for full-time institutional care.

## THE CLINICAL PICTURE OF DELIRIUM

The disorientated confusion and the, often highly, disinhibited behaviour of delirium are accompanied by hallucinatory experiences (see p. 67) and appropriately heightened emotional responses – usually of fear or anger. The whole picture is much more dramatic than that of dementia, and often occurs in the course of recognizable medical illness. Acute infections, the aftermath of anaesthetics, and the withdrawal of alcohol from the heavy drinker are the most likely causes of delirious reactions which will meet the ASW, although drug abuse is becoming a common factor in some areas. And the delirious potential of even minor infection in an old person whose diet is inadequate and who may have sought solace in modest amounts of alcohol should not be overlooked.

The management of any delirium should always include medical assessment, and will almost always require careful consideration of hospital admission so that suitable sedation, appropriate treatment of the underlying illness, and nursing care can be given (and the patient guarded against the effects, on himself and others, of his disinhibited emotions and behaviour).

## The primary psychoses

### The schizophrenic psychoses

If 'dementia' conjures up, wrongly, the picture of an old person, then with more justification 'schizophrenia' carries with it an assumption of adolescence and early adulthood. It is indeed the psychiatric scourge of youth, even though its manifestations may extend well into middle-age. Its causation (genetic or acquired, metabolic, psychological, or sociological) remains a fruitful field of argument, and its definitive diagnosis a matter of contention even amongst psychiatrists. Few, however, would argue about the central phenomena. There is, essentially, an alteration and disruption of the very process of thinking itself, and a blurring of the distinction between 'self' and 'not-self'. The appreciation of what to others is reality becomes altered, emotional responses become inappropriate ('incongruous'), and communication with others becomes difficult, so that there occurs a withdrawal into fantasy and away from the world of hard fact and interpersonal relationships. Often these disturbances are associated with hallucinatory experiences and delusional beliefs – but it is important to avoid the error of assuming that everyone who describes hallucinations or expresses delusions is automatically suffering from schizophrenia. Many schizophrenics do indeed describe both, but schizophrenia is not the only condition in which they occur.

The 'otherness' of the schizophrenic's personality, and the bizarre nature of his thoughts and behaviour, isolate him from others; and being thus isolated, he no longer has need of socially conventional behaviour. His social skills atrophy and this still further increases his isolation – a vicious circle of events. The social rehabilitation of the schizophrenic whose symptoms have remitted may be more arduous than the medical treatment of the illness itself.

## THE CLINICAL SUBDIVISIONS

Traditionally there are four major subdivisions of schizophrenia – simple, hebephrenic, catatonic, and paranoid – but it is doubtful if more than half of all schizophrenics fall easily into these categories; and is possible to produce an almost unending list of clinical varieties. To the social worker it is probably not very important. The thing that does matter is to recognize the disturbed and disconnected thought processes, the incongruous emotions, the inability to relate to others, that lie behind these academic niceties, and to recognize them quickly. The sooner treatment can be initiated the better the chances of remission without irreversible loss of social skills.

## THE QUESTION OF TREATMENT

There is no space here to do more than stress the impact made on schizophrenic patients in mental hospitals in this country over the past thirty years by the phenothiazine group of drugs. The scene in such hospitals has, quite literally, been transformed. Whether one can validly talk of 'cure' or only of full remission of symptoms is still debated, but conscientious adherence to prescribed medication undoubtedly represents by far the best chance a schizophrenic has of regaining a normal life in society.

## The paranoid psychoses

To be 'paranoid', or to suffer from 'paranoia', is to be 'deluded', or to have 'delusions'. Often, but not always, such delusions are accompanied by 'hallucinations'; and it is convenient to discuss these two common psychiatric symptoms under their own heading, even though many psychiatrists would consider the various 'paranoid states' to be but one of the many manifestations of schizophrenia. Definitions are important.

DELUSION

Essentially here we are dealing with the difficult matter of 'belief'. A delusion is:

(a) a false belief, which cannot be altered by what most people would regard as a logical demonstration of its falsity, that is it cannot be altered by an 'appeal to reason' (if it could, it would simply be a mistaken belief); and which is

(b) out of keeping with the holder's cultural background, intellectual ability, and general life experience.

Any such belief is 'paranoidal', irrespective of its actual content. It is indeed the case that many delusions are of a 'persecutory' nature, but the common equation of 'paranoid' with 'persecutory' is invalid: many delusions are 'grandiose' in character, and others have to do with beliefs of 'passivity' (that is the belief that you are being manipulated or operated upon by forces alien to yourself), or with the depressively coloured conviction that you are irrevocably worthless and evil, or that your body has become diseased and corrupt, or undergone bizarre transformations.

Not all delusions show themselves immediately for what they are. The client who believes himself to be visited each night by a messenger from the planet Jupiter travelling in a chariot of fire will not present much diagnostic difficulty; the man who claims his wife is unfaithful may well do. Some wives are unfaithful, some paranoid beliefs revolve around non-existent infidelity. Listen carefully to the whole tale, and wherever possible check it against the objective situation. Remember at all times that, sooner or later, a paranoiac will act on his delusional beliefs – for him, they are true. Listen carefully, ask for clarification, but do not argue. To do so is both discourteous and utterly futile, and will prevent you ever hearing the full story.

HALLUCINATION

An hallucination is an altered sensory awareness which arises in the absence of the external stimulus that normally produces it. Normally, a voice is heard speaking only when the tongue of another person has made the appropriate movements, and we expect that that same voice will be heard at the same time by anyone else present with us who is not deaf. If the voice is hallucinatory, there will be no tongue making movements and those around will hear nothing. The same sort of situation obtains whatever mode of sensory awareness is involved – auditory, visual, or tactile (to list the commonest). There is insufficient space to go into the psychopathology of hallucination: suffice to say that it is a symptom of many conditions (schizophrenia being but one) and that it does not necessarily carry grave clinical significance. Indeed, there are those who would say that it does not necessarily carry *any* clinical significance. Many delusions are, in fact, attempts to explain and come to terms with pre-existing hallucinations ('I believe I am being followed by the police because I hear someone broadcasting my every action'). It is probably rare to be hallucinated and not to have delusional notions (even though one may never express them); it is probably not uncommon to be deluded without ever being hallucinated, which raises the next topic.

## PARANOIA, PARAPHRENIA, AND PARANOID SCHIZOPHRENIA

These terms are in common use. They may or may not identify valid clinical categories. One definition is as follows:

*Paranoia*   A condition in which the delusional beliefs occur without hallucination and in connection with which there is no personality deterioration.

*Paraphrenia*   A condition in which the delusional beliefs are accompanied by vivid hallucinatory experiences, but without any great degree of personality deterioration.

*Paranoid schizophrenia*   A condition in which the obvious delusions and hallucinations are but part and parcel of a schizophrenic illness, leading to marked personality deterioration.

It has already been said that there is no such thing as a perfect classification!

## The affective psychoses

'Affect' means that which has to do with 'mood' – the very basic biological process by which the 'pleasure' of biologically successful behaviour tends to be repeated (to the advantage of the individual and of the race of which he is a unit), and the 'pain' of biologically unsuccessful behaviour tends not to be. A very primitive mechanism indeed – we share it with earthworms. An 'affective psychosis' is a condition in which the dominant feature is an irrational and unacceptably intense 'mood-change', either, and in practice more commonly, towards the 'pain-ful' state of misery (that is, depression) or towards that of elation (that is, mania). As its name suggests, 'manic-depressive' illness envisages both extremes of mood occurring, at different times, in the same person; but not all depressive illnesses are of this type, and those that occur as over-intensive 'reactions' to genuine adversity may be of a different order of things. Certainly, people who have experienced both have no difficulty in distinguishing the one from the other.

Five considerations call for the urgent attention of any social worker:

1 Depressive psychosis produces a profound change in the whole personality of the sufferer. It can radically affect physical health, and carries a substantial risk of suicide.
2 The combination of anti-depressive medication and ECT offers real prospect of betterment but, at the height of the illness, the afflicted person may feel so worthless, defeated, and hopeless as to see no point in seeking help.
3 Most psychotic depressions are essentially endogenous – they arise from causes that have nothing to do with external, environmental events (although such events may precipitate, and colour, the surface manifestations). It follows, therefore, that they will not be significantly helped by an alteration of the external environment, and attempts to do this may create more problems than are solved. To change jobs as a means of overcoming a depression is a pointless gesture if the dissatisfaction with it stems from a depressive illness rather than from any basic problem in the job itself. On the other hand of course, a depression which is a genuine reaction to environmental adversity (that is which is exogenous) may be much alleviated by suitable modification of circumstance. However, all too often the state of affairs that caused the reaction does not lend itself to modification (such as bereavement).
4 The clinical picture of depression may in some people be dominated by bodily discomfort and dysfunction, rather than by mental anguish. There exist, indeed, profoundly depressed patients whose smiling faces effectively mask the true state of affairs.
5 In addition to the misery (which may be a blank apathy or an incessant agitation) most depressives will describe loss of interest in all that previously enthused them, much difficulty in taking decisions, disturbed sleep, diminution of sexual appetite and aptitude, feelings of guilt out of all proportion to wrongdoing (if any), and a host of bodily aches, pains, and malfunctionings. It is an all-pervading symptomatology; do not over-emphasize the importance of actual sadness. And do not ask depressed clients to take difficult decisions: they can't. Likewise, do not accept a depressive's judgement of his actual situation, it is likely to be adversely affected by his altered mood.

The elation of mania is an easier thing to recognize, and the accompanying overactivity, the 'expansive' and 'grandiose' thinking and conduct, the inability to sustain concentration, make an almost immediate impact. Even the lesser state of hypomania soon becomes apparent. Very few people come to have their elations treated; almost all are brought to the attention of doctors or social workers by long-suffering relatives or friends whose patience has been exhausted. The substance Lithium, now used in the treatment of any affective disorder which swings between the two extremes (the term 'bi-polar' is useful in this context), found its initial use in the treatment of the manic phase of manic-depressive illness. But a well-developed manic patient will need to be admitted to hospital, usually against his vigorously expressed wishes, in order to permit skilled nursing and the administration of psychotropic drugs which (even if he condescended to take them at all) lie outside the scope of domiciliary care. Be wary of accepting the good intentions expressed during a phase of elation – through no fault of the patient, they are unlikely to persist. And remember that the elation can quickly change to potentially dangerous anger in the face of minimal frustration.

## The neurotic illnesses

In the context of the ASWs' involvement in mental health legislation, neurotic illness plays a much smaller role than psychosis. However much undoubted suffering and anguish they produce, neurotic illnesses very rarely need or permit compulsory hospital admission – although it should be remembered that being neurotic is no insurance against becoming psychotic; the two conditions are not mutually exclusive.

Traditionally, and still validly, the neurotic states are held to comprise the following: anxiety, obsessional, and hysterical states.

## The anxiety states

Without doubt the commonest of the neuroses, and indeed, perhaps the commonest of all psychiatric illnesses, an anxiety state manifests itself in two interlocking ways, psychologically and physically (or, more correctly, 'somatically').

### THE PSYCHOLOGICAL MANIFESTATIONS

Basically, one is frightened, but the fear is 'irrational' in that there is no external danger, and therefore no escape-behaviour into which the energies released by the fear can be channelled. This fear tends to show itself in one of two inter-connected modes:

*Generalized or 'free-floating' anxiety* In which any of the potentially threatening events of everyday life (if only read about in a newspaper or overheard in casual conversation) becomes a focus for fearful appre-hension which, when assuaged by medical advice or friendly counsel, is speedily replaced by some other source of worry – 'I am greatly relieved, doctor, that you tell me I have not got a brain tumour; would you please have a look at my heart.'

*Situational or 'phobic' anxiety*  In which the fear, amounting at times to unendurable and blind panic, is triggered off by specific objects or situations. It is to the Greek word for these objects and situations that the suffix '-phobia' is commonly added, thereby producing an impressive list of what can be mistaken for separate illnesses. Common sense alone dictates that one keeps away from situations likely to produce overwhelming panic, and thus phobic anxiety almost inevitably results in the emergence of 'phobic-avoidance' reactions, which can at times radically alter for the worse the ability to lead a normal life.

In both these manifestations sleep tends to be disturbed by the appearance, in the form of dreams, of the emotional conflicts underlying the anxiety: a conflict which, even in the dream, disguises itself in the symbolisms associated with psychoanalytical theory. Occasionally the emotions spill over into muscular movements, and somnambulism (sleepwalking) and 'fugue-states' emerge, although against the total numbers involved this is not common.

THE PHYSICAL MANIFESTATIONS

The raised pulse rate, beating heart, altered requirements of bladders and bowels, nausea, sweating, muscular tensions – these more obvious accompaniments of fear do not need elaboration. In the presence of external danger attention is so focused on appropriate 'flight or fight' reactions that these entirely proper physiological changes pass almost unnoticed; in the absence of such external danger they assume a major role in consciousness. If they are then misinterpreted as indicating the existence of pathological illness the scene is set for still further fear to be added to the picture, thereby augmenting the physiological changes, thereby confirming the suspicion of illness, and so on *ad infinitum*.

In many instances it is these somatic manifestations that dominate the clinical presentation. And in this respect one point must be made clear: the disease from which the patient may believe himself to be suffering can be thought of as 'imaginary', *but* the physical symptoms that have led him to that belief *cannot*. It is possible to imagine you have a bad heart; it is not possible to imagine that you have palpitations.

**The obsessional states**

An 'obsession' is an irrationally repetitive thought which is recognized as irrational but which grows stronger the more one attempts to ignore it. A 'compulsion' is the same situation applied to an action. Often they go together, and the term 'obsessional–compulsive neurosis' is commonly used for the combination.

One way of looking at the matter is to envisage a forbidden or unaccept-able emotional drive seeking expression by attaching itself to some outwardly neutral object which somehow symbolizes, or stands as substitute for, the forbidden one. This neutral object then receives the full force of the diverted emotion, often with incongruous, if not positively bizarre, results. But, as the object is only a substitute, it fails to discharge the emotional energy involved, thereby necessitating repetition. The result may at times assume the appearance of psychotic behaviour, but the sufferer is only too well aware that what is happening is irrational. He may indeed regard himself as 'mad', but his 'insight' protects him from a psychotic label.

## The hysterical states

There is only one safe guide in dealing with the vexed and chaotic topic of hysteria. If the term is to be used at all it should be for those states in which emotional conflicts are, purposively but unconsciously, 'converted' into symptoms of 'disease' by the mental process of 'dissociation'. Such states do exist and can be recognized, which is more than can be said for many of the other pieces of human misconduct to which the term has been applied.

The key to understanding the actual conversion is to remember that it is the patient's idea of what constitutes disease (in the widest sense) that determines what happens, not the doctor's. The leg that is totally para-lysed but which moves when its patellar tendon is tapped, or the eye that can see nothing but whose pupil reacts briskly when light is played upon it, are examples. Because the conversion can be thought of as having provided, albeit at an exorbitant price, some solution to the underlying conflict, hysterical patients often show remarkable sang-froid in the face of sometimes appalling disability (the 'belle indifference' of the text books). It would, however, be wrong to imply that the sufferer likes being as he is or that he has deliberately engineered his own predicament. Motive there may be, but it is unconscious.

It is not necessary for the conversion to result in purely somatic dis-ability; hysterical amnesias do occur, as do the rare but intriguing 'multiple personalities' in which – by a process of massive dissociation of mental activity which is probably not available to all of us – the conversion has resulted in a realignment of basic personality components.

## Clinical management of neurosis

Theoretically, and if there were time and opportunity, it would be pleasant to envisage all neurotic illnesses being tackled psychotherapeu-tically, with the basic emotional conflicts being identified and subse-quently resolved by adult readaptations to the conflictual drives. In practice, most neurotics need to be content with symptomatic relief obtained from one or other of the many 'tranquillizing' drugs now available, and in many instances the relief will be substantial. It is easy to deride the swallowing of Valium and Librium – and, like anything else, they can be abused – but the derision tends to come from those who are not themselves neurotic. The 'de-conditioning' techniques of the behavioural psychologist offer real benefit to some anxiety states, but are not always readily available; and superficial psychotherapy (of a simple explanatory type) may have wider uses than perhaps is given credit for.

## Psychopathy

In the Mental Health Act 1983 the concept of *psychopathic disorder* is defined with legalistic rigidity, and needs to be equally rigidly adhered to: the term 'psychopathic disorder' should not be used to indicate anything else. But, if it is so used, then the bulk of what are casually regarded as 'psychopaths' will fall outside that definition. Psychopathic disorder is but a fraction of the total field to which most of us would apply the term *psychopathic personality*, and the two need to be kept separate in the mind of anyone concerned with administering current legislation. The term 'psychopathy' has some use in denoting the whole of the clinical phenomena of which the 'disorder' and the 'personality' are elements.

It would, however, be a brave individual who claimed to be able to delineate these phenomena with any exactitude; the topic is a contentious one both in respect of what it should include and of what are its origins and causes. On a purely descriptive level the old tag that a psychopath is 'not subnormal, not psychotic, not neurotic – but not right' does at least remind us that the original concept was that of a 'moral imbecile' whose anti-social and amoral conduct was held to be a central characteristic of the clinical picture (loud echoes of which are to be encountered in the 'abnormally aggressive or seriously irresponsible conduct' phraseology of current legislation). Like the hippopotamus, a psychopath may be much easier to recognize than to describe.

It may be helpful to think of a psychopathic personality as one which shows traits and features that, while of the same kind as those we all possess, are so altered (in a statistical rather than a pathological sense) they have become either abnormally active or abnormally dormant. This has the advantage of avoiding theories of causation as part of the definition; psychopathic traits can be regarded as arising from genetic factors or as the result of psychodynamic maladjustments during formative years due to a variety of environmental and interpersonal adversities, or as a combination of both. It may of course be the case that our present concept of 'psychopathy' comprises conditions of a radically differing nature, and that no single explanation will cover all cases.

Bear in mind that, although by common consent 'psychopathy' is not 'psychosis', there is nothing whatsoever to prevent a psychopath suffering from psychotic illness. Likewise, many psychopaths show neurotic features, and vice versa. The total clinical picture of mental disorder can be simple and straightforward; it can also be a complex amalgam of many elements.

There remains another aspect of human behaviour, which is thought of as 'medical' but which, rather like 'psychopathy', does not fit easily into our categories of mental disorder: the matter of alcoholism and drug dependence/addiction.

## Alcoholism

Biochemically, alcohol is a slow-acting cerebral poison which puts out of action the more recently acquired mental functions before those of a more primitive nature. As most of the former are intellectual and inhibitory in character, the result of drinking alcohol is to release from control our basic drives and desires, thereby producing behaviour patterns and attitudes that are more spontaneously primitive and uninhibited than normal to the particular individual, while at the same time reducing self-criticism. This is why most of us drink it, and it is foolish to deny that it has its uses, and its pleasures.

The actual behaviour that then emerges is a reflection of the individual, not anything specific to the alcohol. Some of us will laugh, some weep; some will become aggressive, others lustful, some will just go to sleep; loosened tongues will tell normally guarded secrets – *in vino veritas* – and loosened muscles will do things normally not done (however much they may have been contemplated in private). But whatever happens, it only happens because some aspect of the brain has been inactivated by what is an agent of destruction.

At some stage in this process – the timing of it varies widely because of what are probably genetically determined differences in the body's ability to 'detoxicate' the alcohol – at some stage, the pleasures and advantages that were initially derived will be rendered unimportant by the emergence of the ill-understood phenomenon of addiction. At this stage an individual is no longer drinking because he wishes to but because he must; not to do so causes distressingly unpleasant, and potentially lethal, withdrawal symptoms. He is 'hooked', and widespread deterioration in physical health, in mental acuity, in social and occupational functioning, and in moral sensibility will ensue. Indeed, much of this may have started beforehand, but the addiction will set the seal on it.

For some alcoholics the support and therapeutic techniques of Alcoholics Anonymous provide a life-line which nothing else can; others prefer the more clinical approach of therapeutic groups run by various bodies both within and outside the NHS. For yet others the use of substances (such as Antabuse) which when mixed with alcohol in the human body produce effects of great unpleasantness but are otherwise inert, offers a safeguard at least against impulsive drinking. Many will need admission to hospital for periodic drying-out (detoxication under conditions which minimize the risk of withdrawal symptoms, and permit the replacement of depleted vitamins more effectively than can be achieved by oral medication), and very many will require counselling in respect of their shattered social lives. Some, of course, will add to their problems by falling foul of the law because of uninhibited behaviour or because of theft committed to finance the drinking.

## Drugs

Sedative drugs (such as the barbiturates) produce an effect which is basically comparable with alcohol, and although the highly addictive opiates (morphine, heroin, and their derivatives) produce a pleasantly euphoric lifting of mood they, too, are fundamentally narcotic (i.e. sleep-inducing) agents, in spite of their very useful analgesic (i.e. pain-reducing) effects.

Others (such as the relatively mild cannabis derivatives, and not so mild amphetamines, and the far from mild cocaine type of substances) produce a stimulant and euphoric effect. Still others (of the hallucinogenic group which includes lysergic acid, mescaline, and psilocybin) cause marked disturbance of mental functioning with, as their name suggests, vivid visual and auditory hallucination as a prominent feature.

What all of them offer, at any rate initially, is a blurring of reality and/or a heightening of fantasy which appeals to those whose lives are without aim or meaning, or are environmentally unpleasant. There is much evidence linking drug abuse with personality disorders to which the term psychopathic is appropriate but, once a drug-scene is established, many will be drawn into it by the pressure of peer groups, amongst which refusal to experiment may result in loss of status. The end result may be frank (though often reversible) psychosis; it will certainly be an inefficient life of social degradation, and for many there will be the need to turn to crime as the only way of obtaining their supplies, either by stealing the stuff directly from doctors' surgeries or chemist shops, or by stealing money with which to buy it 'on the street'.

With support and sympathetically firm supervision, some drug-abusers may be weaned away from their drug, either abruptly ('cold-turkey') or slowly and with the aid of intermediate substitute substances. For many, though, it is more often a matter of ensuring that supplies are obtained from (and to that extent regulated by) some authorized source. In any case, whatever is attempted, it can only be with the co-operation of the addict; there is no provision at law for the compulsory treatment either of alcohol or of drug dependence. Why this should be is an intriguing matter for private speculation.

### Suggested reading

Curran, D., Partridge, M., and Storey, P. (1975) *Psychological Medicine*. Edinburgh: Churchill Livingstone.

Sim, M. (1981) *Guide to Psychiatry*. Edinburgh: Churchill Livingstone.

Trick, K. L. K. and Obcarskas, S. (1983) *Understanding Mental Illness and its Nursing*. London: Pitman.

Leigh, D., Pare, C. M. B., and Marks, J. (1972) *Encyclopaedia of Psychiatry*. London: Roche Products Ltd.

Priest, R. G. (ed.) (1982) *Psychiatry in Medical Practice*. Plymouth: Macdonald & Evans.

Trethowan, Sir W. and Sims, A. C. P. (1983) *Psychiatry*. London: Baillière Tindall.

# 6

# Social perspectives
# of mental disorder

## M. Rolf Olsen

Fisher *et al.*, in their study, *Mental Health Social Work Observed* (Fisher, Newton, and Sainsbury 1984), concluded, 'With few exceptions, social work practice was not directly concerned with the alleviation of the mental health problem; rather, effort was directed at ameliorating the environmental stresses associated with it.' ' "Amelioration" took several forms: the provision of practical services and financial or material help; liaison, co-ordination or advocacy designed to facilitate the provision of help from other agencies, or to improve communication and understanding with some of the client's social relationships; and the provision of advice or information to the client or to other family members' (p. 193). Whilst the value of this ameliorative work is noted, the authors reach the important conclusion that such work 'fails to contribute to the resolution of underlying problems or to prevent the recurrence of social difficulties. Thus it tends, in effect, to perpetuate needs, so that social work resources become absorbed in long-term and aimless work to the exclusion of new referrals' (p. 193). The authors attribute this failure to a variety of factors, including client expectations, lack of training in therapeutic skills, and lack of confidence in working with the mentally disordered. Whatever the reasons, the authors were in no doubt that 'there remains a need for a more therapeutically-orientated service' (p. 194).

It is my belief that a more therapeutically orientated social work service is in large part dependent upon a clear understanding of the possible contribution of social factors to the onset, maintenance, and management of mental disorder. The aims of this paper are briefly to consider the questions raised by Fisher *et al*. before moving on to examine the evidence which shows that mental disorder can be interpreted not only according to clinical and psychological perspectives, but also according to social factors and as a consequence of disruptive interactions with others.

## The question of social work

Much of the criticism contained in the findings of Fisher *et al*. relates to the failure of social work to define its objectives, to describe its techniques, to determine its worth, or to measure its effectiveness in meeting stated goals. The severity of the resulting criticism, proffered by the improbable alliance between groups of social administrators, sociologists, doctors, and the *Daily Telegraph*, has taken the profession by surprise and the effect on the individual worker is serious. It compounds the stress felt by many workers constantly faced with large-scale human need and misery, without institutional support, public approval, adequate knowledge and skills, sufficient resources, and the mechanisms developed by the established professions for protecting their members. The result is that the morale of social workers is low, individuals are despondent and bedevilled with a deep sense of frustration and hopelessness; the loss of confidence makes many unwilling to experiment and to announce their achievements; blame is indiscriminately attributed to colleagues and to the hierarchy; overall there is a feeling of powerlessness when attempting to respond to the hurts and privations of their clients; many have taken flight.

Of course the denouncements can be considered in a number of ways: not least that the case upon which the criticism is based has yet to be established; that they are the result of the particular obligation placed upon social workers to represent and advocate on behalf of people who often do not fulfil or respect normal social expectations; in the fact that the question of social work in terms of the complexity of the tasks it undertakes cannot yet be answered satisfactorily; and because no one has yet succeeded in reducing the mass of variables to order, or produced a basic system of classification (for a further discussion of these issues see Olsen 1980). More particularly, however, is the failure of social work to promote a rigorous investigation into the potential contribution of social factors in the aetiology/development and management of mental disorder.

The result is that much contemporary social work responds to frequently changing theoretical fashions, organizational change, and financial and political policies, with the consequence reported by Fisher *et al*. (1984).

## The social perspectives of mental disorder

In spite of these doubts the answers to the question of social work with the mentally disordered should remain optimistic. Whilst social work has no 'Morrison's Pill for curing the maladies of Society' (Carlyle 1843), we have at least made the issue explicit, and recent research suggests that we need not remain ensnared in inherited solutions. I want to discuss four of the main hopeful areas of investigation which indicate the importance of social factors in mental disorder and suggest the potential efficacy of social work in its management.

### THE EFFECT OF THE LIVING GROUP ON MENTAL DISORDER

For the past twenty-five years it has been thought that the readmission of psychiatric patients is related to the type of living group that the patient went to on discharge. To test this hypothesis Brown, Carstairs, and Topping (1958), and Brown (1959), in a study of 156 discharged long-stay male schizophrenic patients, found that the liability to return to hospital was related to the type of living group to which the patient went, and to the amount of contact with others at home.

Brown, Monck, Carstairs, and Wing (1962) designed another study to examine these findings further by testing two hypotheses:

1 'That a patient's behaviour would deteriorate if he returned to a home in which, at the time of discharge, strongly expressed emotion, hostility, or dominating behaviour was shown towards him by a member of the family.'

and

2 'That, even if a patient returned to such a home, relapse could be avoided if the degree of personal contact with the family was small.'

A group of 128 male schizophrenics, aged between 20 and 49 years, was followed up for one year after discharge, or at the time of readmission if the patient returned to hospital before the end of the year. During the year, 55 per cent deteriorated, and three-quarters of these were readmitted at least once.

The first hypothesis, 'that patients returning to a high emotional involvement would deteriorate more frequently than those returning to low emotional involvement', was confirmed. Of the patients who returned to high emotional involvement, 76 per cent deteriorated in behaviour compared with 28 per cent of those who went to a low involvement. The statistical significance persisted when readmission to hospital was used as an alternative criterion of outcome.

The second hypothesis, 'that less deterioration would occur in high emotional involvement homes if the amount of contact was small', was also confirmed in patients who were moderately or severely disturbed on discharge. My own research (Olsen 1976b) and that of others supports these findings and conclusions.

## SOCIAL FACTORS IN PRECIPITATING BREAKDOWN

These avenues of research led to further consideration of the significance of life events as precipitators of breakdown. Brown and Birley (1968) demonstrated such a link by investigating the life events preceding the hospital admission of a group of schizophrenics compared with a sample of people working in factories. Subjects in the study and control groups were asked about events that had taken place in the 13-week period prior to admission or interview. Included in the list of events were change of job or home for subject or close member of family, deaths, marriages, disappointments, and fulfilment of goals. The results were highly significant and led the authors to conclude that key social factors can precipitate a breakdown. It also emerged that regular medication did not appear to prevent relapse in certain stressful situations, though it may help to delay it.

## THE EFFECT OF LIVING IN FAMILIES WITH HIGH EXPRESSED EMOTION

During the study Brown and Birley (1968) also noted that the amount of tension in the living group appeared to affect the course of schizophrenic illness, and that patients admitted from homes experiencing 'long-term tension' were much more likely to have experienced a life event during the three weeks prior to the onset of the illness. To test this suspicion they joined Wing to conduct a further study designed to test the hypothesis that 'a high degree of expressed emotion is an index of the characteristics in the relatives which are likely to cause a florid relapse of symptoms, independently of other factors' (Brown, Birley, and Wing 1972). Using a formalized interview schedule which rated the emotional response to a series of questions of relatives, both by content and form of speech, they found a significant association between relapse and being a member of a high expressed emotion (EE) family. Also, the deterioration was particularly marked where the patient spent more than thirty-five hours per week in face-to-face contact with his relatives.

Vaughn and Leff (1976) replicated this work and found that their findings closely matched those of the earlier study. They also found that unmarried male schizophrenics were the most vulnerable. Such men were most likely to have stopped taking medication, to have more than thirty-five hours' contact per week with their families, and were twice as likely to relapse as women. They also showed that of those patients who had become socially withdrawn or who avoided their families, two-thirds were found to be well at follow-up.

## SOCIAL ORIGINS OF DEPRESSION

Brown and Harris (1978) in a meticulous sociological study of the part played by psycho-social influences in depression in women provided further evidence of the importance of key-variables, or 'provoking agents', in mental disorder. But other psycho-social factors involving more fundamental aspects of a woman's life, also emerged as vital determinants of her vulnerability to these events. The vulnerability factors are:

1  Loss of mother before the age of 11 years.
2  Three or more children in the family under 14 years of age.
3  The lack of a confiding partner.
4  The lack of paid employment.

It was found that working-class women were four times more likely to present with a depressive illness than middle-class women. This difference in incidence is accounted for by the greater probability of working-class women experiencing vulnerability factors. Brown and Harris conclude that these life experiences can predispose or protect a woman in relation to the impact of stressful life events.

## Unemployment and mental disorder

The research into the value of work and occupation in the institutional management and rehabilitation of psychiatric patients, particularly chronic patients, has a long history. Most researchers agree that occupational rehabilitation is of value in improving symptoms and behaviour of patients in hospital, although there is evidence that suggests that progress is not maintained once the stimulation of work or occupational therapy is removed.

After the Second World War the British interest in work and occupational therapy led to a number of experiments which contributed to the understanding of the needs of the long-stay patient, and stimulated an optimism in his rehabilitation. This optimism was confirmed in a number of studies (notably Carstairs, O'Connor, and Rawnsley 1956; Baker 1956; Wittkower and Tendresse 1955; Wing and Giddens 1959; Wing and Freudenberg 1961) and by Donald Early (1960) through his success in providing employment in factory-like conditions within the Industrial Therapy Organization (Bristol), set up in 1958.

The significance of employment in the successful discharge of short-stay and long-stay psychiatric patients, schizophrenic in particular, has also been evaluated by a number of researchers. A number support the conclusion reached by Mandelbrote and Folkard, in a paper that considered the social outcome and adjustment of 288 schizophrenics referred to a psychiatric service, that 'The achievement of a satisfactory work perform-ance is one of the primary aims in the rehabilitation of psychiatric patients' (Mandelbrote and Folkard 1961: 232).

Stringham (1952), in a follow-up of thirty-three male patients discharged after at least 4½ years' continuous hospital care, felt that gainful employment and being self-supporting were important factors in half of the successful cases.

Cohen, in a study designed to examine the relationship between work and rehospitalization, found that 'having a job to go to, and having a crystallised vocational plan, are both (significantly) related to remaining out of the hospital', and that 'those who obtained employment remained out of hospital longer than those who did not obtain employment' (Cohen 1955: 31).

Monck, in her description of the employment experiences of 127 male schizophrenics, one year after discharge, considered that whilst,

'The results of this study cannot be used to show that the fact of being employed favourably affected the frequency or severity of symptoms shown by the patients in the home; nevertheless, it was observed that for a small proportion of the patients employment was a necessary condition of staying out of hospital.'

(Monck 1963: 109)

The evidence clearly shows the gains to be made by successfully placing patients in employment or occupation, not least in providing the patient with the opportunity to re-establish his identity as a person, which gives structure and purpose to his life, provides ego satisfaction, social status, and financial reward, and improves the morale of relatives.

## Conclusions

The importance of the research into the significance of social factors, interpersonal relationships, life events, and employment in the onset and maintenance of mental disorder, is apparent for the social worker. How-ever, the findings must be interpreted with caution. Whilst at first sight the association appears compelling, it might be coincidental or non-specific, it may also be mainly due to a retrospective conclusion that the event was important to the subsequent disorder, or social factors might have been experienced as significant or stressful simply because the patient was already ill at the time. On the other hand, attempts to over-come the methodological problems, particularly by the use of control groups and by attempts to separate out events that are independent of the illness, and responses of healthy individuals to the same experiences suggest that, whilst the evidence is not yet complete, it accurately describes many of the situations told by the clients of social workers, and is sufficiently strong to indicate the 'facts' which the social worker should look for.

The question is, where should the social worker start looking for 'facts' capable of determining or influencing the onset of mental disorder? This brief summary of some of the current lines of investigation provides important clues on how we should proceed in the collection and recording of data, indicates our therapeutic priorities, and suggests the most appropriate design and provision of services. Hudson convincingly argues that the social worker occupies 'a unique position to amass the sorts of knowledge which could influence the services which clients receive' (Hudson 1982: 174). But as found by Fisher et al. (1984) such opportunities are currently squandered with the result that too often social workers at best rely on informed intuition to guide their understanding and actions. The result is that the meeting between client and worker is often no more than contact in which the client is unaware of the social work aims or purpose, and the worker fails to state objectives or to measure outcome.

Social work in general, and the ASW in particular, must promote an understanding of mental disorder which is rooted first in social perspectives and second in epidemiological study of the distribution of their clients in terms of such key factors as age, sex, social class, occupations, living group, ethnic origin, etc., in the tradition of Durkheim's study (1952) which attempted to demonstrate the social causality of depression.

# 7

# A critical appraisal
# of the medical model
# in psychiatry

*Brian Sheldon*

Calls for better inter-professional co-operation in the field of mental health
– the callers usually glaring admonishingly at the called – are now so
frequent as to go almost unheard by those who are supposed to respond.
Not that the issues are unimportant from the patient's point of view. There
are very few studies indeed that show a single profession achieving better
results than when it acts in concert with other relevant disciplines. The
sense of resignation has more to do with the widespread assumption that
all that is required is willpower. In fact, the distortion of social service
priorities created by the scandal-hungry popular press over child abuse
and the different pattern of theoretical assumptions about insanity held by
psychiatrists and social workers, stand as serious and definite obstacles to
co-operation. The first problem has been well aired but remains intractable, the second we may be able to do something about, since many of our
differences are based upon misapprehensions. We could at least begin by
looking our differences in the eye, examining their origins, and seeing
whether our respective points of view have any empirical backing. This is
the purpose of this chapter. It is an attempt to clear the ground of myths
and stereotypes to see whether a new basis for inter-professional co-
operation could emerge out of research into the nature of mental disorder.

## The medical model: origins and effects

Mention the 'medical model' on a post-experience social work course and you will hear a kind of background hissing once reserved for the characters in black hats in silent movies. Only slightly more restrained reactions occur when social scientists (complete with bulging folders of data on rare Polynesian tribes which apparently prize the hallucinatory experience) and psychiatrists foregather. We come from different places on this issue, as they say in California. Social workers tend to regard the medical model as an over-applied metaphor which has dangerous consequences for civil liberties. However, they are usually forced by circumstances to work within it. Most psychiatrists take it for granted.

Let us look now at the origins of the idea, beginning with its main assumptions:

1 Many forms of mental disorder are physical in origin, but we have not yet discovered their causes. After all, it is not so long ago since patients received psychoanalytic treatment for ulcerative colitis. Similar developments are expected in much of the rest of psychiatry.

2 People who show marked deviations from accepted patterns of behaviour may be regarded as sick; if not in the physical sense, then mentally sick. Such conditions follow a similar pattern to physical illnesses and require a similar approach to diagnosis and treatment, and similar training. It was once fashionable to extend this model to certain categories of social problems. Reiner and Kaufman (1969) linked personality disorders and the various problems of slum life – not the other way round. Mercifully, such excursions into foreign territory are increasingly rare.

3 As a corollary to the above, behavioural symptoms are said to fall into recognizable clusters, and from these patterns it is possible to determine something about the underlying process of causation.

4 The process of diagnosing such disorders can be almost as value free as the process of diagnosing physical disorders and is expected to get better and better.

5 Assessment decisions based on the medical model have an acceptable level of validity in reliability. Syndromes can be clearly identified, and this makes a difference to both treatment and outcome.

6 Direct intervention to deal specifically with symptoms may occasionally have a palliative effect but is more likely to result in the re-emergence of symptoms – perhaps in a more pernicious form. This is the idea of symptom substitution which is supposed to be a limitation on the application of behavioural methods. Medical treatments that seek to isolate and treat the underlying cause run no such risks.

7 The identification of these underlying causal processes and intervention with specific remedies requires a high level of professional expertise,

and are not processes to be meddled in by relatives, 'para-professionals', and 'laymen', although they may have a subsidiary part to play if closely supervised (Brewer and Lait 1980).

This is very broadly how the proponents of the medical model view things. However there are several problems associated with this formulation of abnormal behaviour, whether applied to psychiatric, psychological, or social ailments. The foremost of these is the problem of tautology. While it seems reasonable at first glance to suggest that just as excessive coughing (symptom) may result from a germ-infected larynx (cause), excessive cleanliness (symptom) can similarly be seen to be the result of a 'guilt-complex' (cause); and delusional talk (symptom) can be taken to be merely the outward expression of an underlying 'schizophrenia', things are not this simple. The overriding idea here is that just as biochemical abnormalities in the Islets of Langerhans can result in excess blood sugar and lead to the condition we know as diabetes with all its consequences, so Mrs Brown's 'poor social functioning' can be said to stem in an equally direct way from her 'inadequate personality'. But there is a heavy element of circularity here. In the case referred to above, the existence of the schizophrenia is inferred from the symptom, which is the only evidence in existence. Therefore, Mr Smith's paranoid behaviour is said to be the result of his schizophrenia, which we know he has because of his paranoid behaviour, which is a primary symptom of schizophrenia, and so on. Likewise, Mr Jones's unscrupulous behaviour stems directly from his 'personality disorder', which we know he has because unscrupulous behaviour is one of the main symptoms of personality disorder. Similarly, Mr Hardcastle lacks assertiveness *because* he has an 'inferiority complex'. Now although it may seem on the face of it that we have accomplished something by classifying certain troublesome behaviours as indicative of say a 'neurosis' or an 'inferiority complex', in fact we have achieved very little because naming is not explaining. Unless we can establish testable hypotheses and shed light on a relevant causal sequence we delude ourselves if we think we have done more than roughly to classify. Bandura (1969) indicts this process of circular reasoning about psychological and behavioural problems as having clogged up our thinking on such matters for decades. Macrea's observations are also relevant here:

'A name can act as a myth . . . as the declaration and charter of the readiness to act. Lots of subjects in natural science, as well as social science, begin as names, claims on areas and methods of which we are in fact yet ignorant, promises and programmes to which credence can be attached. And names, too are fences – devices by which people can be excluded as illegitimate trespassers on a territory staked out as private property, even if not, in fact, explored and tested for ore.'

(Macrea 1970: 59)

One of the main effects of the primitive medicalization of problems (which *may* one day turn out to be medical in fact) is to exclude these subjects from the curricula and the research project outlines of other types of investigator. After all, laymen and relatives have little to say about the origins, prognosis, and treatment of acute appendicitis, so, by implication, relatives are given little say in the management of mental disorder. Are relatives and friends to ignore delusional talk when it occurs in the hope that it will die away, or are they to investigate its origins with the sufferer and provide opportunities for him to 'get it off his chest'? Many relatives discover that they have an important part to play only through contact with voluntary organizations and self-help groups such as the Schizophrenia Fellowship.

But the medical model has brought other side effects with it too; in order to understand these, we need to look at its historical context. Its origins lie in the Enlightenment in the eighteenth century, when those concerned with the confinement, control, and, in the case of a few well-off patients (later to include George III), the treatment of lunacy, attempted to bring the problem into the province of science. Other factors included: the desire for a more humane approach to the day-to-day care of the insane (Hogarth's engravings give some idea of the prevailing practices); revulsion at the treatment of witches (Szasz 1971); and a desire to do for the mentally afflicted what medicine was apparently doing for the physically ill. I say apparently, because the really substantial reductions in mortality came later, and were due rather more to the activities of water engineers and public health boards.

Alongside these early hit-and-miss attempts to establish lunacy as a problem worthy of scientific study (a book on the causes of insanity citing masturbation as the main influence went to eighty editions between 1716 and 1764), social reformers such as Conolly in England and Pinel in France fought to improve the appalling physical conditions in which the insane were kept. But the move to have insanity defined as a kind of sickness, though in time bringing with it important humanitarian changes, also introduced a pattern of crude experimentation which was in effect anything but humane.

The mentally disordered became victims of spinning machines (centrifugal force was expected to expel whatever noxious 'humours' the body might be host to); mechanized cold water douches; scalding baths; purging and bleeding; deliberate infection by malarial mosquitoes to induce pyrexia; injection of chemicals (such as camphor) to induce convulsions; overdoses of insulin to induce coma; and more recently, electric shocks to the brain. Now this is not just a random pattern of well-intentioned abuse. If we look closely three trends are discernible:

1   The theme of *shock*, going through a *crisis*, or experiencing a *jolt*, sufficient to bring the patient to his senses, is obviously present. In fact, it pre-dates medical experimentation, and was first advocated in the *malleus malefactorum* (the hammer of witches), a kind of torturers' guide to the extraction of confessions and the expulsion of demons (see Szasz 1971). Advocates of the restorative properties of such violence were to be found well into the nineteenth century: 'Terror acts powerfully on the body through the medium of the mind, and should be employed in the cure of madness', argued the 'reformer' Benjamin Rush in 1812.

2   The disease-entity theme is strongly present. Sociologists and critics have probably made too much of the similarities between theories of demonic possession and modern conceptions of mental illness. However, the general point remains that when the dominant institution in society was the Church, this form of deviancy was interpreted by means of religious explanations. As scientists, and more recently psychiatrists, have come to replace bishops as authorities on normality and abnormality, madness has been understood through a series of medical analogies. In some cases this 'illness' model seems to work quite well, in others our suspicions are sometimes aroused that patterns of deviancy, or problems of living, or – in some societies – politically inconvenient behaviour, are being tidied up with medical explanations. I am writing these paragraphs in Moscow, where the all-pervasiveness of such ideological influences is quite breathtaking. Here dissent against what is so *obviously* in the best interests of the people (whether they know it or not); or against the 'forces of history', becomes itself a sign of psychological abnormality and is treated accordingly. The parallels between psychiatric abuse in the USSR and the excesses of the mediaeval Church, *are* quite striking and the following quotation shows this very clearly. It is a reply by a Soviet psychiatrist from the Serbsky Institute to a question from John Wing on the exact nature of an item in the Soviet diagnostic catalogue: 'delusions of reconstruction and reformation' (or 'Solzhenitsyn's disease', as it might be more economically called). It is given here in the belief that such views deserve all the publicity they get.

> 'The patient thinks it necessary to reform the system of government control in this country. He thinks that he himself is capable of undertaking leadership; that it is necessary to review theoretical problems of social science and that he himself is capable of explaining the theory and practice of Soviet industry and reconstruction. His ideas are so essential (he believes) that he should leave the Soviet Union and disseminate them in all the countries in the world.'

(Wing 1978: 189)

Lest the reader think that this style of thinking is a recent phenomenon,

Peter Chaadayev, a Russian nobleman who, in 1836, wrote an article (in French) suggesting that Russian culture was rather backward, was sent for by a scandalized Tsar and thrown for his heresy not into jail, but into a lunatic asylum (Chaadayev *Memoires of a Madman*).

The point here is that we must be on our guard against the influence of taken-for-granted and natural-seeming assumptions about the origins of deviancy: that delinquents are the products of broken homes; that families *cause* schizophrenia or that the shortcomings and inconsistencies of the role of women in our society are the exclusive cause of depression in females. Such factors may operate to some extent, but ideologies exert a powerful pressure on the 'up to a point' reactions with which we are naturally equipped. Therefore it now seems unarguable to some that a bolt of electricity to the head will be useful in cases of depression. The only trouble is that experimental work comparing real ECT with a fake variety (where only the anaesthetic is given) generally reveals a very substantial placebo effect (see Johnstone *et al.* 1980). Rather than seeing this as a troublesome side effect which gets in the way of valid physical procedures, such influences deserve close investigation in their own right. Yet the physical component (the electricity) would be very hard to give up, as the correspondence columns following the publication of research into its effectiveness show. I venture to say as someone who has taken part in the administration of ECT – kept a clean white coat for the occasion; helped carry unwilling patients to have it for their own good; enjoyed the resuscitation procedures because they were more like what I was trained for (psychiatric nursing) than other routine things (like talking to patients about their worries) – that the reason for the popularity of these ECT machines is that they are the nearest thing mental hospital staff have to the laser scalpel. Therefore, although possibly the technique may have only limited use in certain well-defined types of patients (Royal College of Psychiatrists 1977) its widespread, and rather indiscriminate, use is likely to continue.

3   Psychiatric treatments tend to reflect the state of technological development and the technological preoccupations of their times. This is not only true of physical treatments – the link between psychodynamic notions of repression, symptom substitution, the 'leaking out' of unconscious material and steam-age 'hydraulics', should be obvious. Thus, as we have seen, in the eighteenth century patients were confined, spun, purged, and bled. In the late nineteenth and early twentieth centuries (perhaps as a result of the experiences of empire) they were infected with tropical diseases. In the case of ECT, it was noted that few epileptic patients in captivity seemed to be schizophrenic, and so perhaps the convulsions had a kind of 'purgative effect'. Therefore, when the technology was available, 'fits' were induced, first chemically, and then electrically. When the action

of insulin was understood, it too was pressed into service. After the rough geography of the brain began to be understood, bits were sliced out with rather dubious results (although the position is now rather better). When the physiology of low-level infections carried in the blood from 'septic foci' was understood, whole wards full of patients had their teeth removed. This sequence follows the general drift of scientific development, through Newtonian mechanics; through early experiments with chemical compounds; through an understanding of bacterial and hormonal action; the harnessing of electricity, and so forth. The revolution wrought by the introduction of phenothiazine drugs is the happy exception to this pattern – but it too is now in danger of betrayal through indiscriminate use.

Sometimes these crude technological adaptations are justified on 'empirical' grounds, that is they seem to work, though we do not as yet know why. Examples of physical diseases where this was the case are usually cited in defence of such procedures, but it is usually forgotten that the time-scale in the present case is well outside anything encountered in physical medicine this century. It is true that more recent developments may, in part, justify this experimentation (I use the term loosely, for fashions in the physical treatment of mental illness have, until very recently, had few of the features of genuine experiments). The justification may come from the increased level of understanding, now being obtained through drug trials and biochemical experimentation, of the mechanisms which control mood, and certain aspects of schizophrenic behaviour. The identification of receptors in the brain for many of the compounds commonly employed in psychotropic drugs suggests that pharmacologists are on the right track. However, in general, biochemical research into the origins and treatment of mental disorder has yielded rather disappointing results. Clare (1976) has drawn the attention of psychiatrists to the extent of experimentation in this field, and the low level of concrete results actually obtained, but biochemists themselves confirm his views:

> 'There have been many attempts to identify a biochemical abnormality in the schizophrenic diseases. None to date has stood the test of time, possibly because of the diffuse nature of the schizophrenias, and the extreme difficulty of reaching any agreement over diagnosis.'
>
> (Bender 1975: 143)

More recent developments in this field seem more promising, but gains in understanding are slow because of the complexity of brain chemistry and the enormously labour-intensive nature of such research. In which case, the present mood of 'psychiatric micawberism': the feeling that something biochemical will definitely turn up soon, though understandable, is difficult to defend on empirical grounds.

## Patterns of disease

We must next examine the proposition, implicit to the medical model, that maladaptive and troublesome behaviours fall into well-defined groups. Diagnosis is now no different from any other decision-making process: selective perception, and the necessary human tendency to impose patterns on discrete or even random events, can mislead us into thinking that we are applying objective criteria or merely describing or systematizing 'what is there'. Often, we are guilty of looking for data to confirm our own implicitly held theories about what *should* be there. This is a process not of discovery, but of invention. A classic paper by Heine (1953) demonstrated that the factors accounting for change in psycho-therapy clients, plus many of the details of each case record, could be accurately predicted just by knowing the theoretical leanings of the therapist. Studies of this kind have led many psychologists and socio-logists to view insight-giving therapies and other conversational approaches to the treatment of deviant behaviour, as having more to do with labelling and social conversion (to the therapist's point of view) than they have to do with the resolving of deeply buried conflicts.

In addition to questions of validity, there is the problem of the reliability of the various problem classification schemes built upon the medical model. For example, do psychiatrists, when confronted with the same or very similar case material, assign it to the same broad category? Most of the available research on this topic has been done by psycholo-gists, using psychiatrists and their subjects (see Ullman and Krasner 1969). Research into diagnostic reliability throughout the helping professions has in the past yielded consistently disappointing results. The pattern revealed in *Table 7.1* is typical, and shows levels of concordance between psychiatric observers which fall well short of the level of approxi-mately 80 per cent agreement usually thought necessary.

Another study of diagnostic observation (Temerlin 1968) was based on tape recordings of actors conversing normally. When panels of volunteer psychiatrists and psychologists were asked to assign these people to one of the mental illness categories, they went merrily ahead. Inter-observer ratings were disappointingly low as usual, but, more seriously, only 7.6 per cent of the psychiatrists (n = 95) decided that there were no signs of pathology! Categorizations were strongly influenced by a suggestion of vaguely defined 'mental problems'. The psychologists did better, but barely trained psychologist students did best of all – they knew no better.

However, there are two rather more positive trends at work in this literature. First, investigations into diagnostic reliability conducted here in Britain, show better results (see Kendell 1973). Second, the later the study, generally speaking, the better the reliability ratings. This latter finding is probably due to the increasing use of more systematic

*Table 7.1*  Percentage of agreement among psychiatrists for twelve different categories

| category | number of calls | % agreement |
|---|---|---|
| all categories | 910 | 57 |
| schizophrenics | 170 | 74 |
| mental deficiency | 40 | 73 |
| personality disorder | 205 | 66 |
| chronic brain syndrome | 56 | 66 |
| psychoneurosis | 223 | 56 |
| acute brain syndrome | 40 | 46 |
| psychophysiologic reaction | 25 | 40 |
| manic depressive | 45 | 36 |
| involutional psychotic | 59 | 26 |
| psychotic depressive | 33 | 22 |
| psychotic reaction, other | 4 | 17 |
| paranoid reaction | 10 | 13 |

*Source:* Sandifer, Pettus, and Quale (1964). Copyright 1964 The Williams and Wilkins Co., Baltimore. Reproduced by permission of the publishers.

approaches to the question of diagnosis – paradoxically, pioneered by the Americans with their Diagnostic and Statistical Manual, a kind of check-list of symptoms. We are still left with the conclusion, however, that diagnosing mental disorder is not at all like diagnosing whooping cough. The problem is that some medical personnel have convinced themselves that it is.

A further problem associated with diagnosis is that the treatment procedures applied to various categories are not as differentiated as might be supposed. Great effort is expended in trying to decide what patient X is 'suffering from' when, broadly speaking, the specificity of the diagnosis cannot be met by any parallel specificity in treatment.

The point here is that although social workers would be foolish to disregard the opinions of their medical colleagues, a healthy suspicion about the predictive capacity of the diagnoses attached to the patients who come their way, is no bad thing. Without this we are all in danger of fulfilling our own prophecies.

### The influence of genetic factors

Next to the disease-entity model of mental disorder, social workers have most difficulty with the idea that inherited factors play a large part in causation. The probable reasons for this are as follows:

1 Ideas of fixed and inherited potential or of hyper-sensitivity to environmental stress have a rather 'undemocratic' flavour, which, rightly or wrongly, runs counter to the established values of the profession. Social work depends for its existence upon the (predominantly American) notion that individuals, even those who fail to function as society might wish, nevertheless have a massive, untapped potential. Anything that threatens this view is regarded with great suspicion, and examined (as to some extent it needs to be) in political and sociological terms.

2 The scandal over Sir Cyril Burt's work on intelligence (see Eysenck vs Kamin 1981) has allowed a generation of students to dismiss *all* genetic research. However, research into the genetic patterns underlying certain forms of mental disorder, though it uses similar techniques – twin and adoption studies – is quite a different kettle of fish (see Tsuang and Vandermey 1980).

3 Psychiatrists anxious to counter the sporting environmentalists of the mid-1960s, rather overplayed their hand. The number of methodologically adequate twin studies available then was quite small, and certainly insufficient to justify the claims based on them. Therefore, there was an 'immunization effect' which, unfortunately, has lasted until the present day – even though research of this kind has improved substantially both in quality and quantity.

Separating out the relative contribution of genetics and environment in the production of mental disorder is an extremely difficult business. It has all the problems of the Nature versus Nurture debate which so preoccupied personality and developmental psychologists two or three decades ago. The basic problem is that parents who confer their genes to their offspring usually confer the environment in which they are brought up as well. There are two kinds of research which have tried to separate out these broad influences: developmental research conducted mainly by psychologists; and research into inheritance factors in particular diseases, conducted by geneticists.

Let us look at the psychological variety first. A classic study by Thomas, Chess, and Birch illustrates the scope of this. These authors sought to investigate the hypothesis – favoured by parents everywhere but rather out of fashion in the 1960s when this study was undertaken – that babies are *different* from birth. That is, they arrive in the world already equipped with well-marked temperamental and behavioural predispositions. The reasons given for embarking on such a study will strike a chord with most social workers:

'As physicians . . . we began many years ago to encounter reasons to question the prevailing one-sided emphasis on environment. We found that some children with severe psychological problems had a family upbringing that did not differ essentially from the environment of other children who developed no severe problems. On the other hand, some children were found to be free of personality disturbances although they had experienced severe family disorganisation and poor parental care.'

(Thomas, Chess, and Birch 1968: 1)

After a considerable amount of field work, the authors developed techniques for classifying and analysing behavioural differences in very young children, things such as the extent of motor activity, adaptation to new circumstances, distractability, responsiveness, and so forth. The validity of these observations was checked later by panels of independent adjudicators. They identified nine characteristics that could be scored reliably on a three-point scale (low-medium-high) and found that they could identify 'behavioural profiles' in children as early as two months. They next selected a sample of 141 children whose families were free from serious personal and environmental problems, and carried out tests and observations of the kind described. They then followed up this sample over a period of many years using methods such as: direct observation of children; scheduled interviews with parents; scrutiny of school and other records. They were also at pains to investigate what happened when a particular temperamental style came into conflict with environmental factors. The following pattern of results emerges:

1 The temperamental characteristics of the children remain stable over the years: active outgoing babies tended to grow into active outgoing teenagers.
2 Discrete classification of children into categories such as 'easy', 'slow to warm up', or 'difficult' had considerable predictive value. For example, about 70 per cent of the 'difficult' children developed behavioural problems, whereas only 18 per cent of the 'easy' children did. Similarly, of the 42 children referred by parents for psychiatric help, by far the greatest proportion came from the 'difficult' group, with the next largest proportion coming from the 'slow to warm up' category.
3 Temperamental–environmental clashes were readily understandable in terms of the child's early temperamental profile, and were often reversible once a 'with the grain' environment was produced. For example, active, outgoing, easily distracted children did not do well in very controlled environments, e.g. classrooms run on formal lines. 'Difficult' children had great difficulty over frustration-control in many spheres.
4 Attempts by parents to counter temperamental tendencies were often effective. However, the more established the temperamental tendency, the greater the effort required to modify the environment so as to bring this under control.

The last item points to one of the more interesting features of the Thomas, Chess, and Birch study, namely, its refusal to consider separately the possibilities of genetic *versus* environmental influences. Instead, it stresses the *interaction* between these two sets of variables. It shows how 'difficult' children born into tolerant, caring, patient homes learn to cope with their tendency to fly off the handle; similarly, 'slow to warm up' children could often overcome their reticent behaviour given a higher than usual level of encouragement by parents. Conversely, 'difficult' children born into 'difficult' families inherit a situation of double jeopardy. This study, and others like it, point to the likelihood of personality and temperament being shaped by the constant interplay of innate and external environmental factors. Such conclusions are also very much in line with modern developmental research in psychology and provide as well a model for genetic research into specific forms of mental disorder. Moreover, they are consistent with the work of personality theorists (see Eysenck 1957, 1961) who have attempted to bridge the gap between the two fields; with Eysenck's early (and remarkably robust) findings on the introversion–extroversion continuum of personality (introverts are stimulus-shy, easy-to-condition individuals; extroverts are stimulus-hungry, hard-to-condition individuals) and with the findings of Soviet psychologists (see McLeish 1975) on the influence of excitation and inhibition at the level of nerve cells in the brain. All such research points to an inherited, physiological basis for temperament, and for certain fundamental patterns of behavioural consistency which we call personality. However, it should not be overlooked that these researchers all point to the large influence of environment in modifying such tendencies – notably through learning experiences.

## Patterns of genetic research

We will now consider research designed to elucidate the extent of any genetic component in specific forms of mental disorder. Three main approaches are used: family studies, twin and separated twin studies, and adoption studies.

### FAMILY STUDIES

Consanguinity between particular mental patients and their traceable relatives is used to predict the risk of a given type of mental disorder. Large samples are used, sometimes with control groups of relatives with no members suffering from mental disorder. This type of research investigates whether the closer the biological connection, the greater the risk is of attracting a diagnosis of mental disorder. It provides pointers as to whether mental disorder runs in families, but cannot pinpoint the exact influences. The possibility of a 'cycle of deprivation' or of particular groups of relatives or families coming under the same kinds of environmental stress, cannot be ruled out. However, over large samples, and with detailed statistical work, strong trends supporting the idea of inherited predispositions do emerge.

## TWIN STUDIES

This kind of research takes advantage of the biological fact that whereas *monozygotic* (MZ) twins (identical twins from a single egg) have an identical set of genes, *dizygotic* (DZ) twins (non-identical twins which have developed simultaneously in the same womb, but are the products of two fertilized eggs) have only 50 per cent of their genes in common. If mental disorder does have a strong genetic component, then the brothers or sisters of MZ twin mental patients should run a high risk of attracting a similar diagnosis. In the case of DZ twins, the risk should be approximately half as strong. Here again, the fact that twins also share a similar environment rules out the absolute attribution of any findings to an underlying genetic pattern and the results of these studies must be regarded as suggestive only. If the fact that twins inevitably have a different life experience to children born singly were in any way causal or contributory to the acquisition of mental disorder, then we should expect to find a disproportionate number of twins in the mental health statistics. This is not the case.

## SEPARATED TWIN STUDIES

Studies exist of MZ twins who were separated at birth and reared apart. Such research cancels out the effects that might be due to environment. This is a very strict test of the presence of inherited factors, but the problem is that separated MZ twins are very rare, and consequently samples tend to be small. However, better record-keeping by national authorities means that larger numbers of separated MZ twins are now available for study. Similarly, data from small studies can be 'pooled' and subjected to cross-analysis.

## ADOPTION STUDIES

Adoption studies are the most satisfactory method for measuring the relative impact of genetics and environment on predisposition to mental disorder. Three levels of comparison are possible in such research: between biological parents and adopted-away children; between adopted children and their adoptive parents; and between biological and adoptive parents themselves. The results of studies of this type are important for social workers to know about, not because of what they can *do* with the information, but rather what they might decide not to do on the strength of it. They might decide, for example, not to follow half-baked Laingian notions and look for 'double binds' in the discourse between schizophrenic patients and their relatives, thereby transmitting an unspoken accusation that the relatives somehow caused the condition. A generation of such people have yet to forgive the 'helping professions' for their excursion into 'flower-power' psychiatry in the late 1960s.

## Results from genetic research

*Table 7.2* contains evidence from pooled data studies (collections of research which are then cross-analysed). These reveal MZ/DZ concordances of 45.6 per cent and 13.7 per cent respectively (Tsuang and Vandermey 1980).

*Table 7.2*  Level of risk to relatives of schizophrenics

| relation | risk(%) |
|---|---|
| *first degree relatives* | |
| parents | 4.4 |
| brothers and sisters | 8.5 |
| brothers and sisters, neither parents schizophrenic | 8.2 |
| brothers and sisters, one parent schizophrenic | 13.8 |
| fraternal twin, opposite sex | 5.6 |
| fraternal twin, same sex | 12.0 |
| identical twin | 57.7 |
| children | 12.3 |
| children – both parents schizophrenic | 36.6 |
| *second degree relatives* | |
| uncles and aunts | 2.0 |
| nephews and nieces | 2.0 |
| grandchildren | 2.8 |
| half-brothers/sisters | 3.2 |
| *third degree relatives* | |
| first cousins | 2.9 |
| general population | 0.86 |

*Sources:* Based on figures from Slater and Cowie (1971), Zerbin-Rüdin (1967), and Shields and Slater (1967) after Tsuang and Vandermey (1980).

Results from *Table 7.2* may be interpreted as follows: if schizophrenia is a genetically transmitted disease, we would expect three patterns of family risk to emerge: (a) a higher rate of schizophrenia among relatives than among the general population – this is obviously seen; (b) higher rates among near relatives than among distant ones – this pattern too appears; and (c) in Tsuang and Vandermey's words, 'a striking leap in risk' for children of two schizophrenic parents – this pattern is clearly present (Tsuang and Vandermey 1980: 71–2).

On the basis of this evidence and of other research (for example half-sibling studies which control out pre-natal influences), it is reasonable to conclude that even given the problems of diagnosis and genetics (researchers go to considerable lengths to get these judgements confirmed on stricter criteria than would normally be applied), the schizophrenias have a strong predisposing genetic component. Similar conclusions can

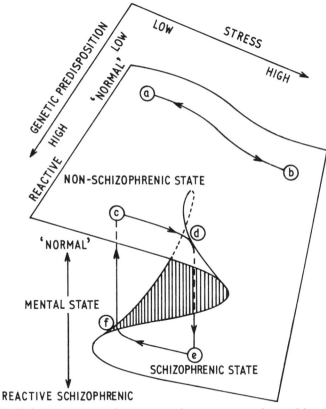

Figure 7.1  Relative impact of genetic and environmental variables in reactive schizophrenia. This model encompasses the suggestion that a high level of genetic predisposition requires only a middling level of environmental precipitation to produce a strong risk of the disorder (c–d–e). Similarly, a middling level of genetic burden requires a high level of precipitating stress to manifest the disease (a–b). When the stress is relieved the patient returns to a period of relative normality (e–f–c). *Source:* From Woodcock and Davis (1978). Reproduced by permission of the publishers.

also be drawn for mood disorders (Winokur 1970), and for alcoholism in males (Goodwin 1976).

However, as with the findings of developmental and personality research, we are talking here about an *interaction* of biological and environmental variables. It should be noted that in the case of schizophrenia, the role accorded to environment approaches 50 per cent. The most convincing attempts at mapping the nature of this interaction have come, not from psychiatrists, but from mathematicians. The three-dimensional graph (*Figure 7.1*) gives some idea of the relationships involved. This diagram needs to be thought of as a piece of paper with a fold in it, and three axes: one along each edge, displaying respectively, genetic and environmental/stress variables; and one *through* the surface of the paper, displaying the level of schizophrenic symptoms and the point of precipitation where the individual, as it were, *slides down* into the disorder.

In the case of neurotic reactions, the role of genetic factors is much less clear cut. It seems likely that in the psychoses a small group of genes interact with environmental stress to precipitate the disorder. In the case of neuroses, such genetic factors as may be present have their influence through a much broader range of emotional and behavioural predispositions – through the personality and temperament of the individual. Here, the most convincing work is that of Eysenck who is clear that the two groups of disorders are quite distinct, and that the neuroses, which may on occasion be equally crippling (though rather more self-limiting in their cause), are problems of living (Eysenck 1976). They are examples of broadly predisposed maladaptive behaviour; in other words, they are largely learnt reactions. Human beings can acquire self-hatred, or profound anxiety in the face of ordinary everyday decisions in exactly the same way as they can learn to tell lies, or to honour their fathers and mothers.

## Environmental variables

In the case of psychotic reactions, the problem in considering the influences that make up the environmental 50 per cent of the equation stems from the fact that the field is rich in conjecture and short on hard evidence. 'Stress' is usually indicted as the villain of the piece, but this is a very broad concept indeed. As shown by Olsen in Chapter 6, two or three pieces of work stand out as exceptions to this rule, including that of Brown, Birley, and Wing (1972) and Vaughn and Leff (1976). These attempts to refine the nature of stress and particularly family stress and its association with precipitation and relapse, have resulted in the concept of *expressed emotion*. Empirical work so far confirms broadly that emotional over-stimulation, or the overloading of individuals whose genetic make-up makes them hypersensitive to such influences, stands in direct relationship to the rate and intensity of relapse.

## Implications for social work

On the basis of the trends and evidence reviewed in this chapter, it seems appropriate to conclude here that the psychoses are a group of disorders possessing a considerable biological component and are therefore worth considering as mental illnesses in the true sense. Social workers are dealing here with a group of vulnerable people and their hard-pressed relatives, who require not only patience and understanding, but also an active approach to the *management* of their problems. A useful parallel can be drawn here between psychotic and stroke patients. Patients suffering cerebro-vascular accidents as a result of primarily physical causes, can none the less have their condition exacerbated by environmental stresses. They benefit not only from medical treatment, but also can have their recovery speeded (or hindered) by the quality of rehabilitative and after-care services they receive.

In the case of a psychosis there is a clear role for social workers, as providers of social support for patients and their relatives, and as people who can offer advice on how best to control the living situation of patients so as to minimize the risk of relapse. Evidence also suggests that careful attention to precipitating factors in families may also help to prevent the emergence of symptoms in the first place. Therefore there is a preventative role too and the re-emergence of schemes that attach social workers to health centres and GPs' surgeries may mean that they are once again well placed to do some good at any early stage (Ashurst and Ward 1980).

As for neutroic disorders, the field is wide open. There is a place here for social workers to develop a primary therapeutic role alongside the other helping professions. The evidence for behavioural approaches in work of this kind is very compelling indeed (see Rachman and Wilson 1980).

The clearer view that is emerging from empirical research of exactly what we are dealing with in the field of mental disorder, ought to make effective inter-professional co-operation more possible by inhibiting tendencies to medical, and for that matter, social, 'imperialism'. Were we to learn to take practical experimentation as our reference point in sorting out our demarcation disputes then power would lie with the rational majority in all our professions.

# 8

# Perspectives of mental handicap

## Derek Thomas[1]

This chapter is about people we call 'mentally handicapped', their needs and the kinds of services they require, but it is also about the rest of the community and the changes we will have to make if those with a mental handicap are to become valued members of society.

Despite the evidence of MIND (1978) and others arguing the exclusion of mental handicap from this legislative provision, people with a mental handicap have *not* been excluded from the Act. Consequently, a person with a mental handicap who *also* shows other kinds of 'abnormally aggressive' or 'serious irresponsible' conduct may be legally classified as 'mentally impaired' and compulsorily detained or admitted to guardianship. ASWs will have the powers and obligations outlined in Chapter 3 which relate to all categories of mental disorder. If they are to exercise independent judgement, and discharge their very important responsibilities fairly to the handicapped person and the community, they will need to develop knowledge and skills through generic and specialized practice.

This chapter is therefore addressed primarily to ASWs or those preparing for the official examination. However, it should also be of value to other social workers who may need to refer to an ASW, contribute to an

---

[1] I would like to acknowledge the help of Margaret Turner and Frances Brown in the preparation of this chapter.

assessment, or provide the mandatory follow-up services now required for those discharged from a compulsory treatment order (Section 3).

As with the Mental Health Act 1959 there are implicit and explicit expectations that care should be provided wherever possible in a community setting and that for each person efforts should be made to develop the 'least restrictive alternative'. It is clear therefore that neither the ASW nor the social services departments are expected simply to wait for crises and then to organize admissions to hospital. The Mental Health Act 1983 is an opportunity for social services departments and social work practitioners to undertake a radical review of the ways in which they provide services to handicapped people. Even when crises occur, it is important that social services departments begin to develop a capacity to offer alternatives to compulsory admission to hospital. Social services departments could have a central role in the provision of high-quality, cost-effective services and in creating positive changes in public and professional attitudes toward those with a mental handicap.

The purpose of this chapter is not to tell social workers 'how to do it' – such learning is essentially experiential – but to provide some per-spectives which will help social workers to be aware of the excitement and challenge that can be involved in working with mentally handicapped people, their families, and the community. It also touches on some of the practical issues which the ASW is likely to encounter in interviewing those with a mental handicap and in deciding on the best course of action following incidents of 'aggression' or 'irresponsible' behaviour.

## The developing policy context

Most of the community-based services in England and Wales today and the significant reduction in the number of people living in mental handicap hospitals, are directly attributable to two major policy initiatives.

The first entitled Better Services for the Mentally Handicapped, published as a White Paper (DHSS 1971a), argued for a major shift away from sub-regional hospital care to care in the community. It set, for the first time, definite targets for residential and day services places to be achieved over 15–20 years. This central initiative, backed as it was with promises of capital and revenue finance, can be seen largely as a response to the mounting criticism of institutions from research studies, journal-istic exposés, and complaints by parents and concerned citizens. These resulted in a number of Public Inquiries, whose reports were well publicized. Here was a good example of a 'climate for change' being created by a small number of people and events.

Subsequent ministerial decisions to establish a multi-disciplinary team in 1975, the National Development Group 'to provide advice to the

Secretary of State on policy and strategy' and a National Development Team to advise field authorities, were political decisions within the 'Better Services' framework to sustain the momentum for change towards community-based services. It was also intended that they would promote better practice in both existing and new services and collaboration between health authorities and the local authorities.

The second initiative, which occurred in 1970, was the implementation of an Education Act which made 'education' a right to *all* children in England and Wales. No child could now be regarded as 'ineducable' or 'unsuitable for education'. Consequently, the education of those who previously had been left at home, together with those attending junior training centres or hospital schools, became the responsibility of the Department of Education and Science (DES) and local education departments. However, whilst this Act recognized a right to education it did not propose a right to special education in ordinary schools. It also perpetuated the idea of two qualitatively different kinds of people, mildly handicapped and severely handicapped. Within education the main development occurred seven years later through the Warnock Committee's Report (DES 1978) and the subsequent Education Act 1981 which introduced the idea of special educational needs, removed the categories ESN(S) and ESN(M) (educationally subnormal severe/mild).

The consequences of these two major policy developments should not be underestimated. In combination there is little doubt that they provided the ideas, organizational structure and finance that have affected both the level and quality of provision at both national and local levels.

The reorganization of the health services in 1974, with its principle of conterminosity of boundaries (local authorities and health authorities), in turn made it practicable for central guidance to be issued about joint care planning teams and specialist mental handicap planning groups (DHSS 1977). Joint finance, an arrangement whereby health services' money could be made available to local authorities to start up new community-based services, provided an extra spur to joint planning, and significant amounts of this money were spent on services for people with a mental handicap. (In 1983/84, one-third of the £94 million joint finance allocation in England.)

More recently there has been a central push to get mentally handicapped children out of hospital (Jenkins 1980); small amounts of money earmarked to start up community provision (DHSS 1981a); arrangements that extend joint finance to housing and education (that is not just social services) (DHSS 1983a); and a most important mechanism which allows health authorities to transfer money *in perpetuo* to local authorities if they will take people out of hospital (DHSS 1983b).

In addition to these financial initiatives, designed to promote local services, there has been a general extension of the individual benefits available to all handicapped people and their families (for example non-contributory invalidity pension (NCIP), constant attendance allowance, mobility allowance, as well as social security payments, which are payable to people living in the community but not to those in hospital). There is also legislation which extends the duties of local authorities to all disabled people (HMSO 1970) and which requires housing departments to accord priority to people such as those who are mentally handicapped and living in hospital due to the lack of suitable accommodation (DOE 1977). These moves to promote care in the community, together with the reorganization of local authorities, also led to the establishment of the Jay Committee (HMSO 1979) which made recommendations for a common training for local authority and health services staff working in residential care with mentally handicapped people. These were not adopted and recently there have been more modest proposals for shared training, made by a joint Nursing Council/CCETSW working group (CCETSW (GNC) 1982; CCETSW 1983), and the introduction of a revised syllabus in England and Wales for mental handicap nurses (GNC 1982). In the field of education there has been a major staff training effort.

In summary, what we have witnessed is a decade of positive discrimination at a national level towards people with a mental handicap, which has directed priorities at a local level. Reorganization of NHS and local authority services has provided the possibility of collaboration between the two, and an opportunity for better co-ordination within an integrated social services department. Important changes have also occurred in the structure, content, and commitment to staff training.

But in parallel with these official policies there has been a sustained criticism of the service models advocated and of their likely benefits for handicapped people. Determined efforts have been made to demonstrate alternative models of care. Sometimes these alternative models and strategies have been treated with hostility. At other times, as with the initiative to get children out of hospital, official and 'alternative' views have eventually converged or at least the proposals of outsiders have been assimilated into mainstream policy.

Even before 'Better Services' was published, Townsend produced an anticipatory critique. In a postscript to his paper, Townsend argued that:

'the Government offers no sustained analysis of the social and residential needs of the mentally handicapped . . . much depends on whether or not [these homes] resemble *private housing* in urban localities. What the nation does not want is a system of minor isolated barracks put up by Local Authorities in pale imitation of the larger Victorian barracks which are at present run by hospital authorities. Yet the White Paper makes this an all too likely possibility.'
(Townsend 1970: 208–09)

Because the policy-makers and planners had a philosophy that was at best incomplete and without operational definition, it was possible first to argue that homes should be 'homelike' and that mentally handicapped people should not be segregated from non-handicapped people *and* second, and in contradiction, to 'advocate' the buildings, twenty-place hostels, multi-purpose ATCs, and segregated special schools, often on the outskirts of the community. This resulted in the perpetuation of the idea that there are two categories of mentally handicapped person, those who *need* to live in a hospital and those who can live in the community. Consequently a number of small mental handicap hospitals have been built and large amounts of capital spent on upgrading existing hospitals.

More important, planners have perpetuated the damaging perceptions of the mental handicapped as people who are 'sick' and therefore need nursing care, as people who may be frightening and therefore should at least live on the edge rather than in the middle of things, and as people who are 'perpetual children' in need of lifelong training. There was continuing confusion as to who were the primary consumers – people with a handicap or their families. Care in the community could simply mean discharge to lodgings or a boarding-house, or a 'group home', again sharing your life with other handicapped people and getting little appropriate support.

The criticism of residential and day care services was sustained during the early 1970s, in particular by the Campaign for Mental Handicap (CMH 1972, 1973), a London-based pressure group. It was extended and legitimized by the Jay Committee (Jay 1979), who outlined an alternative model of residential care involving smaller groups, more sharing between handicapped and non-handicapped people, and the use of ordinary houses and flats. The establishment of the project group which produced 'An Ordinary Life' (King's Fund 1980), together with a series of conferences and widespread dissemination of the report, ensured that the alternative view continued to be heard and debated.

In education there was a quiet undermining of the official position. Beresford and Tuckwell in 'Schools for All' (1978) challenged the accepted wisdom about segregated special education and more recently the Advisory Centre for Education (ACE 1983) is ensuring that parents know their rights under the Education Act 1981 to be involved in the assessment and placement of their child and that the arguments for educational integration are put to local education authorities.

Coming right up to date, what we now see is a reluctance to 'blue-print' from the centre and to retain mechanisms which would continue to exert pressure on Ministers to push local authority priorities towards services for mentally handicapped people. This vacuum has been filled to some extent by the Independent Development Council (1981, 1982) and by *ad hoc* working groups, one of which produced the influential report 'An

Ordinary Life' and its successor 'A Vocational Service' (King's Fund 1980, 1984). It has also been filled by regional local working groups. These include the All Wales Working Party (Welsh Office 1982), with its politically and financially backed report and strategy documents, and groups in various other regions (for example South West Thames RHA 1983 and the North Western RHA 1982).

Within this alternative framework there are now many examples of good practice, such as the early intervention programmes which bring support and advice to parents on teaching approaches in Manchester (described in Cunningham 1983), and home teaching programmes which have been introduced in other parts of the country including Wessex (Smith *et al.* 1977). Following initiatives in Somerset, Leeds, and Northumberland, programmes in which another family offers short-term care to handicapped children now exist in many parts of the UK (King's Fund 1981). Similarly, there are now many community support teams consisting of social workers, mental handicap nurses, psychologists, and sometimes speech- and physiotherapists working with handicapped people, with families, and with residential and day care staff. There are other schemes in which professionals act as advisers or facilitators, or sometimes just as group members in self-help groups of parents (Richardson 1984), and the work with groups of handicapped people undertaken by the Avro Students Council in Southend is increasingly seen as important (Williams and Shoultz 1982). Ann Shearer (1981) has described the wide range of alternative residential services available to handicapped children, ranging from professional fostering to specialized 'staffed homes'. The range of options for severely mentally handicapped adults now includes staffed houses (Felce 1983), boarding-out (Penfold 1980), flat and house sharing with non-handicapped volunteers, as well as unstaffed group homes. Many of these residential services are part of initiatives to resettle people who have lived for many years in hospitals.

Employment programmes include individual supported placements in open employment, and various enclave arrangements. In education there have been pilot projects to integrate mentally handicapped children into ordinary schools in London, Cambridge, Derbyshire, Wolverhampton, and Oxford (ACE 1982).

## Principles and practice

The policy context is important. It provides the framework of ideas, legislation, resources, and organizational structure within which social workers will have to operate. Concern about the damaging effects of many of our services and visualizing alternative possibilities are prerequisites for innovation and change.

What are some of the major needs of people with a mental handicap and their families? What sort of programmes are likely to meet individual needs and how are they to be evaluated? What sort of skills will social work practitioners require? Is there a model or framework that can integrate sociological and psychological perspectives and various levels of consumer, professional, and political action?

## PEOPLE WITH A MENTAL HANDICAP

Who is mentally handicapped? Nearly all legal and administrative classifications incorporate the idea of intellectual development that is very much below average and impairment in personal and social competence, sometimes referred to as adaptive behaviour. While such labels may have value when referring to a group, for example in making distinctions from mental illness or physical handicap and in providing a focus for selective 'positive discrimination', it is important to stress that such terms convey little useful information about a particular individual. Second, many people with a mental handicap do not like to be so described. The term 'developmental delay' preferred by many parents with young handicapped children or Warnock's 'special educational needs' represent moves towards more generic and dynamic descriptions and hopefully much greater access to generic services. Whilst there are probably as many as one million people in Great Britain with an IQ less than 70, less than half will come to the notice of statutory agencies as being mentally handicapped. In England there are probably 120,000 who might be described as severely mentally handicapped. The corresponding figure for a local authority with a population of 250,000 would be 600 people of whom 200–250 would be children under 16 years.

The vast majority of severely mentally handicapped children (90 per cent) live with their families, but many live apart, 2,000 in mental handicap hospitals, 2,500 in local authority and voluntary homes, and perhaps another 1,000 in residential special schools often as five-day boarders. About 15–20,000 (40 per cent) adults live with their parent(s) (many of whom are aged), another 20,000 live in local authority and voluntary homes, and 40,000 are still living in hospital. There are now 45,000 places in ATCs in England.

Whereas severe mental handicap is fairly evenly distributed across all social classes, mildly mentally handicapped children are very much more likely to be found in social classes IV and V. The link with social disadvantage is well established as is the fact that these children can be helped by comprehensive approaches which bring employment opportunities and support to parents at an early stage as well as additional infant stimulation (Garber and Heber 1977). Up-to-date information about the degree and nature of disabilities of those with a mental handicap is scarce, especially on those who live at home. Generally those in hospital have more severe disabilities than those in hostels in the community, but one-third of those *in hospital* can walk, have no recorded behaviour problems, are continent, and can feed and wash themselves (DHSS 1980).

However, such statistics provide only one side of the story. One third of severely mentally handicapped people have Down's Syndrome or other conditions which draw negative attention to their appearance. Many have epilepsy, which can sometimes be very severe and life threatening. Many have additional physical handicaps such as cerebral palsy, and many have visual or hearing impairment. Recurrent respiratory illnesses are common and 'mental illness' is not uncommon although notoriously difficult to diagnose in those who are severely mentally handicapped.

Both severely and mildly mentally handicapped people have serious learning difficulties. There are various theories or explanations about why this should be so, which include poor memory and poor attention. This is a major disadvantage when it comes to learning more complex skills such as speech, literacy, and numeracy, but also in acquiring important social skills.

Often the descriptions of some of the common characteristics of those with a mental handicap end here. But they should not because there are some other common experiences which taken together can become life defining and confining and which compound their learning problems.

The first one is the experience of segregation, which is usually accompanied by congregation. Most of our services by design seek to separate handicapped people from families, friends, neighbours, and communities. Most seek to group large numbers of handicapped people together. Many mentally handicapped people have experienced severe discontinuity of place and relationships (from one school to another, from one home to another) and have experienced multiple caretaking. These are not the natural transitions involved in a move from primary to secondary school or a change of job involving a house move, but often quite gratuitous moves which reflect the needs and inadequacies of agencies and professional staff rather than the handicapped person. Added to this is a limited choice about where you live and who you share your life with (hospital, hostel, group home, parental home). Most mentally handicapped people are unemployed. Educational opportunities are few, particularly in adult life. In residential services, despite the fact that most mentally handicapped people are single, they usually share a bedroom with someone else who is not a chosen partner. It is important to note that for many, if not most, none of these options is the '*least* restrictive alternative'.

Despite the fact that we now know a lot about the effects of different kinds of physical and social environments and which teaching programmes can be most effective, such programmes are very rarely available or sustained. Lack of community presence and lack of relationships with non-handicapped peers lead to few opportunities to learn from others. Limited range of experience can contribute to poor skill development. But mentally handicapped people have the same kinds of biological and psychological needs as non-handicapped people have; similar values and aspirations despite their social disadvantages. They have many skills, competences, and personal characteristics that are valued. As with non-handicapped people there are individual differences. People with a mental handicap experience similar life crises to others and for example have similar reactions and feelings towards starting school, the death of friends or relatives, and unemployment.

## THE PRINCIPLE OF 'NORMALIZATION'

It was against the background of superimposed disadvantage that people began to look for a value-based model that would incorporate psychological and sociological perspectives. It was Neils Bank-Mikkelson who first talked of 'letting the mentally retarded obtain an existence as close to the normal as possible' (Bank-Mikkelson 1969), and Nirje who advocated 'making available to the mentally retarded patterns and conditions of everyday life which are as close as possible to the norms and patterns of the mainstream of society' (Nirje 1969). But it was Wolfensberger (1972, 1980) who was to elaborate and explain the concept and its implications as 'the utilisation of means which are as culturally valued as possible, in order to establish, enable or support behaviour, appearance and interpretations which are culturally valued as possible'. It was also Wolfensberger and Glenn (1975) who developed a technique for the critical evaluation of human services called Programme Analysis of Service Systems (PASS).

'Normalization' is concerned with how we should behave towards those we define as mentally handicapped. As such, it is not in itself an empirical statement. However, it is in no way inconsistent with current empirical knowledge and, indeed, if it is to be applied, requires knowledge of prevailing culture and of ways of maximizing the development of personal and social skills in handicapped people. The principle is concerned with both process and goals, with particular emphasis being placed on the process. We are encouraged to give careful thought not only to the development of adaptive behaviours by the handicapped person but also how we are to encourage and facilitate these behaviours. We are encouraged to make informed choices about the methods and approaches we adopt and to recognize that images can create barriers and a 'mutual handicap'. For these reasons it is important that mentally handicapped people are presented or interpreted to others in a culturally valued manner, that is as people with hopes, expectations, abilities, and as members of society with a contribution to make, rather than as people without worth. For Wolfensberger, these ideas are expressed by the proposition that there are two major dimensions to 'normalization'. One concerns our *interaction* with mentally handicapped people, while the other concerns the way in which they are *interpreted* or presented to others. He also suggests that we can think of the application of the principle at three levels, the personal, primary and intermediate social system, and societal.

'Normalization' is compelling as a basic principle. However, it requires intelligent elaboration and application. It is a concept that is easily mis-interpreted and therefore runs a constant risk of being rejected. If accepted it has major implications for social work. Services should be planned around the needs of identified clients, and field-based practitioners must be given the authority to use financial and human resources in a flexible way. Social integration should be seen as both a means and a goal. Most services should be local and use should be made of ordinary community resources, houses, neighbours, shops, volunteers, and leisure facilities. Where buildings are required, careful attention should be paid to location, size, appearance, and the number of handicapped persons served in one place. Attempts in adult services to abandon language, environments, and teaching approaches that convey powerful images about children should be made. Community services should be planned for all people with a mental handicap, not just the most able. Partnership with consumers would become an essential safeguard to political momentum and quality.

## DEVELOPMENTAL AND PROSTHETIC APPROACHES

In addition to understanding normalization, the social worker also needs to know about the way that physical environments can be adapted to compensate for disability. They also need to be informed about major advances in medical, behavioural and psychotherapeutic 'treatment' techniques. Matson and Mulick (1983) provide an up-to-date review of these three treatment approaches together with more focused reviews of language training, the teaching of self-help skills, and vocational training. Mittler (1977) provides a useful overview of research that is influencing practice. Breuning and Poling (1982) summarize what is known about behaviourally active drugs and their use with those with a mental handicap, and Betts (1982) provides a good readable chapter on psychiatry and epilepsy.

There are now, for example, a wide range of aids available to improve mobility, posture, grasping, feeding, toileting. Social workers need to know about these and some of the ways in which computer technology, hardware and software could further revolutionize the quality of life of people with all degrees of mental handicap.

As argued by Sheldon in Chapter 20, for learning to be most effective, precise teaching goals must be set; some skills will have to be broken down into incremental steps whilst others are best taught as a whole behaviour. Additional cues can be helpful. Gold, for example (1972), taught the very handicapped a complex assembly task through the provision of additional colour cues. Overlearning is helpful, and careful attention to consistent reinforcement of successful performance is important.

Social workers should know, for example, what aids for feeding are available or where to direct parents for advice. It is now not uncommon for a speech therapist and physiotherapist to combine to help a child develop better posture, more relaxed muscle tone, and improved mouth and tongue movement. The use of prosthetic devices to correct or compensate for spinal defects and leg calipers to assist standing and walking is becoming more widespread as are various forms of orthopaedic operations which surgeons were not previously prepared to do. The importance of voluntary or passive exercise of limbs for those with physical handicap is now recognized. Mobility allowances and a willingness by parents and carers to spend time teaching means that many physically handicapped people can now move about in motorized wheelchairs.

Hearing and visual impairments are nowadays much more likely to be diagnosed and attended to in the community and in mental handicap hospitals. The widespread introduction of Makaton, a signing vocabulary derived from the British Sign Language, has been a major breakthrough not just for those with sensory handicaps but for many severely handicapped people with little or no speech.

Social workers also need to know about the use of various medicines, particularly those which alter mood and behaviour and those which are used to control epilepsy. The introduction of more flexible technology allows 24-hour waking EEG recording to be undertaken and is improving diagnosis. There is now a wide range of drugs available for its control and clinicians are less reticent about discussing the possibility of sub-clinical epilepsy which may heighten irritability and contribute to aggression in children and adults with a mental handicap.

Social workers need to know about the range of techniques now available to direct carers and to parents which can make the teaching and retention of new skills more likely and can be used to minimize maladaptive behaviours.

Goal planning (Houtts and Scott 1975) in which a strengths and needs list is drawn up – key activities or skills are identified and a programme designed which utilizes preferred objects and interests and relationships in their personal development – is now an essential part of residential and day services. Individual programme plans in which checks on progress are reviewed, long- and short-term goals set and responsibility assigned to various members of an inter-disciplinary team are to be found in many localities (see for example Blunden 1980).

## SOCIAL WORK IN PRACTICE

The opportunities and challenges in the 1980s, for social work with handicapped people are quite different from those of the 1970s. There is a much wider range of local community-based services available. Many people with a mental handicap wish to move to less restrictive alternatives. Better information, new philosophies and technologies have contributed to raised expectations all round. Many social workers now have an opportunity to work more closely with community nurses, psychologists, and remedial professions.

A number of quite distinctive contributions are emerging and being recognized. One is a counselling role with handicapped people as they attempt to move into the mainstream and to establish relationships with non-handicapped people. Support, advice, and good teaching are essential if such efforts are not to be misinterpreted and crushed by parents or direct care staff. Sexual counselling (Kempton 1973) is something that many professions find very difficult but social workers are taking it on and developing experience and skills. Similarly ongoing individual support is often required by families who have a continuing need to talk about their feelings and the difficulties they have had with professionals.

Another role seems to be as a person who is in a good position to create links. For those families who have difficulty in creating their own 'structure for coping' (Bayley 1973), social workers may be able to suggest strategies to allow them to help themselves. Often the role is as one who communicates for or 'advocates' on behalf of the person with a mental handicap. Groupwork, as another vehicle for self-help of the kind described in another context by Dunn and Moss (1978) is proving to be an essential technique.

Finally, there are now many examples of social workers using their experience as practitioners and knowledge of individual clients to contribute to a new style of service planning that is more personal, more local, and involves assessment of community resources as well as individuals.

## Mental impairment

Living as part of the community and in the least restrictive environment is a right, which brings with it certain obligations and risks for the handicapped person and occasionally to the community. These risks include the risk of prosecution and punishment for aggressive behaviour or behaviour which endangers others.

The inclusion of those with a mental handicap in the scope of the Mental Health Act 1983 means that ASWs have an important part to play in minimizing the risks of wrongful or inappropriate prosecution or compulsory admission to a hospital, and aiding successful and valued participation by handicapped people in the life of the community.

Although recommendations and decisions about whether an individual is 'mentally disordered' in terms of the Act will be made by doctors, the ASW will be expected to exercise independent professional judgement without undue influence from doctors or the local authority. Sometimes the social worker will have to initiate the referral for medical opinion. At others he will be asked by a GP to make an application. Sometimes the social worker may not agree that such an application should be made, at others he may agree to the application but may wish to comment on the recommendations made (for example to record that admission to a hospital is not necessary but is required because of lack of community alternatives).

The following illustrations indicate the wide range of possible behaviours and situations that may face the ASW. A GP may have been called out during the night to see a severely mentally handicapped person living with her aged mother, now in her sixties. The person may or may not be known to the local social services department. She has attacked her mother or has perhaps destroyed furniture and possessions in her home. The GP refers the case to the ASW with a recommendation for a hospital admission. A man who has lived for most of his life in a mental handicap hospital has now been living for two years in a local authority hostel. He has been accused of and may have admitted to a sexual assault on a teenage girl and is being held in a local police station. A severely mentally handicapped teenager living in a local staffed home has assaulted a young child or member of staff. A young man has set fire to some rubbish in a bin in a leisure centre. A young woman has been found wandering on the main railway line. A teenager, running away from a mental handicap hospital where he was an informal patient, has stolen a boat and lit a fire to keep warm.

First, there is the duty to interview in a suitable manner. This is a central and legal obligation. A number of decisions and judgements will have to be made – is the person mentally handicapped; what behaviour has occurred; has the person done what is alleged; what are the circumstances; what is known about previous behaviour and what kind of care and treatment is appropriate? In some ways, social workers may face similar problems to those of the police and discussed by Hewitt (1980, 1983). The person may not have any speech or speech may be unclear and complicated by physical handicap. The person may have additional sensory handicaps. He may not be able to write out his own statement or to read what has been written. Being able to sign your name is not evidence of reading ability. It may be that the person has so far been unable or unwilling to communicate with others at all and the social worker may need to start here, if corroboration of particular behaviour is required. The person may not understand what is being alleged or the seriousness of the situation and/or his legal rights, and may have confessed to something he did not do. Even where there is no doubt about the offending, evidence of *mens rea* may not be sought in court.

The encouragement of age-inappropriate play by parents and by carers in handicapped adults may mean that they are more likely to be found close to or in the company of young children and consequently more at risk of accusation should an assault take place.

Generally the social worker should try to interview the person in surroundings that are familiar and to involve other people, family or professionals, who know him well. He should seek as much independent corroboration of the alleged behaviour and information about the abilities and interests of the person from other people if mental handicap is suspected. Where there is serious hearing impairment, it may be necessary to get in someone who can communicate using British Sign Language or other sign vocabularies such as Makaton (Walker 1981).

Second, there is the issue of aggressive or irresponsible behaviour. Is the aggression abnormal or the behaviour seriously irresponsible? Such behaviour should be judged against the norms and values of the community in general. In this respect the handicapped person is on the same footing as those of average intelligence.

Where there is little doubt that the person did behave in a particular way the social worker may need to establish the circumstances; whether there was a trigger; was it an atypical event or part of a persistent pattern of aggression? Is there drugs or drink involved? Sometimes benzodiazapines can induce aggression in certain individuals. Is there a history of epilepsy? Such questions will be of particular importance with regard to treatability if the classification is mental impairment.

Third, there is the definition of the two categories of mental impairment. The Act refers to incomplete or arrested development of the mind, but since this is an abstraction or inference, the central concepts here are 'significant impairment of intelligence and social functioning' and 'severe impairment of intelligence and social function'. How is the approved social worker to operationalize such concepts? What criteria is he to use and what sort of reference or comparisons are to be made in determining significant or severe levels of impairment? The Act is silent here. It does not require standardized assessment of intelligence or social functioning.

Whilst there are many valid arguments about the socially divisive effects of intelligence assessment in general, and the stigmatized and low expectations encouraged in others towards mentally handicapped people in particular, there is a case for their use, particularly where there is some doubt about whether impairment or severe impairment is the appropriate classification, or where there is a belief that the person's intellectual abilities may be within the average range. In these cases and when time permits, referral to educational or clinical psychologists could be used by social workers to prevent inappropriate classification and detention in a hospital. It is by no means certain that medical practitioners will seek such safeguards. Where such standardized assessment is not possible, the social worker is on his own. The first advice has to be to base his judgement on the behaviour of the person, both directly observed and reported by others. In an interview with someone whose verbal abilities are limited and who finds himself in stress-inducing situations it will probably require the presence of someone else, perhaps a relation or another social worker or professional who knows the person well. Probably the social worker would first want to establish the level and complexity of the person's language. What sort of understanding is there of what is being said in reply to questions? What sort of vocabulary does the person have, how many words, how varied? Are whole sentences used? Ability to read a newspaper might be indicative of normal intelligence, but a lack of literacy would not prove the converse. Numeracy and ability to handle change might also be assessed. Perceptual motor ability might be assessed by getting the person to copy various shapes or to draw a figure. Generally care should be taken to rule out hearing or visual impairment which may interfere with performance and to make due allowance for physical handicaps, which for example may make speech very indistinct in a person who is not intellectually handicapped.

As for social functioning, the same kind of advice applies. Wherever possible social workers should use an informant who knows the person well to complete one of the several social skills check lists that are readily available (Gunzburg 1976; Nihira 1974). Such assessment might also be used in follow-up to monitor improvement (or deterioration) in personal and social skills.

The 1983 Act requires the social worker to satisfy himself that detention is the *most appropriate* way of providing care and treatment. This obligation has major implications. It assumes a knowledge of the kinds of settings and services that are likely to be of benefit. It also assumes knowledge of various medical and psychological approaches to treatment of aggressive or troublesome behaviour. For those who are impaired rather than severely mentally impaired, it involves judgement about whether such treatments are likely to 'alleviate or prevent deterioration of the condition'. Personal knowledge of the local services, inside and outside the hospital (mental handicap and mental illness), is also required. An assessment should be made of the strengths and needs of each service.

The pros and cons of various kinds of special units have been debated by the Jay Committee (HMSO 1979) and in a new DHSS publication (1984). Jones (1983) has described a treatment unit which relies on behaviour modification approaches and Day (1983) has described a unit in which medical approaches play an important part. A King's Fund publication (Firth 1982) takes the view that all people, including those with difficult and disturbed behaviour, can live within the community, providing appropriate supports are made available. This was a principle that those in Eastern Nebraska endeavoured to put into practice (Thomas, Firth, and Kendall 1978). It is important because of the puzzling and intractable nature of some behaviours that we do not invent a special 'group' just as a decade ago 'Better Services' invented groups which would need 'constant medical and nursing care'. If our goal is to protect the community then we should say so. Most of what has been said in this chapter suggests that segregated care in hospitals whose organization is highly centralized and medically dominated is unlikely to be an effective setting for people to unlearn maladaptive behaviours and acquire the skills needed to live as part of the community.

Behaviourally based programmes are the most likely to succeed with those whose actions are life threatening to themselves (Hollis and Meyers 1982). Such programmes are most likely to be effective if the physical and social environment provides a setting in which other adaptive behaviours are encouraged, in which experiences are varied, and relationships are possible. Similar comments could be made about aggression directed against others. Whatever is decided it is essential that there is multi-disciplinary management; that there is an individual programme plan which sets clear goals and specifies who is to take responsibility for various parts of the programme.

Space does not permit discussion of where guardianship might be used. Under the 1959 Act there had been a drop in its use from 207 in 1976 to 101 in 1978. However, it is possible that this might become a preferred option to hospital admission.

### Conclusion

The Mental Health Act 1983 brings with it considerable promise and potential to promote community-based services for people with a mental handicap. It is likely to stretch the knowledge and skills of all social workers and present particular challenges to the ASW who will have to interpret and apply the Act.

# PART THREE
# ALTERNATIVES TO
# HOSPITAL CARE

# 9

# Residential care

## *Ann Davis*

This chapter reviews the potential of group care in residential units for providing viable alternatives to hospital care. It also explores ways in which ASWs might exploit this potential in carrying out their duties and responsibilities under the Mental Health Act 1983.

### Residential care: problems and potential

It is often the problems associated with residential care rather than its potential which engage social workers in the mental health field. This stems from the fact that the main contribution to this form of care still lies within the walls of large specialist hospitals. Most of the studies and official reports of hospital-based residential care have pointed to its defects. It has been described as an 'institution-oriented' rather than a 'resident-oriented' service (King, Raynes, and Tizard 1971). Its prime concern appears to be with the efficient, smoothly running ward which maintains a daily routine impervious to the needs of residents. Characteristically too, this approach is one where activities such as feeding, toileting, and bathing are organized on a group or 'block' basis and little space is given for residents to have personal possessions, privacy, or opportunities to initiate activities which are personally important. Contact with the surrounding community is limited and the social distance between residents and staff is considerable. As a consequence this kind of care has been shown to de-personalize, depress, demoralize, and so disable those who are exposed to it for any extended period.

Many vivid accounts, often in diary form, exist of the routines and regimes which have evolved over decades of institution-orientated care (Oswin 1973; Ryan and Thomas 1980). All of them chronicle the heavy costs that residents bear. These costs are clearly seen in,

> 'apathy, lack of initiative, loss of interest more marked in things and events not immediately personal or present, submissiveness, and sometimes no expression of feelings or resentment at harsh or unfair orders . . . a lack of interest in the future and an apparent inability to make practical plans for it, a deterioration in personal habits, toilet and standards generally, a loss of individuality, and a resigned acceptance that things will go on as they are – unchanging, inevitably, and indefinitely.'
>
> (Barton 1966: 47)

Sustained efforts have been made in some hospital units to change this traditional approach to caring, and create more 'resident-orientated' regimes. Where these innovations have been successful they have resulted in environments that respond to resident need and increase the participation of both residents and staff in the daily life of the community (Towell and Harries 1979).

But social workers also express doubts about the worth of providing residential care on a more 'resident-orientated' basis when the thrust of policy and practice in the services is towards helping people manage and resolve their difficulties in their *own* homes. The experiences of 'segregation' and 'separation' which occur on entry to residential care appear to be at odds with the declared intent of 'community' care to support individuals in their 'normal' environments and to mesh professional help with the usual life-style of an individual.

These doubts rest on a firm belief in the positives offered by social networks and the negatives offered in residential units. The comparison is often made between the individualized care provided in emotionally secure social networks, and the more public and regimented world of the resident unit which promotes dependency and isolation from the outside world.

I have discussed elsewhere (Davis 1981) the problems of this over-simplistic comparison and have suggested that it stems from a lack of understanding of the complex and contradictory relationship that exists between family care and residential care. This relationship is constantly bedevilled by the fact that,

> 'residential solutions not only remove prime responsibility for caring

for the private sphere of family life to the public sphere of welfare and social work, but can also be a complete substitute for family life. In a society which stresses that the individual and the family should take prime responsibility for welfare, such provision must pose a threat, as well as offering a source of relief.'

(Davis 1981: 24)

For this reason the point needs to be made that while relatives, friends, and neighbours make a major contribution to the care, control, and support of people suffering from mental disorder, there are costs. Individuals and their networks can use more 'time out' than our services allow and we need to acknowledge this more openly.

Residential care offered outside hospital can offer a positive response to the crisis and breakdown in people suffering from mental disorder. It can encourage personal independence and enhance an individual's ability to manage his life and resolve the difficulties which face him.

Crisis and breakdown occur in two, related ways. First, at a personal level in the way an individual feels, behaves, and functions. Second, at an interpersonal level where it is the relationships between an individual and others that are at risk or have disintegrated. Workers in residential units for people with mental disorder and mental handicap have to recognize and work at both of these levels. Indeed, Ward argues that it is intervention by residential workers at these levels which shapes the two main aspects of the residential social worker's task.

'(i) Working with individuals in the context of the group inside the residential unit and
(ii) with the residents individually and through the group across the unit's boundaries.'

(Ward 1977: 25)

The response made by any residential unit to crisis and breakdown in mentally ill and mentally handicapped individuals and their social networks, will vary according to the combination of a number of factors. These include the skills and interest of the staff group. The mix of the resident group, and the availability of other residential resources and alternative accommodation. However in most local services there is such a dearth of residential care available outside the health service that residential social work staff who are pioneering a unit may find themselves, initially, with considerable scope in determining the aims and objectives they will employ. In reaching what are often difficult decisions about the kind of residential care they are going to provide staff need to consider the characteristics of their potential residents as well as the skills and experience that the staff group possesses.

Obviously the scope given to staff to influence the type of residential resource that is going to be provided will depend on how far the local authority or voluntary organization has a particular mandate to satisfy. An example of this can be found in Race and Race's (1979) fascinating account of a residential scheme for mentally handicapped adults which evolved in direct response to the concern expressed by a group of elderly parents about the future of their handicapped offspring. The scheme developed was specifically designed to be used when family care began to be difficult for parents to maintain. It provided a short period of stay in a hostel during which groups of residents learnt basic skills of day-to-day living and were encouraged to get to know one another. Following this phase residents were moved on to live in an unstaffed 'group home' supported by hostel staff and community-based social workers. For individuals or couples who could move on a further link in the chain was added – ordinary housing in the community.

## Approaches to residential care

Four main residential care approaches to crisis and breakdown in individuals and their networks can be currently identified within specialist residential units run by local authorities and voluntary organizations: crisis work; therapeutic communities; rehabilitation work; long-term care.

### CRISIS WORK

Work with individuals and families in crisis is a regular part of the social worker's caseload. Not all of this work is tackled by single practitioners. There are some well-established crisis intervention services which use specialist social workers alongside nurses and psychiatrists. Olsen in Chapter 19 shows that these aim to intervene on a time-limited basis with the individual in trouble and his social networks. Most crisis teams try to support individuals in the community, but if risks are involved residential care may be used for limited periods. The usual residential resource that such teams have to offer is a hospital bed, but this does not have to be the only option. Local authority or voluntary residential units staffed by social work care staff can also offer viable residential alternatives to such teams, providing a base from which individuals can review their predicament and work with unit staff and members of the crisis team towards some alternative solution of their problem.

Crisis work in the community can be combined in a variety of ways with residential care. An example here is the Crisis Service established in 1983 by Coventry social services department. This is based in a large detached house in a residential area of the city. A team of specialist social workers take referrals (from psychiatrists) of individuals in crisis and work with them in whatever way they decide is most appropriate. The house has a few residential places which can be used for a very limited period by individual clients. This residential provision is managed by the workers in the team and access is determined by them. This residential facility aims to provide an opportunity for clients to look at the problems which have resulted in crisis and make decisions about the direction of their lives. The emphasis here is on problem-solving rather than the treatment of illness, with a short break from family and friends being used constructively, either as a breathing-space for all concerned, or by using the house and its workers to meet together on neutral territory to re-negotiate relationships (*Community Care* 1983).

Using residential care as an integral part of crisis work presents a considerable challenge for the social workers involved. It calls for expertise and confidence in working with individuals, families, and groups in a variety of settings. It crosses the traditional boundaries between field social work and residential social work. It requires that the workers involved share aims, objectives, and information and can weather the ups and downs involved in managing a limited resource in the face of con-siderable demands.

As Olsen shows (Chapters 3 and 4) in his interpretation of the duties laid on the ASW by the 1983 Act, one source of referral to units offering a crisis facility could come from ASWs. In order that the potential of this kind of resource can be fully exploited in situations where hospital admission is being considered, local authority departments need to involve residential social workers and managers and their field work counterparts in review-ing the use made of existing residential places. Questions need to be asked about the criteria which individuals in crisis will have to meet in order to gain entry to this form of care, and the 'mix' of residents which a unit could be expected to accommodate. It might be that existing residential units that are not part of a crisis service may be able to offer a limited facility alongside their mainstream work. Such imaginative use of existing resources will depend not just on formal arrangements but on the commitment and joint working of residential workers and ASWs in the field, to break new ground.

## THERAPEUTIC COMMUNITIES

This approach is a well-established part of our mental health services in Great Britain. Both inside and outside hospitals, therapeutic communities have developed on the premise that it is helpful for individuals with psychological problems to live in a group where they are encouraged to confront and share their difficulties with others. Such communities have been organized on the basis that all aspects of the daily routine provide therapeutic opportunities, as do all encounters between members of the group – whether they are residents or staff. Some of the benefits of this form of residential care have been described as providing individuals with experiences that help minimize distortion of reality; encourage communication and participation; reduce anxiety; and increase self-esteem and insight into the causes of individual difficulties. It is claimed that a period spent in such a community can result in growth and development and therefore long-term changes in behaviour and ways of relating to others (Hinshelwood and Manning 1979; Jansen 1980).

As Muir (Chapter 16) shows, the ideas and practices that have shaped this kind of residential care in Britain are well documented and have been used with a wide range of resident groups. However this has not been a popular model in local authority residential units. It has been left to voluntary organizations such as the Richmond Fellowship to experiment with and develop this approach. Obviously, the access of an ASW to a voluntary residential unit of this kind is limited by departmental policy and the availability of finance. In the current economic climate this might mean an under-use of existing communities.

It is interesting to speculate why local authority units have not embraced this approach more fully. Large psychiatric hospitals have not proved a very fertile soil for the spread of this form of care, for implicit in the practice of the therapeutic community is a critique of the way in which staff power and authority is traditionally exercised in such institutions. It is probable that such a critique is applicable to the traditions of staff–client interaction which have become part of local authority social services departments.

The success of the therapeutic community approach relies on paid staff opening up as individuals and avoiding professional roles which distance them from residents. This 'closing of the gap' between staff and residents challenges some of the well-established ideas that residential staff hold of the capabilities of residents. Jansen considers that in the majority of residential units in England that provide an alternative to hospital there is an 'underestimation of the resident's capacity to take responsibility and (a) corresponding need for staff to assume a parental role. There are often strong elements of patronage: "see how well my monkeys can perform tricks", or the kind of pride parents display in the child who begins to walk and talk' (Jansen 1980: 378). Such attitudes are, of course, antithetical to a therapeutic community approach. In addition the organizational form that such communities take is one that stresses democratic participation. This does not 'fit' well with the bureaucratic structures of local authority social services departments. While local authorities remain unable to accommodate therapeutic communities within their residential services, it will be left to voluntary agencies to continue to demonstrate the value of this alternative to hospital care. This effectively prevents an approach, with considerable potential, entering the mainstream of provision for the mentally ill.

## REHABILITATION WORK

The use of residential care to rehabilitate mentally ill and mentally handicapped individuals has proved a much more popular approach in local authority residential units for the mentally disordered. The focus of this kind of residential care is also to use the intense experience of communal living to enhance the abilities of individuals to cope with recurring or long-term difficulties. But the emphasis here is not on 'feelings' but on 'doing'; on improving specific skills by practice and graded learning opportunities in order that individuals can survive more successfully in the outside community (Morgan and Cheadle 1981).

Work in such units is usually based on individual assessment of handicaps or problems. Unit programmes are then used so that individual and group activities focus on the areas highlighted. More recently some rehabilitation units have begun to work on modifying the environment to which individuals will return, but usually the focus is on individual change and adjustment.

Rehabilitative work has been used with a wide range of groups: those suffering from the effects of years of institutional care can be trained to live independent lives again; elderly, mentally frail people needing help in coping alone with daily routines; people leaving their families and struggling to achieve a measure of independence in order to live alone or with another group of residents.

The emphasis of individual and group programmes is on the social skills needed to cope with life in the community – with personal needs, occupation, and recreation. Crucial to the success of such programmes is that residents are able to transfer the skills learnt when they leave the unit. To help individuals manage such transitions some units build in phases through which each resident must move. These may culminate in a period in a flat attached to the unit, where an individual or group is expected to manage with minimal support from the unit. Access to a range of housing is crucial to the focused working of residential units of this kind. Without such access, units will find that they are having to provide a roof for individuals long after they have completed their programme.

For the ASW this kind of unit can be an invaluable resource in plans to support individuals who need to establish more independence from their families or re-establish routines of daily living. They can also provide, as the earlier example showed, a base from which couples or small groups can learn what it means to live together before attempting to do so in ordinary housing. The use of a guardianship order becomes a more viable option if this kind of focused residential care is locally available.

LONG-TERM CARE

Some residential units provided by the local authorities and voluntary organizations offer by design or default a permanent home for mentally disordered and handicapped people. In some instances such care is provided because of a lack of viable alternative accommodation in the community. In other instances hostels or homes become 'silted' because of the lack of a focused programme which helps residents move on to ordinary or sheltered housing. But for some individuals group homes, boarding houses, or their own home will be too difficult to manage – a staffed and structured residential unit of a permanent kind is the most appropriate response to their needs.

Unfortunately, as Tyne (1977) points out, most of the alternative residential provision that has been developed in recent years has met the needs of the least-handicapped groups. Those who are in greater need of staffed, long-term provision are still to be found in hospital care. There is no reason to suppose, however, that community residential units would be unable to provide a home for the most disabled mentally handicapped and mentally ill clients. As the Jay Committee, in considering the provision of long-term care for mentally handicapped people, stated,

'We do not wish to deny that many mentally handicapped people will need very intensive and highly skilled staff support, nor that some mentally handicapped adults will be unresponsive or difficult and that interactions with them may often be unpleasant and may bring little direct reward to the staff caring for them, but our model requires that the residential accommodation which we offer to the more severely and indeed profoundly handicapped person . . . should be small, should serve a local community and, wherever possible, should use suitably adapted ordinary houses. The homes we envisage should also be capable of acting as a resource to the families in the locality.'

(HMSO 1979: 49)

Wing (Wing and Olsen 1979) amongst others has suggested that the same type of provision would be beneficial for the most disabled mentally ill people.

The approach adopted by staff in long-term care units should be informed by a respect for the dignity and worth of each individual resident and a wish to maximize opportunities for moving towards personal independence. In other words it should be 'resident-orientated', encouraging participation by residents and contact with the surrounding community.

The work of Raynes et al. (1979) is very pertinent here. In comparing three residential facilities for mentally retarded people, they considered four dimensions of caretaking: daily living, speech used by staff to residents, contact with the surrounding community, and the physical environment of the units. The findings suggested that a participative, resident-orientated style of care is not guaranteed by a small-sized unit. Crucial to developing and sustaining this kind of care are residential staff who feel supported and involved in their work and have a high degree of autonomy and responsibility in responding to residents' needs. If local authorities and voluntary organizations are to rise to the challenge of developing long-term residential care which provides a good quality of life, they must pay attention to organizational structures, in particular,

> 'participation in decision making, formalisation, the role of the middle-line manager, promotion systems and communication. All of them have implications for the care staff *and* the care they provide. Without a supportive organisational structure for care staff innovations to improve the quality of care will neither endure or contribute much to raise the standard of care.'
>
> (Raynes, Pratt, and Rose 1979: 160)

Again the provision of this kind of care in a local district should influence significantly some of the decisions that an ASW can make about the placement of disabled individuals, who seem to require the support of long-term care.

## Combining approaches

The approaches discussed so far are not self-contained options, in certain situations a 'mix' of approaches can be developed to great effect. Long-term units can be linked to a small flat or bedsit in order to provide a limited rehabilitation facility. A crisis unit can adopt therapeutic community techniques in helping residents confront their problems.

Importantly too, each of these approaches can be combined with a wider residential service comprising unstaffed group homes and independent households. Such combinations serve to ensure that units do not 'hold' residents unnecessarily and can also provide a support service to vulnerable people from a residential base in which they have formed relationships.

In some instances residential units can be used productively to support families and the informal networks which are providing care in the surrounding community. This 'care-sharing' approach has been developed to good effect in relation to mentally handicapped children. The unit staff can provide relief care for parents and children and share skills and ideas for coping with difficult behaviour. McCormack (1970) describes one such unit, 'Field End House' in London. This unit offers long-term care, short-term care, and day care to children with multiple handicaps. Admission to the unit is conditional on parental involvement.

Family members are expected to share the care of their relatives with staff. Some parents are also involved in the management of the unit, sharing decision-making with staff.

This kind of initiative can be adopted for use with adults. However it opens up another area of uncertainty for residential staff and managers. It increases the visibility of workers' practice and attitudes, and demands that they consider not only the regime of the unit but what is happening in the residents' family situation.

## Conclusions

The majority of those who work in local authority and voluntary residential units have no qualifications in social work. Indeed most care workers have no relevant qualification at all. Research shows that care staff develop ways of relating to clients and running programmes that are heavily influenced by the 'care style' of the head of the unit in which they are employed (Tizard, Sinclair, and Clarke 1975).

Currently most heads of units for mentally disordered and handicapped people who are qualified have been trained as nurses. The provision of residential care that is going to offer a viable alternative to hospital care and that is going to be of positive value to ASWs and their clients requires staff who are trained and supervised in their work. Training and support must become a priority within both local authority and voluntary services if the full potential of residential care in this field is to be realized.

# 10
## Day care

*Ann Davis*

Day care is a well-established part of the services available to mentally ill and mentally handicapped people. It fulfils a wide range of functions for its users and their families, yet it remains a relatively underdeveloped form of care. This is partly because it is provided on a limited basis – current day care places for mentally ill and mentally handicapped people fall far short of government-recommended targets (MIND 1981). It is also because it has been developed in a rather *ad hoc* fashion with little thought given to how it might link to other services. Finally, scant attention has been paid to training staff to work in day care units with the result that the full potential of this form of provision remains unrealized.

This chapter reviews the current pattern of day care for mentally ill and mentally handicapped people, and considers the ways in which day services can be used to expand the available alternatives to hospital care.

### Day care for mentally ill people

The provision of psychiatric day care as an alternative to hospital care has been part of health service provision since 1946, when the first day hospital in the UK was opened in London. Social services departments and voluntary organizations also contribute to this form of provision, but it is health service day units, usually called day hospitals, that continue to dominate the day care scene. Carter's national survey of this form of care for mentally ill people estimated that 75 per cent of day units were provided by the health service with local authorities providing 20 per cent and voluntary organizations the remainder (Carter 1981).

Despite the fact that psychiatric day care has existed for almost forty years, there is still scant data which can be used by those asking questions about what this form of care can offer and what kinds of individuals can benefit most from it. As one consultant psychiatrist, who has spent decades working in this area, puts it:

'It seems doubtful whether we can establish policies and norms until we have more information and more reliable data. There are still large areas of ignorance and uncertainty and hence a continuing need for limited experiment. . . Most people do not really understand day services; it takes time to train and accustom hospital and social services staff to day treatment and we have few day places in which to train them.'

(Bennett 1981: 551)

In this situation of uncertainty and doubt the statement on day care made in Better Services for the Mentally Ill (DHSS 1975) stands out. This White Paper which recommended national guidelines for the provision of psychiatric day care distinguished between the functions of day hospitals and day centres. The former, provided by the health authority, were described as offering treatment, group and individual therapy, and also providing a wide range of occupational and rehabilitation activities, while the latter, provided mainly by local authority social services departments, should aim to meet users' 'immediate needs for shelter, occupation and social activity' as well as helping them with 'difficulties in forming or maintaining of personal relationships . . . adjusting or readjusting to the demands of work' and encouraging them to realize their 'potential' (DHSS 1975: 35).

A further DHSS circular on this subject was able to make similarly clear statements about the most appropriate client groups for each form of day care. The day hospital service was particularly suited for 'two groups of patients, those who need more intensive treatment than can be given as out-patient treatment and those for whom day care is a step in the process of rehabilitation after in-patient treatment' while the service provided by day centres should aim at providing 'relatively short term rehabilitation for those likely to return to open employment or domestic duties, and long term, perhaps permanent, work or occupation for those whose chances of return to employment are poor' (Bennett 1981: 552).

In practice, as Carter's (1981) survey of thirteen area health authorities demonstrates, this distinction has not been adhered to. The programmes that existed in both day hospitals and day centres showed considerable overlap. They included social activities such as cards and table tennis; physical treatments provided by doctors, nurses, or therapists; arts and crafts; education classes; group and community meetings; and industrial and domestic work. As for the users of the service: 'close resemblances were found in the users of the two main sectors of day services for the mentally ill. Their views of their mental health were similar. Their perceptions of their physical health had a great deal in common. They were remarkably uniform in their age, their sex, marital status and living circumstances' (Carter 1981). There were, in fact, only two major differences in the backgrounds of users. Of day centre users 50 per cent had spent more than a year in hospital, compared with just over 20 per cent of the day hospital users. Referral paths differed too. Most users of day hospitals had been referred by hospital doctors and most users of day centres had been referred by social services social workers. Self-referrals were uncommon except in the voluntary sector.

Given such a degree of overlap in programmes and users' backgrounds it is not surprising that there was a shared view of the purposes of day care. Most of the heads of these day care units described the primary aim of their programmes as keeping users out of hospital although few had any evidence of how effective they had been in achieving this.

## Day care for mentally handicapped people

The provision of day care for mentally handicapped people has a longer history than psychiatric day care. The 1913 Mental Deficiency Act imposed an obligation on local authorities to provide training, occupation, and supervision for 'defectives' in their area and this resulted in the gradual spread of 'occupation centres'. Expansion of this form of provision was stimulated by the shift to 'community care' heralded by the report of the Royal Commission on the Law Relating to Mental Illness and Mental Handicap (HMSO 1957; discussed more fully in Chapter 1), and the duties of local authorities spelt out in the Mental Health Act 1959 and subsequent legislation (NDG 1977b).

As this history would suggest almost all current day care for mentally handicapped adults is provided by local authority social services departments in ATCs. Carter points out that this makes it a unique form of day service – 'a virtual monopoly' of one agency. ATCs provide a service for a wide range of people. As the National Development Group (NDG) for Mentally Handicapped People has stated:

'the potential users of day services do not constitute a homogeneous group. There will be people who are mildly mentally handicapped whose problems are often instability and immaturity who will need help only in certain areas such as communication or other social skills to enable them to lead an independent life in the community. There will be others who are severely mentally handicapped and who will require long-term help in many different areas, but who can progress towards greater independence and competence although they may always need a supportive environment. A proportion of mentally handicapped people in any day centre will also be multiply handicapped. Between these extremes there will be people whose learning abilities, though limited, will enable them to acquire a wide range of work, social and self-help skills.'

(NDG 1977b: 8)

The characteristic approach to meeting the needs of this diverse group has been, as the title 'Adult Training Centre' implies, that of social and occupational training. In Carter's national survey of day services for adults, it is clear that the form this training takes is modelled on the world of commerce and industry rather than education or therapy. This is partly a reflection of the background and experience of staff in the centres. The majority of managers and instructors have come from industry and commerce, with only one third having undergone training related to work with the mentally handicapped. This is a distinct contrast to staff in psychiatric day units, where nursing qualifications predominate.

The size of the training centres also plays a part in the type of training adopted. Since the birth of local authority social services departments there has been a marked increase in the number of centres provided. Three out of every five ATCs in Carter's survey had been opened since 1970 and the average size of these new centres had increased to 120 places. The background of staff and the size of these day units result in a very distinctive form of organization.

'Centres . . . are nearly always organized in a hierarchy. There are so few staff trained in other disciplines to incorporate into the running of the centre and instructors. . . form a hierarchy which extends from the most junior member of the centre to the manager.' 'Coming as they do from the factory, or from positions in the office, most managers and instructors are used already to working in hierarchies. The transfer from the factory or office to working to ill-defined objectives about people is a formidable task of thinking and practicality.' (Carter 1981: 57–8)

It would appear, then, that the response to the needs of the wide range of users of ATCs is an alarmingly homogeneous one. Fairly static user populations spend most of their time engaged on contract or industrial work supplemented sometimes by domestic work in the centre or outside in the gardens.

The National Development Group for the Mentally Handicapped, in their report *Day Services for Mentally Handicapped Adults* (1977b), outlined a radically alternative concept of day care designed to meet more fully the wide-ranging needs of mentally handicapped people. The 'Social Education Centres', which the NDG proposed should replace ATCs, have four major elements:

1 An admission and assessment section, which would provide for each entrant a multi-disciplinary assessment of needs on which his programme in the centre could be based.
2 A development and activity section, which would be the main section of the centre and incorporate many of the features of the current ATCs, providing education and training in literacy and social skills and a range of work activities.
3 The special care section, for entrants with severe handicaps, in need of constant care and attention.
4 The advanced work section, to provide entrants with realistic pre-work experiences.

It was envisaged that these elements would be used flexibly on the basis of individual need so that some entrants might move directly from assessment to advanced work while others would move to development and activity or special care.


## Approaches to day care

It is obvious that there are clear distinctions, as well as some areas of overlap, between the day care currently provided for mentally ill people and that provided for mentally handicapped people. However it is possible to identify in both kinds of day services three main kinds of provision. First, the provision of treatment and training designed to improve individual functioning. Second, the provision of work experience and preparation for work in paid employment or the home. Third the provision of opportunities to pursue educational, recreational, and leisure activities in the company of others.

There is little evidence to suggest that the 'mix' of the above ingredients in any day care unit's programme is shaped by design and assessment of users' needs. It is usually the interest and experience of care staff and the orientation and qualifications of the head of the unit that determine daily programmes. Very few units operate on the basis of a clear agreement between staff and users about what aspects of the programme might be most useful to each individual. More systematic thought needs to be given by day care staff, and those planning the service, to what each of these elements has to offer to individual users and their families. Consideration also needs to be given to the scope available for using this form of provision as an alternative to hospital care.

## Treatment and training

The non-physical treatment or training that is available in most psychiatric day units is based on the group therapy and rehabilitation
techniques which have already been outlined in Chapter 9. The use of
these techniques in a day care rather than a residential setting, opens up a
whole new range of possibilities. Day care provides more limited contact
between staff and users and greater opportunities for users to test out new
skills and ideas in their own homes. This should mean that staff work to
maximize the impact of treatment or training sessions by devising programmes which encourage users to apply new skills outside the unit. Such
programmes should build in 'feedback' sessions where users are
encouraged to share their experiences of changing their behaviour or
taking on new tasks in their living situation.

Using the potential that day care offers to effect change in 'real' life
situations, may mean that staff have to work on the reactions of those with
whom the user normally lives. For example a rehabilitation programme
designed to increase the independence of clients may well threaten the
long-established patterns of interaction between some clients and their
families. A study (London Borough of Wandsworth 1976) of the views of
mentally handicapped people attending ATCs in a London borough is
pertinent here. This study revealed marked discrepancies between the
ideas which some 'trainees' had about their capabilities and their future
lives and the ideas of their parents and training centre staff on these
topics. There was a tendency for some parents and staff to view the
trainees as children. In contrast, many trainees wished for more independence or a recognition that they were adults who could make decisions
and take responsibility. With client groups such as these, day training
programmes that work towards increased independence must incorporate
sessions for relatives. Otherwise those users engaged in the programme
will be left to negotiate contradictory messages from their relatives and
centre staff.

## Work and retraining

The emphasis in some day centres (particularly those for the mentally
handicapped) on work, or retraining for work, stems from two traditions.
The first is to provide a sheltered alternative to work for groups who will
not be able to find employment in the open market. The second is to
increase clients' chances of finding suitable employment by establishing
or re-establishing work habits and teaching new occupational skills.

In most day centres, staff views about the purpose of the work that the
users pursue are muddled. This muddle has increased in recent years as
unemployment has risen and the chances of mentally ill and handicapped
people entering open employment have diminished. The response of

some centres to this has been increasingly to provide a substitute for paid employment for a number of individuals who in the past would have used the centres for short retraining periods.

The problem of this response is that it can have some very negative consequences for users.

'Increasingly we are seeing withdrawn people in our psychiatric day centres and high ESN(M) people in our mental handicap centres. By their attendance in our day centres, these people are unwittingly undergoing a labelling process which switches the focus from the external reality of no jobs to the person's internal, emotional or intellectual shortcomings. Thus, the day centre is quite important in deflecting attention from what actually needs changing – inadequate economic opportunities – to the inadequacies of the individual.'

(Bender 1983: 20)

Charles Patmore has argued that current unemployment levels pose a major challenge for day centre staff who need to think again about the work element of their programmes. In discussing psychiatric day centres he suggests that there are at least two positive options which they could develop. The first is to adopt ways of working which help the more coping users develop 'independent support systems outside paid employment'. To this end he suggests that,

'it is not enough to run within the centre social or survival skills groups to prepare clients for life away from the unit. The crucial step is to enable clients to actually transfer part of their week's routine from attendance at the centre to regular involvements in the community of the sort that may fulfil some of the myriad support needs which are often met indirectly as a result of employment.'

(Patmore 1981: 567)

Examples here would be voluntary work of a structured and regular nature.

The second option which day care units could pursue is the reorganization of existing resources 'to provide low-intensity, long-term support networks for less coping clients in settings that are as close as possible to the work and social life for which they substitute' (Patmore 1981). Again, decisions need to be taken so that the amount of day care available to any individual user is organized to have the maximum impact, given that individual's needs.

## Recreation and education

Picking up the challenge that unemployment poses for some centre users will obviously influence the content of the third main area of work in day care – opportunities to pursue educational, recreational, and leisure activities in the company of others. It is significant that studies of day centres that have asked users how they spend their time have found that a major and positive activity for most users is talking to other users. For a significant minority a day hospital or centre provides their only social contact outside of the home and for relatives a welcome break from caring (Carter 1981; Peace 1980). Recreational and educational opportunities that provide social contact and stimulation are therefore a valued part of day care and staff could usefully consider the boundaries of their contribution here.

There are very few examples of day centres that use the potential of users to manage and direct daily programmes. Where such experiments have occurred, for example in a day centre pioneered by Knowlseley social services department, there is evidence that users have not only gained a great deal from their time spent at the centre, but have through the centre established personal relations with others which have been helpful in managing their lives outside centre opening hours (Brandon 1981).

The Brecknock Community Mental Health project was a unique experiment in user involvement. Centred in a housé in inner London, its aims were to provide a place where people with mental health problems could come together for support, generate a network of support to combat stress and isolation, and demonstrate ways in which psychiatrically disabled people could improve their relationship with the local community. The project centre, open six days a week, provided a wide range of responses to help users who were in crisis or difficulty as well as providing an informal, warm atmosphere which was highly valued by many users (Jowell 1981).

It is not just the relationships between staff and users that could be usefully reconsidered in order to make greater use of the social contact which centres can promote. The relationship that exists between the unit and the surrounding community needs to be thought about. A number of studies have shown that day centres can provide 'institutionalizing' environments despite the limited number of hours they are used (Carter 1981; Bennett 1981). If users live the rest of their days in isolated and unstimulating surroundings, then this kind of day care will compound difficulties rather than provide a positive experience. To counteract such tendencies staff and clients need to make full use of the educational, recreational, and leisure facilities in the surrounding community. Examples here might be mentally handicapped people using a local college of further education for courses (NDG 1977a), or groups using the swimming baths regularly. There is also considerable room to experiment with opening centre facilities to community groups and providing day care in non-specialist community facilities.

## Conclusion

Day care has the potential of becoming a major focus of activity, treatment, and care in any local service designed to meet the needs of mentally disordered and handicapped people within their own communities. This potential can be developed not only by increasing the range and quantity of day care available, but also by day care staff focusing more clearly on the needs of their users and the rationale behind the programmes they offer.

For ASWs seeking to help individuals and families in crisis, day care can offer a great deal. It can provide intensive therapeutic help; supplement the care being provided by relatives and friends; break the isolation and loneliness experienced by clients; help individuals tackle the problems of long-term disability and develop more independence; and it can make the difference between having to arrange hospital admission, and working with the client and day care staff to manage a crisis in such a way that the client maintains contact with his normal way of life.

# 11

## Boarding-out and substitute family care

## M. Rolf Olsen

In Chapter 1 Davis showed that since the 1950s successive governments have announced their preference for community- rather than the institutional-based care of the mentally disordered. This notion has received widespread professional support. Generally, this alternative solution is interpreted to mean care by the family. However, in Chapter 6 I reported the evidence that shows that relapse is related to the type of living group in which the patient resides and in particular to living groups in which the patient experiences high emotional involvement. These findings indicate that it is not always in a patient's interests to be discharged to a living group in which he encounters close emotional ties. This paradox suggests we must promote other less hazardous living environments in which patients may reside without additional burdens being placed upon them with the risk of relapse or deterioration. Alternatives, such as hostels, group homes, boarding houses, and substitute family care.

This chapter examines the evidence for two of these alternatives – boarding-out and substitute family care – and argues not only for their proper development within a range of provision which should be made available, but also for their use in guardianship in appropriate cases as an alternative to compulsory admission to hospital.

### Boarding-out and substitute family care

I have shown elsewhere (Olsen 1976a, 1976b, 1979a) that in psychiatric care the terms 'family care' and 'boarding-out', although not really synonymous (in that the first implies foster or substitute family care and the second a physical or economic arrangement), are used to describe a system of care in which discharged psychiatric and mentally handicapped patients are cared for in non-institutional living groups which are not their own. Under this arrangement patients may be placed with families or in similar residences such as boarding-houses, either singly, in small groups, or in quite large groups of thirty or more.

The first recorded system of family care was in Gheel, Belgium, where it has been continually practised since the seventh century. However, in spite of its long history and its successful adoption in a number of other European countries, it has not, since the nineteenth-century revelations which publicized the 'trade in lunacy' and the wretched condition of many lunatics living in private houses, been favoured in English or Welsh psychiatry. However, the Mental Welfare Commission for Scotland (1970) have stated that Scotland has had a system of boarding-out for well over a hundred years. The basis of this practice is 'to provide family care' with the intention 'that the boarded-out person should be absorbed into the life of the guardian's home, and as far as possible into the life of the community'. The system arose out of the 1845 Poor Law Act when paupers became chargeable to the Parish. Those who were insane had to be lodged in an asylum or legally authorized institution; because there was little institutional accommodation, and probably as a result of the scattered population living in a difficult terrain, private houses were licensed.

Wing (1957), during his review of family care systems in Norway and Holland, found that in England and Wales there were some 3,000 mental defectives in the community under the guardianship scheme, many in foster homes. He also discovered that although the system was acknowledged to work well and in spite of the provision for boarding-out certified patients under Section 67 of the Lunacy Act: 'Only 50–60 psychiatric patients are boarded out under it and it is clear that neither the Local Authorities nor the Hospital Management Committees are in favour of using it' (Wing 1957). This local authority resistance may have important implications for the 'guardianship' provisions in the 1983 Act and for the obligation placed upon the ASW, before making application for the admission of a patient to hospital, to 'satisfy himself that detention in a hospital is in all the circumstances of the case the most appropriate way of providing the care and medical treatment of which the patient stands in need' (Section 13(2)).

The lack of enthusiasm in England and Wales compared unfavourably with Norway and Holland where Wing met a keen interest. In Norway he found that 51 per cent of the certified were cared for in mental hospitals, 39 per cent were looked after in families, and 10 per cent were in nursing homes. In Holland, Wing found that many hospitals had some provision for family care. He conveyed the strengths of these different care systems and stressed particularly the humanity and personal liberty they afforded. Their basic weakness was seen to lie in the custodial attitude and the dependence that they created – it is rarely used as a short-term measure. Wing concluded that:

> 'after social and somatic treatment in a mental hospital, and with the support of other social services, there seems no reason to doubt that family care could contribute considerably towards the rehabilitation of many kinds of psychiatric patients.'

(Wing 1957: 886)

In America the boarding-out system was introduced on a small scale in 1885 (Wing 1957), but it was not to gain ground until after the Second World War. Barton (1953), in a review of the psychiatric progress in America during 1953, reported that 'the slow growth in family care continues'. He estimated that the total number boarded-out in his country had risen from 4,937 in 1951, to 6,201 in 1953.

More recent papers from America (Chien and Cole 1973; Fairweather, Sanders, and Maynard 1969; Friedman, Von Mering, and Hinko 1966; Keskiner et al. 1972; Lamb and Goertzel 1971; Sandall, Hawley, and Gordon 1975) show that during the 1970s 'there has been a mass exodus of long-term mental patients from State hospitals' (Lamb and Goertzel 1971); and the 'major thrust in hospital treatment programs during the past two decades has been to release chronic patients to protective community settings' (Keskiner et al. 1972); and that the conclusion shared by many psychiatrists is that 'many hospitalised psychotic patients can live and function in the community if a suitable sheltered environment is provided' (Chien and Cole 1973).

In England and Wales the major drive for the development of boarding-out care of the discharged psychiatric patient followed the Mental Health Act 1959, and the 1962 Hospital Plan for England and Wales, both of which advocated that a greater share of the management of long-stay patients should be transferred back to the community. In the absence of a family or alternative community-based accommodation, those psychiatric hospitals and local authorities who wished to implement the proposal had little option but to improvise and tap into existing community resources.

However, the use of boarding-house care had a slow start: in 1968 the Ministry of Health reported that '76 mentally ill patients were boarded-out'. This estimate, although rightly conveying the overall picture, is grossly inaccurate in that a number of institutions were by that time boarding-out. For example by the end of 1967 the North Wales Hospital, Denbigh, had itself placed 174 patients in boarding houses. In a written reply to me, the DHSS (30 April, 1970) stated, 'We have no statistical information concerning patients boarded-out on discharge from psychiatric hospitals'.

In the absence of any central monitoring it is difficult to estimate the developments in boarding-out with accuracy. However, from 1959 several reports indicated that an increasing number of hospitals and authorities were employing this strategy to rehabilitate and discharge psychiatric patients, including the County Borough of Brighton (1959), Somerset County Council (1960), Severall's Hospital (1963), Borough of Croydon (1962), Exe Vale Psychiatric Hospital (1962), The North Wales Hospital, Denbigh (1964), and the Old Manor Hospital, Salisbury (1974).

## Boarding-out: circumventing and interrupting chronicity or relocalizing the miniature institutions?

The fundamental questions in relation to boarding-out are whether it is an effective and viable strategy in circumventing and/or interrupting chronicity, or whether it represents no more than a relocalizing of psychiatric patients in miniature institutions.

The opinion in the major studies, apart from some minor reservations, suggests that boarding-out is not only a viable strategy but that it also offers the psychiatric patient a number of advantages which would be denied if he remained in institutional care. In particular: the opportunity to return to and be supported by the community; personal family-based care; employment; increased privacy; greater self-determination; a greater dignity from the opportunity to contribute to their own and the well-being of others as opposed to the passive acceptance of institutional care; and avoidance of the worst features of institutional dependence. The hospital and the wider community are also felt to gain from the alleged financial savings and the better use of scarce hospital resources.

There are, however, a number of authors who reject these conclusions and argue that, whilst it is true that hospital populations and the length of hospitalization have been reduced in some institutions, the patients have not achieved the benefits outlined above. Some argue that circumventing a long stay in hospital is artificial in that, whilst it reduces the length of stay, it has resulted in a new disguised chronicity referred to as 'intermittent patienthood' (Friedman, Von Mering, and Hinko 1966). This status and condition is characterized by repeated admission to hospital which leads to an institutional dependency and loss of family ties in much the same way as occurs in the single, long admission.

Others (Fairweather, Sanders, and Maynard 1969; Lamb and Goertzel 1971) argue that, whilst boarding houses have enabled the long-stay patient to be discharged, they have a low expectation of achievement, docility is valued, and little initiative is expected. In consequence, 'the boarding-house group is not really in the community. It is like a small ward moved to a community setting' (Lamb and Goertzel 1971). A view which has been supported by adverse media reports.

Darley and Kenny (1971), during their investigation of the low success rate of a day centre for psychiatric patients, came to the same conclusion that discharge often represents no more than a relocation of the patient in a different institutional setting, or sheltered sub-society in which the patient is 'given the damaging role of citizen-on-probation'. Keskiner *et al.* (1972) also dismiss the alleged benefits of boarding-out care arrangement, arguing that:

'1 Chronic patients lack the social and vocational skills necessary for functioning independently in the community;
2 mental health manpower and financial resources are being utilised to maintain them in miniature institutions; and
3 the community is not providing the acceptance or the assistance essential for the social reintegration.'

(Keskiner *et al.* 1972: 283)

The authors, however, do not reject the principles of community care, rather they argue that if we are successfully to apply them we must construct a resocialization programme which is designed not only to prepare the patient for community living but also the whole 'foster community' – on the lines of Gheel – to adopt 'psychiatric patients as new citizens'.

Whilst the contradictory conclusions contained within the quoted papers point to some of the fundamental problems of family care and boarding-out, none rejects the feasibility of placing chronic patients in non-institutional living groups, or invalidates the concept in any way. Rather they argue for alternative systems within the overall policy to return long-stay patients to the community and raise the major issues which arise out of the strategy.

### Some boarding-out schemes, England and Wales, 1959–75

This optimism is supported by the findings of a number of British investigations which report the outcome to boarding-out discharged psychiatric patients.

For example Smith (1975, 1979), in largely descriptive accounts, relates the success of boarding-out 130 mainly elderly long-stay patients from the Old Manor Hospital, Salisbury, to live either with a family (93) or in a nursing home (37). The emphasis throughout this project was on integrating the patient into a family atmosphere; therefore in only two families were more than two patients allowed to go together, because they had become friends whilst in the hospital and did not wish to be separated. In the first year of the project none of the boarded-out patients had been readmitted and 3 had died – 'all over 80 years of age' – from natural causes (Smith 1975). During the total follow-up period of 3–4 years only 8 (8.6 per cent) of those discharged to a family home and 2 (5.4 per cent) of the 37 who went to a nursing home were readmitted (Smith 1979).

Although readmission cannot be held as a totally reliable indicator of success or failure of the scheme, it does provide information about the small number who were unable to remain in the community. 'The primary complaints which led to readmission were: incontinence, quarrelsomeness, garrulousness, and wandering into other people's rooms and helping themselves to their possessions' (Smith 1979).

Overall, Smith reached three major conclusions. First, that institutional dependence is reversible; second, that supported lodgings are a viable strategy; and third, that family homes are often preferable to residential and group homes which often demand a too high level of achievement.

Slater (1971, 1979), in a similar but larger study, reports that a survey carried out at the Exe Vale Psychiatric Hospital in 1962 'indicated that of the 1,600 patients approximately half no longer required hospital care'; 'they remained there simply because they had no home to go to and no one to care for them'. Arrangements were made to discharge these patients to private homes, and eventually the scheme was extended to include newly admitted patients who could not return to their admission address.

Remarkably, by 1971 the hospital had approved 41 homes providing up to 535 beds in groups ranging between 1 and 41. During the ten years 1962–71, over 1,000 female patients were discharged to the selected private accommodation; of these approximately 8 per cent returned to remain in hospital. In a later report Slater (1979) records that 'During the 15 years under review over 2,000 patients have been discharged to carefully selected accommodation'. The 8 per cent readmission rate had been maintained.

Slater saw the merits of the scheme in terms of it enabling patients to leave hospital without delay; making better use of hospital beds, reducing waiting time for admissions; as a more efficient use of medical and nursing skills; involving the community in a caring role; and making financial savings.

My own study (Olsen, 1976b) into the personal and social consequences, 2–5 years after discharge, of long-stay psychiatric patients from the North Wales Hospital, Denbigh, during 1965–66, mainly to boarding houses, also showed that these residences were successful and resulted in real gains for a significant number of patients and the persons who cared for them. During the six years 1965–70, 22 boarding houses were opened in the North Wales area to which an estimated 504 patients were discharged. A few of the patients were placed singly, most became members of small groups, and some joined quite large groups of thirty or more.

I followed up patients discharged to the first 12 houses to be opened. I found that these houses had admitted a total of 269 discharged patients, mostly with a long stay in hospital of two years or more. By the end of five years 20 per cent had moved elsewhere, a number to an environment which offered greater independence, and in spite of the degree of social and personal handicap which was evident in many on discharge, only 15 per cent had been readmitted. On balance these residences provided a number of advantages over hospital care. In particular they enabled the patient to return to the community, and compared with the conditions in Denbigh Hospital before the discharge policy was implemented, offered a higher standard of care, a greater degree of privacy and independence, and opportunity for self-determining behaviour, as well as the chance of an increased dignity from the possibility to contribute to the well-being of others.

Nevertheless, in spite of these achievements it is important to acknow-ledge that the arrangement was confronted with a number of difficulties, many of which were declared by the landladies themselves. The overall conclusions to be drawn from the landladies' evidence is that in many instances both the landlady and the resident were needlessly disadvan-taged by the enterprise. All but three landladies were thought to give the patients a good standard of physical and emotional care in spite of an almost punitive financial return. The main disadvantages were: having to give constant 24-hour care; a lack of free time and a detrimental effect on family life; inadequate support from the professional services; some hostility from the neighbours; a lack of training and preparation for the task; and having to cope with a variety of behavioural and care difficulties in the patients. The patients also suffered from the disregard for their social and occupational needs, and a very poor income. The net result of these disadvantages was that the houses, as they were operated, primarily served as holding environments, in which there was a low expectation of achievement and initiative, and that as feared we relocalized the patients in miniature institutions when we might well have circumvented chroni-city and achieved rehabilitation.

The blame for this must lie in the exploitation of the landlady and the patient and in the failure of a number of hospital, local authority, and other services to support the venture. It is a sad reflection that twenty years after Wing's (1957) report of the family care systems in Norway and Holland, the care and support given to these boarding-houses completely fails to match the standard which he reported.

## The use of boarding out as an alternative to hospital, and in guardianship

'Before making an application for the admission of a patient to hospital an approved social worker shall interview the patient in a suitable manner and satisfy himself that detention in a hospital is in all the circumstances of the case the most appropriate way of providing the care and medical treatment of which the patient stands in need.'

(Section 13(2), Mental Health Act, 1983)

The findings reported in this chapter show that it is not only possible successfully to accommodate and rehabilitate the mentally disturbed within boarding-houses and substitute family care, but that the arrangement has many advantages over the more traditional solutions of hospital and family care. This raises the question of how far such a strategy might be successfully used to fulfil the requirement laid upon local authorities to provide after-care to patients discharged from treatment orders (Section 117); and the duty laid upon the ASW to satisfy himself that detention in hospital is necessary (Section 13(2)). This last statutory obligation has the dual function of ensuring that the patient's therapeutic needs are met; and, in the absence of judicial oversight, that the patient's liberty interests are protected. The ASW must be satisfied that detention in hospital is the 'most appropriate way' of providing the care and treatment. This implies that it must be the least restrictive conditions possible. What is possible depends of course on what is available. If detention in hospital is not necessary but alternative community-based methods of management like boarding-out are not available, then the ASW's protective function will be subverted and patients' liberty interests will be lost.

The evidence in relation to boarding-out and substitute family care is sufficiently strong to suggest that their use as an alternative to admission to hospital, in guardianship and in rehabilitation, should be actively promoted. However, the results also show that if we are to utilize this therapeutically and economically valuable community resource to the full, it is vital that landladies and substitute families receive the political support and professional interest of which they are currently starved. There are also a number of professional issues to which we must address ourselves. In particular we must ensure that landlady applicants are not accepted without due consideration being given to their motives and suitability to the task; we must undertake careful evaluation of the role of the landlady and of the difficulties which she encounters so that we might devise a suitable 'training'; we must give a fair financial payment to ensure that the caring person receives a proper return, is able to employ help and to avoid overcrowding; particular attention must be given to the selection of patients and ways devised to try to reduce the behavioural and care problems they can present – particularly in relation to the neglect of hygiene which is frequently reported by landladies; the educational, social, and occupational needs of the patients require careful evaluation and the provision of an appropriate range of recreational, occupational, sheltered workshops, and day centre services; the breakdown of continuing support from the psychiatric and social work services should be avoided and greater efforts should be made to promote community acceptance of the houses and integrate the patient into the community. It is only by these efforts and the application of these resources that we will avoid relocating the patients to nasty, sub-standard, large, cold, unsupervised houses or in a sheltered sub-society, and begin to develop the full potential of this primary resource.

# PART FOUR
# ISSUES RELATING TO THE DELIVERY OF SERVICES

# 12
## Developing comprehensive local services

'If we do not have a vision of what we need we will not move
far from what we have at present.'                    (MIND 1983)

## Ann Davis

Knowledge of the resources available to mentally ill and mentally handicapped people is essential for effective social work with this client group.
In any district these resources are not just provided by central and local
government departments; they are also drawn from voluntary organizations, private commercial concerns, and ordinary households. Together
they make up a local service.

The purpose of this chapter is to highlight the essential elements of any
comprehensive local service which is being developed to meet the needs
of people with mental disorder. Particular attention is paid to the part that
social workers (both approved and general) can play in such a service and
the demands which the Mental Health Act 1983 might make of them. This
chapter should be used as a spring-board for individuals and groups to
discuss their own local service and collect information on local resources.

The emphasis throughout is on the needs of people suffering from
mental disorder and the type and style of services which might meet those
needs. Detailed consideration is not given to statistical questions, that is
the quantity of any particular service or provision per 100,000 population.
Such guidelines provided at national level can be unhelpful if not mis-
leading when applied to local district populations with distinct characteristics. It should be part of the task of those with the responsibility of
managing and planning local services to devise targets which take fully

into account the profile of the local population, the use made of existing services, and the available national guidelines.

Of course the majority of people with mental disorder and mental handicap do not use specialist mental health services in times of need. They seek and receive support and advice from relatives and friends. It is social networks based on family, the neighbourhood, or work which make the largest single contribution to the care of mentally disordered people (Goldberg and Huxley 1980). A local mental health service, offering specialist help and drawing on the resources of a range of statutory voluntary and private provision, always operates alongside an extensive informal system of care. It is therefore crucial that any developing local service takes fully into account the way it relates to the informal care system.

## Principles

Local services that are responsive to the needs of people who are experiencing mental distress and disability are not just a mix of particular facilities. Crucial to the success and development of these services are the attitudes and philosophies of the staff involved. Their view of their clients and their own role will play a key part in determining access to and use of the local service. Service initiatives and experiments are always dependent on the drive and enthusiasm of those involved, and on their willingness to take risks and work in situations of uncertainty.

In recent years there has been a growing interest in mental health literature in establishing a set of principles which should inform developments in community-based mental disorder and mental handicap services. This interest has sprung from concerns to formulate a clear, alternative basis from which innovative work can develop. The principles which have emerged (for example those outlined in the Jay Committee Report (HMSO 1979)) reflect particular views about the nature of disability, individual rights to welfare provision, and a commitment to the idea of community care.

The most recent contribution in this area has been that of the Independent Development Council for people with Mental Handicap (1982) and MIND (1983). Building on the Independent Council's work, MIND's *Common Concern* manifesto outlines a set of principles which they argue should underlie the development of any local mental health service.

'A local comprehensive service is one which:
1 Values the client as a full citizen with rights and responsibilities, entitled to be consulted and to have an active opportunity to shape and influence relevant services, no matter how severe his or her disability;

2 Aims to promote the greatest self-determination of the individual on the basis of informed and realistic choice;

3 Aims to provide and evaluate a programme of treatment, care and support based on the unique needs of the individual, regardless of age or severity of disability;

4 Aims to minimise the dependence of the client on professional resources, but which does not allow this as an excuse to withdraw appropriate services;

5 Aims to meet the special needs arising from disability through a locally accessible fully co-ordinated multi-disciplinary service offered by appropriately trained staff;

6 Is easily accessible locally, and delivered, wherever possible, to the client's usual environment;

7 Plans actively for those in institutions to reintegrate into society if they so wish;

8 Aims to enhance the individual or collective capacity to cope with or alleviate distress.'                                    (MIND 1983: 7)

These principles are ones that uphold the rights of the individual client in a form that is highly congruent with the values of social work. They also reinforce the view that where a professional's services are used they should be offered in the least restrictive environment possible and in a manner that does not unnecessarily disrupt the normal life style of the individual client. ASWs who are involved in situations where compulsory detention, assessment, and treatment may be an option, need constantly to review their decisions in the light of such considerations.

### Key elements of a local mental service

People who are mentally disordered receive help, advice, and care from two main sources. First, and most importantly, from their relatives, friends, and neighbours who contribute to the *informal care system* in any local district. Second, from the *formal system*, those welfare services and facilities provided by central and local government departments, voluntary organizations, and commercial enterprises.

The majority of social workers, both specialist and general, are employed in the state services of the formal system and this consideration of the key elements of a local mental health service places particular emphasis on the contribution of these services.

When reviewing the local services of which they are part it can be useful for social workers to think of a comprehensive district mental health service as having three key elements:

1 The contribution made by mental health specialists to the care and treatment of mentally disordered people.

2 The contribution made by a variety of general agencies to the lives of mentally disordered people.
3 The contribution made by mental health specialists to the work of those general agencies that work with mentally disordered people.

In any local service there will be a unique blend of each of these three elements. There will also be considerable variation in the size and scope of each element and the impact each makes on local need. In the rest of this chapter each element will be discussed, in the light of the principles outlined earlier.

## THE SPECIALIST CONTRIBUTION

It is the NHS which provides most of the specialist care available to mentally disordered people. Only 5 per cent of those diagnosed as mentally ill have contact with specialist provision which takes the form of outpatient, day patient and in-patient care. Amongst this 5 per cent are those suffering acute conditions as well as those with severe and disabling illnesses who may be dependent on specialist care for considerable periods of time (Goldberg and Huxley 1980).

A comprehensive local service, informed by the principles outlined in Chapters 3 and 4, would seek to organize this specialist health service care on a community basis. Wherever the specialists' main base was, arrangements would be made to ensure that their services were available to the populations they were serving. Health centres and church halls might be used to provide outpatient consultation or day care, if they were more central than hospital units. In districts covering scattered rural populations, travelling day hospitals or outpatient clinics housed in mobile units might be an option. The frequency of contact of such services would be determined by the location of particularly vulnerable populations such as the elderly, or isolated mothers with young children.

Whatever the choice of location the care and treatment provided should be of a multi-disciplinary nature, calling on the skills and expertise of psychiatrists, nurses, social workers, psychologists, and occupational therapists. Ideally specialist health provision of this kind should not only provide ongoing assessment and treatment but should also offer a crisis intervention service. This service should be available round the clock using multi-disciplinary teams to work with individuals and families in crisis in their own homes, wherever possible.

The range of special need which is likely to be found in any district is bound to include: disturbance in childhood, adolescence, and old age; alcoholism; drug addiction; long-term disability; and disturbed offenders. For each of these groups additional services as well as those available through the specialist team will be required. These additional services should include staff with special interests and training as well as facilities designed to provide particular forms of care and treatment. For example, in meeting the needs of those who have long-term disability, a rehabilitation and resettlement service, designed to enhance individuals' abilities to cope through training programmes and supported housing schemes, would be essential. This service could be based within the health service or within local authority residential provision, but would need to draw on the skills of psychologists, nurses, occupational and industrial therapists, and social workers. In addition, day care in hospital, local authority and voluntary centres would be necessary to monitor progress and provide occupation and recreation, as well as a range of accommodation, both staffed, unstaffed, and supported, and a community psychiatric nursing service.

Local authority social services departments make the second major input to the specialist provision of any local mental health service. Social workers should play an active part in any community or crisis specialist team, and consideration needs to be given to the way in which the local authority organizes this input. Several approaches can be adopted (DHSS/ Welsh Office 1974). Individual practitioners can be placed permanently in every consultant-led specialist team; a group of practitioners based in social service area teams can provide input on a rotating basis to specialist health teams; a team of social workers can be established in a specialist hospital, to be used by health teams inside and outside the hospital; a team of social workers can be based in the community to liaise with specialist health teams on a regular basis.

Apart from a social work service, local authority social services departments should also develop specialist day care and residential units which will make their own distinct contribution to local resources and could provide an alternative basis for the work of specialist multi-disciplinary teams. (The forms that this kind of development can take are reviewed in Chapters 9 and 10.)

## THE CONTRIBUTION OF GENERAL AGENCIES

The majority of people suffering from mental disorder and mental handicap do not become the clients of the specialist services described above. In meeting need outside of their social networks they seek help from the general agencies which are part of any local welfare system. This section considers four areas of need with which general agencies become concerned – health, income, housing, and employment.

*Health*   As far as health is concerned it is the primary health care services which advise and manage most individuals who are mentally disordered. But as Goldberg and Huxley point out (1980), reliance on the skills of the general practitioner in this area is insufficient. The emotional, personal, and social difficulties that are brought to surgeries and health centres require the concerted efforts of a group of health professionals if they are to diminish or be resolved. The contribution of the GP can be usefully supplemented by that of the district nurse, health visitor, social worker, and psychologist. Joint working of this kind can be extended to provide domiciliary assessment and support, drawing on additional health resources such as nursing auxiliaries. It can also be used to improve access to health care for groups who are hard to reach. For example, special arrangements can be made between primary health care teams and night shelters or day centres working with people of no fixed abode.

*Income*   Social security benefits are the main source of income for many mentally ill and mentally handicapped people and their families. There are several reasons for this. Increased levels of unemployment, to which disabled people are particularly vulnerable, have increased dependence on state benefits. The proportion of elderly people and women amongst claimants and the mentally disordered populations has an influence too.

The complexity of the state benefit system is renowned and the most major recent change – the introduction of the housing benefit scheme – has increased the involvement of local authority housing departments alongside the DHSS in its implementation. New administrative procedures designed to help staff cope with the growing number of claimants has resulted in an expansion in the use of forms and written claims for benefit.

Mentally disabled people share the general problems of access to and use of this system. In addition they may also face particular difficulties. The experience of psychiatric illness can bring problems in sustaining regular routines. This can result in loss of benefit when, for example, an individual fails to sign-on regularly at an unemployment benefit office or return a particular form. Periods in and out of hospital or hostel accommodation can lead to considerable delays in receiving full benefit entitlement. Special care or treatment such as attendance at outpatient clinics or day hospitals and centres can add considerably to expenditure. But there is no reimbursement for such costs unless additional claims are made and lack of literacy skills can hamper claimants receiving financial aid.

General advice agencies such as citizens' advice bureaux or welfare rights services can provide the kind of expert help that mentally disabled claimants and their families often need in order to receive the benefits they are entitled to. A comprehensive local mental health service must ensure that clients and professional helpers have knowledge of such agencies and that their staff are fully used. There have been several interesting experiments in this area. Middlewood and Tooting Bec Psychiatric Hospitals have regular advice sessions from their local citizens' advice service. Take-up campaigns in day units for both mentally ill and mentally handicapped people have assessed clients and helped staff and clients claim benefits. What is more they have revealed considerable short-falls in benefit payments. Advice staff have also been used in training sessions to alert both specialist helpers and claimants to changes in the benefit system (Davis and Hayton 1984).

*Housing*   Access to housing can pose problems for people who are mentally handicapped or have a history of mental disorder. Low income increases dependency on the local authority and private sectors of the housing market. Local authority allocation systems discriminate against single people and those who do not have a number of years' residency in a particular area. The private sector provides some of the most inadequate accommodation available – dilapidated, overcrowded, and lacking in basic amenities.

The provision of adequate housing is essential to any local mental health service which aims to promote the independence and citizenship of mentally ill and mentally handicapped people. It is also essential to the success of rehabilitation and resettlement services. As Etherington outlines in his guide for housing workers, housing that meets the needs of mentally ill people must be allocated so that stress is minimized and contact with family or specialist services is preserved. He argues that housing workers have an important role to play in relation to mentally disordered people:

> 'Housing workers should encourage their local authority departments to accept responsibility for patients without a home as potentially homeless persons and should press vigorously for rehousing as a point for this group. This can be done within the framework of the Homeless Persons Act. Other methods of allocation can also be used. A good example of this is the quota system. Under this system a number of houses or flats are allocated by housing departments specifically to mentally ill people. The system is normally administered jointly by housing and social services departments. Patients are assessed by both departments and, once their capacity to live independently has been established, housing is allocated.'                    (Etherington 1983: 34)

Apart from meeting general housing needs, local authorities and housing associations can develop schemes of supported or warden-assisted accommodation to meet special needs.

*Employment*   Both the employment and education services can play a part in helping individuals who face unemployment. A recent Manchester study highlights the considerable difficulties faced by people who have psychiatric histories in the employment field. This study reveals the dearth of advice and counselling available after discharge from hospital and suggests that clients and the specialist services need to be more aware of existing services which might provide occupational and employment advice as well as opportunities to develop recreational and leisure interests (Birch 1983).

Finally, local authority social services departments provide a range of general services which supplement the support provided by informal systems of care. Such help can make the difference between an individual remaining at home or entering residential care. The use of the home help service, meals on wheels, and good neighbour schemes can assist in maintaining an elderly, confused person at home. The provision of child care on a regular basis can be crucial in preventing the hospital admission of a depressed mother.

THE CONTRIBUTION OF SPECIALISTS TO THE WORK OF GENERAL AGENCIES

The specialists who are employed in any local mental health service are drawn from a range of professions. Together and individually, they have an important contribution to make in supporting those working in general agencies through consultancy, education, and supervision.

To take the ASW as one example. A specialist social worker based in a community or crisis mental health team has an important role as a member of that team in working with primary health care professionals. With access to particular resources, such as a day place and regular consultancy contact with the ASW, a primary health care worker may be able to support an individual who might otherwise have required specialist care and treatment. In such cases the social worker would be sharing his skills in working with individuals suffering emotional distress as well as his knowledge of, and access to, local resources in order to supplement the contribution of primary health care professionals.

Similarly, psychiatrists or psychologists from specialist teams can work productively with residential staff of units for children and elderly people, focusing on problems encountered in dealing with difficult or depressed behaviour. Yet other examples might be a community psychiatric nurse who provides a regular advice session for a group of carers or staff working in a night shelter; or Emergency and Accident Units of general hospitals that deal regularly with parasuicide and should be a prime target for specialist liaison and support.

Staff in advice centres, housing departments or housing associations, social security offices, and reception areas of general agencies, are often faced with difficulties in responding to people who behave in bizarre or aggressive ways. Specialist workers can make useful contributions to staff training programmes for such groups of staff and through this improve responsiveness of general services to the needs of people suffering mental disorder.

## Conclusion

It is impossible to cover in a review of this kind all the elements that are essential to the development of comprehensive local services for mentally ill and mentally handicapped people. The areas I have focused on in this chapter need to be considered alongside the contributions that voluntary organizations, informal networks, and the private sector make to any pattern of local provision.

The framework I have provided, however, can be used as a basis for individuals or groups to discuss their own local services and the part they, as specialist or generic social workers, play in it. From such discussions more detailed information can be collected on the local resources available to people suffering mental disorder. In sharing this information individuals and groups should consider what initiatives are needed to improve their local resources and where such initiatives might start.

# 13

# Working with volunteers and self-help groups

## *Ann Davis and Lynne Muir*

Community resources for the mentally disordered are minimal in most areas. Therefore one of the primary tasks of the mental health worker is to develop community-based facilities. This might be achieved through the more extensive use of volunteers and self-help groups.

### Volunteers

Volunteering has a long and respectable history in social work. A number of organizations, such as the Young Men's Christian Association (YMCA), Marriage Guidance Councils, Samaritans, and Family Service Units, were established by and continue to be run by volunteers. Some have the help of a few paid staff (such as MIND), while others are managed by voluntary committees but serviced by paid staff (like Settlements).

Organizations run by volunteers have the advantage of not being accountable to a larger bureaucratic, state-supported agency. This means that they should be able to experiment with new methods of work, identify and meet minority needs and interests, and respond quickly to new demands without the constraints endemic in large organizations. Due to the size, structure, and public accountability with which government agencies must contend, they often are not free to reallocate resources quickly into new areas of work. It is here that voluntary organizations can make a real contribution – and it is unfortunate that some have not moved with changing trends but have calcified at an earlier stage of development.

Large statutory departments can gain some of the freedom of movement of voluntary organizations through the use of volunteers. Because volunteers are not part of the staff allocation, they do not incur costs in terms of salary, pension, and national insurance, and often represent a wider cross-section of the community than does the social work profession.

Unfortunately, in a time of financial restraint, the use of volunteers can become a political issue. Some of the current political arguments that are turned against the use of volunteers include: (a) volunteers are a cheap labour force and should not be exploited; (b) volunteers are brought in to do social work jobs, and therefore frozen posts will not be released if the work is covered by others; (c) social workers have professional ethics regarding confidential information, but this does not apply to volunteers. While some of these arguments may be valid, there is no evidence, particularly concerning the last point, that volunteers are worse than social workers in dealing with confidential material. One has only to think of the number of people in a social services department, from typists to social workers, who have access to the files to realize the weakness of this argument.

The Seebohm Committee (DHSS 1968) stressed the need to 'enlist the help of large numbers of volunteers to complement the teams of professional workers'. This cry was reiterated by the Aves Committee (Aves 1969) which said that volunteers should be 'an extension of and complement to the work of qualified staff'. A 3-year research project (Holme and Maizels 1978) to see how far these recommendations had been implemented was undertaken by the British Association of Social Workers, and the results were published in 1978. They approached 1,220 social workers and 203 probation officers through a postal study, in order to determine how volunteers were being used. While just over 50 per cent of social service workers who replied to the survey used volunteers, for most it was an indirect relationship, which the writers called a supplementary model, with little regular contact between workers and volunteers. They found that about 70 per cent of probation officers who responded used volunteers, and that many were involved in direct personal relationships with their volunteers, which the writers called a complementary model. A tendency was also indicated for social services to use volunteers with groups, while probation used them more for work with individuals. As would be expected, this study supported the findings of other studies that a typical volunteer was a woman; the age range varied from under eighteen to over fifty; and men were more likely than women to give practical services, while women were more likely than men to give befriending help.

A 3-year study commissioned by the DHSS and carried out by the

National Association of Youth Clubs (Muir 1983) looked at ways of utilizing volunteers in the development of intermediate treatment provision. This project, carried out in Brixton, Devon, and Birmingham, was based on the idea that volunteers may be effective with young people in trouble because (a) the volunteers 'do it because they care' (as one young volunteer said) and not because they are paid to care, so that young people were seen as people and not cases; (b) the volunteers recruited often had a similar cultural and socio-economic background to the young people so that class differences that may exist between social workers and young people were not a problem; (c) the use of local people as volunteers involves the community in taking responsibility for its own members, rather than abdicating this role to others; (d) volunteers can provide continuity of care as they often move less frequently than social workers.

This project used volunteers in a variety of ways, from individual befriending to running small interest groups, to working within youth clubs. While it is difficult directly to link a drop in re-offending rates to the participation in the project, both Devon and Brixton found that the rate for reappearing in court for those who had gone through the programme had dropped.

Workers sometimes hesitate to consider the use of volunteers for a number of reasons, including the debate over the motivations of volunteers, the problem of selecting people with the qualities needed to work with the client group, the time needed to train and support volunteers, and the resources needed to sustain a volunteer programme. Yet there are many successful groups now being run in the community for a number of client groups, including the mentally disordered. Some are self-help groups organized by recovered mentally disordered people, while day centres, run by MIND and others, use volunteers extensively. The potential of the volunteer community is discussed by Schindler-Rainman and Lippitt (1977) who outline some goals for an ideal volunteer community. They include extending the range of places and ways in which volunteers can serve the community; developing voluntarism in such critical and underdeveloped areas of service as cross-age, cross-talent, cross-sex, cross-race, cross-social class, and cross-economic status; increasing the knowledge of men, women, and children in all parts of the community about the opportunities for volunteer service, and increasing their motivation to offer their services; and developing the necessary knowledge, skills, and resources to find, recruit, train, place, and support additional volunteers for service throughout the community.

### Self-help groups

Of course involving others in helping people who suffer from mental disorder is not just a matter of recruiting and supporting volunteers.

Professional social workers in the mental health field often ignore the potential their clients have for helping others as well as themselves. This blindness stems from a tendency to work from the negatives, shown in the social workers' preoccupations with the difficulties and problems of clients and their past and current failures to resolve them. Professional skills in focusing on the positives – the clients' abilities to survive despite emotional and social suffering, their willingness to share with and help other people – often become eroded.

The preoccupation of social workers with 'client weaknesses' often results in a professional blindness in which clients appear to have over-whelming problems in coping with life: they are in crises, they are suffering, and they are asking for help. Yet in accepting and working within this agenda mental health social workers can confirm their clients' worst fears – that they are failures, a race apart, a group with such great problems that they need expert help, and in the world of mental health that help can carry with it a profoundly stigmatizing label.

In a series of interviews undertaken with people coping with long-standing disabilities arising from mental illness or handicap, or the effects of living for years in institutional care, reference was often made to the disabling effects of some contacts with professional helpers (Davis and Davis 1982; Towell and Davis 1984). The men and women interviewed had all negotiated rehabilitation schemes and were successfully settled in the community, mainly living in group homes. This experience, described by one woman in her mid-fifties, of the nurses who had cared for her in hospital was echoed by others:

'They meant well, don't get me wrong. I'm not criticizing them. They thought it was all for the best, for our own good, but they treated us like children. They made your mind up for you and you stopped thinking for yourself. They said we could not be expected to cope with the ups and downs of life. It did me no good, I lost my confidence altogether.'

A man in his early sixties:

'I don't think it helps, being told what you can't do. We all can't do everything. Some are better than others. But on the rehabilitation unit it was what you couldn't do, not what you could do, that seemed to count with the staff.'

All of us know that having our lives held up to critical scrutiny by others can generate anxiety, aggression, depression. It can sap our confidence in our ability to cope. Yet knowing this, social workers at times put their clients through these experiences in one-to-one encounters, family work, group work, or rehabilitation programmes.

An antidote to this tendency amongst professional workers is the self-help group. Such groups, as their name suggests, are organized on the basis that there is a potential within people who share a common experience to help each other. That potential stems from an experience that they all share, and the effect it has had on them as individuals. Such groups differ from groups organized and led by social workers or volunteers in one crucial respect: they are groups wholly comprising sufferers, who are both seeking and giving help to other group members.

Apart from providing an alternative to professional help (self-help groups can begin as a protest at the lack of help given by professionals), self-help groups can also be important in tackling isolation. Many people who struggle with emotional distress and mental illness feel isolated from others. The feelings which overwhelm them when they are depressed, anxious, or agitated can cut them off from others, and the struggle to cope with their feelings and manage their life becomes a lonely battle. It is not easy to share such experiences. Others might 'empathize', but if they have never had such experiences barriers may be erected which compound feelings of shame and loneliness. Self-help groups can provide opportunities to share common troubles, and for some people this kind of contact can be very positive indeed.

As a member of a local 'Depressives Associated' group put it,

'People have said that they found it helpful to go along and speak to others who are in the same boat, because unless you have suffered from a depressive illness you have no idea how devastating it can be. All the light goes out of life, and sometimes it is just a case of hanging on to life by sheer will power, even hope seems to die. And to go along to other people who say "Yes, I know exactly how it feels", and particularly to see people who are getting better, or who have got better, it is very encouraging to be able to do that.'

(Central Birmingham Community Health Council 1979)

Self-help groups do not just have a therapeutic potential. Some are formed around issues that affect the lives of members as profoundly as their emotional problems. Lack of adequate provision in health and social services, social security, housing, and transport systems also disable and isolate individuals and their families. Campaigns to improve provision or provide a much needed service on a self-help basis have always been part of the tradition of the self-help movement in this country. Examples abound. Two women met one day on a bus as they were making their long and difficult journey to visit their elderly relatives in a large, isolated psychiatric hospital. Finding that they shared the problem of maintaining regular contact in the face of a rapidly contracting public transport system, they began to speculate on how many others might be in a similar position. Using the notice-boards of the hospital and an interested social worker, they formed a 'relatives group' which proved successful in running a regular visitors' bus and car service on a self-financing basis.

'Sitting' circles, organized on a mutual-aid basis, which give members a few hours away from the care of elderly dementing relatives, exist in various parts of the country, initiated by individuals who found that no such help was available from existing statutory and voluntary organizations.

The defining characteristic of a self-help group is that its members organize themselves on the basis of mutual experience and interests. Because of this it is often difficult for social workers to work out their role. In districts where such groups exist, social workers can usefully point potential members towards them, but is that the only useful contribution which social workers can make? The dilemma facing any social worker interested in encouraging self-help is how far his contact with such groups will undermine rather than enhance the mutual aid that lies at their heart.

There are, we think, four main ways in which social workers specializing in mental health can work with self-help groups: by encouraging potential founders; increasing knowledge of existing self-help groups; providing 'low profile' support; and using self-help groups.

## ENCOURAGING POTENTIAL FOUNDERS

Amongst the clientele of social workers are people who are suffering or have suffered from mental disorder and have a great deal to offer others. There are also those who have experience as carers of relatives and friends, who could both use and give mutual support. Social workers can encourage such people to channel their potential and interests in establishing a self-help group. Encouragement of this kind does not mean playing a leading role in creating a group, but providing an informed and sympathetic ear to those who are pioneering this work.

## INCREASING KNOWLEDGE OF EXISTING SELF-HELP GROUPS

A useful job can be done at a local level by specialist social workers in collecting up-to-date information about active self-help groups to share with clients and colleagues. Nationally there are organizations that exist to encourage local self-help groups around such problems as bereavement, tranquilizer use, alcoholism, postnatal depression, and the burden of caring. Such organizations can provide useful information for local groups, and specialist social workers should also keep an up-to-date directory of them. Finally, a great deal can be learned from the experiences of groups in other parts of the country. The 'Good Practices in Mental Health' project (IHF 1979), initiated by the International Hospital Federation, has accumulated a wealth of information about self-help groups, and social workers could usefully tap this source in order to increase their knowledge of work in this area.

## PROVIDING 'LOW PROFILE' SUPPORT

Some self-help groups have discovered that it is useful to be able to draw on the services of outside helpers or consultants such as social workers to sustain their work. Outsiders play a useful role by being available for a group to call on for suggestions, encouragement, and specific resources. But maintaining a 'low profile' is essential for the group's life, and this may mean resisting pressures to take over and direct certain groups. For some groups continuous support of this kind may be vital because of the particular background of the members. For example, self-help groups of people suffering from depression have found that at times when all members are at a low, someone from outside 'who can help to provide suggestions, to build up what little initiative is there, to encourage' (Central Birmingham Community Health Council 1979) can make all the difference. Groups with little previous experience in decision-making and organizing themselves can also be helped by regular support of this kind. As an outside helper involved with a group of young adults who had suffered from schizophrenia and met for social activities put it: 'I think people who have had a lot of things done for them, like the people in this group, need encouragement to be able to actually do things and organize things for themselves. So we stay in the background, supporting, saying "You can do this if you want to"' (Central Birmingham Community Health Council 1979).

Of course a social worker is not the only source of outside support of this kind. Volunteers who understand what is required and are sensitive to members' concerns can make a valuable contribution here.

## USING SELF-HELP GROUPS

Social workers are potential members of self-help groups. They are not exempt from the life crises and emotional pressures that their clients face. They have particular needs, too, as professional workers coping daily with the distress and disturbance of other people. Mutual support organized through groups of this kind can both provide help for the individuals involved and improve professional functioning. Social workers could usefully direct themselves as well as others to create and explore this form of help.

## Conclusion

In considering the development of community resources for the mentally disordered, social workers need to look at a wide range of possibilities. This chapter has discussed the involvement of volunteers in developing services, as well as looking at the relatively untapped potential of self-help groups. Brandon says, 'The foundation of genuine helping lies in being ordinary. Nothing special. We can only offer ourselves, neither more nor less, to others – we have in fact nothing else to give' (Brandon 1982: 8). When social workers are tempted to be precious about their professional expertise, they need to reflect on this advice. There follow some guidelines on the steps that a social worker may consider when planning the involvement of volunteers in work with the mentally disordered.

# Guidelines for using volunteers

### Pre-recruitment

1  For what tasks do you want to use volunteers?
   (a)  Befriending (home visiting, day centres)
   (b)  Administrative (filing, typing)
   (c)  Practical help (car-driving, tea-making)
   (d)  Specialized activity (skills)
   (e)  Group leaders
   (f)  Ethnic contact.

2  Why do you want to use them?
   (a)  Additional resource
   (b)  Demystify mental illness in the community
   (c)  Normality of volunteers
   (d)  Linking ex-clients with current clients.

### Agency preparation

1  What do you need to find out from
   (a)  Management
       (i)  Resource availability – travel allowance, accommodation, telephone, project money, clarification of legal issues (insurance), use of existing resources (minibus, secretarial help).
       (ii)  Accountability – supervision, training, and support of volunteers.
   (b)  Co-workers
       (i)  Will they refer clients?
       (ii)  What degree of involvement by volunteers would they accept?

(iii) What help will they offer in recruitment, selection, training, and support of volunteers?

## Recruitment

1 What resources have you in the community? Prepare a list of existing networks, key people, and organizations, as well as potential sources.
2 What methods will you use to recruit volunteers?
  (i) Standard ways – local papers, volunteer bureaux, friends of friends, local organizations, relatives of clients, schools and colleges, radio and TV.
  (ii) Unusual ways – open public meeting, supermarket notice-boards, video of hostel or group, talk show on local radio, unions.

## Selection

Referral or initial contact
↓
Complete application form, consult references → reject
↓
Individual interview → volunteer withdraws or is counselled out
↓
Introductory meeting → withdrawal
↓
References followed up → reject
↓
Group meeting
↓
Visits to practical venues → withdrawal
↓
Matching volunteers to tasks
↓
Ongoing training/support

## Training

1 Pre-service:
  (a) Basic understanding of client group
  (b) Define tasks and expectations
  (c) Draw up a working contract.
2 Start-up support:
  (a) Regular meetings, group or individual
  (b) Provide opportunities for volunteers to meet other volunteers to share experiences

   (c) Use recordings or other material that the volunteers present

3 Ongoing support and supervision:
   (a) Provide opportunities for more specialized training
   (b) Give feedback on their progress.

4 Reviews:
   (a) At specific points, review the initial task and contract
   (b) Transitional training – if the volunteer is ready to move on to other tasks, present opportunities to do so.

# 14
## Teamwork

## *Lynne Muir*

Teamwork is currently seen as a desirable goal within British social services. Its attainment, however, is somewhat more problematic. Social workers often imply 'team work' when they talk about their team, whereas in fact they are referring to a group of workers who occupy the same office space, perhaps share some social activities together, and attend weekly staff meetings; but each member independently carries out his own work without reference to the other members. A team, as differentiated from a work group, requires that the group shares some common objectives, works together in carrying out the tasks of the organization, and co-ordinates the different specialisms and interests within the team. If there are no common objectives or pooling of skills then it is unlikely that teamwork exists. If this level of co-ordination is not present and the time spent on team meetings does not produce more effective services for the clients, then the idea of a team as a modern holy grail needs to be reassessed and other models of organization examined.

There are many definitions of a team, ranging from groups of people interacting together to accomplish the work of the organization, 'a group of people who possess individual expertise, who are responsible for making individual decisions, who hold a common purpose, and who meet together to communicate, share, and consolidate knowledge, from which plans are made, future decisions are influenced, and actions are deter-mined' (Brill 1976: xvi), to 'an instrument for carrying out the work of the organization' (Payne 1982: 13).

It is the intention of this chapter to look at some of the various types of teams to which the ASW may be attached; to discuss some of the dis-advantages and advantages of such an arrangement; to examine the evolution of a team in order to see how its success can be enhanced; to identify some common problems which can lead to team conflict; and to propose some methods for building an effective team.

In social work, as in other professional activities, most teams are sub-systems of a larger organization. Therefore it is necessary to look at the total structure and goals of the host organization in order to understand the functioning of a team within that larger system. If this is not done, then a team may try to implement ideas and practices which are not sympa-thetic to the organization, and which therefore do not receive backing or resources and support. This can create frustration and low morale within the team. Brill (1976: 112) suggests four conditions that should exist for a team to operate effectively within a larger organization:

1  A clear commitment to the overall agency and team purpose, with recognition that the methods of achieving objectives will vary;
2  there should be clear provision for channels of communication between the host organization and the team;
3  the professional judgement of the team members should be respected in that they should not be expected to implement policies which they have not been involved in formulating;
4  there should be provision for the accountability on the effectiveness of the team to the host organization.

The application of the unitary approach in organizations has been difficult to achieve. In part this is due to organizations persisting in allocating work on an individual basis with the result that workers are not encouraged to examine their workloads on the basis of shared problems (such as the number of depressed single parents in an area).

Evans argues that 'unitary models can only be implemented by social work teams working as groups rather than by separate individuals' (Evans 1978: 20). These two different approaches, the individual versus the team, have implications for the mental health worker who may be trying to identify common needs in a client group in order to develop new community resources, yet have difficulty acquiring the necessary infor-mation because of the style of work within the organization. This means that mental health workers will need to look at the structure, policies, and decision-making processes of the host organization as it affects the organization of their work. The result of this may be that the new ASWs will find themselves working within a team as a specialist and also focusing some attention on persuading the host organization to look at the ways in which work is structured and allocated.

Hey (1979: 27) draws a helpful distinction between team and network. The former refers to continuing interaction between a small, clearly bounded group of the same people who share a common task, similar values and who hold distinctive knowledge and skills; the latter is composed of a range of people with different knowledge and skills, who may meet infrequently with a changing constituency, yet who work on a common task when the occasion demands. An example of a team, using this description, would be a mental health specialist team within a social services department, while a network might comprise a mental health social worker, nurses, doctors, and occupational therapists on a hospital psychiatric ward. It is important to distinguish between team and network as frustration arises from confused expectations as to what *should* happen in a team/network as opposed to what *does* happen; some of this confusion arises from a lack of clarity on the functions and structure of both.

*Table 14.1*   Taxonomy of teams (adapted for mental health teams)

| Tasks (jobs the team must do) | Skills or roles (abilities of team members available to do jobs) | |
|---|---|---|
| | homogeneous (members have similar abilities) | heterogeneous (members have different abilities) |
| homogeneous (jobs are rather similar) | 1 Emergency duty team<br>2 Specialist mental health team in social services department | 1 Psychiatric hospital social work team with different grades of staff<br>2 Day centre teams<br>3 Social workers attached to psychogeriatric team |
| heterogeneous (many varied jobs to be done) | 1 Area specialist team with hospital-based social workers and divisionally-based social workers | 1 Primary health care team<br>2 Generic patch team with an ASW as member<br>3 Staff employed in hostels for mental disorder who are part of area teams |

A taxonomy of teams was developed by Webb and Hobdell (1980) and adapted by Payne (1982: 10) which offers a cognitive framework for the mental health worker (*Table 14.1*).

All these teams share the common concern of working with the mentally disordered but their skills may vary (such as a day centre with trained and untrained staff of social workers, nurses, occupational therapists, and teachers); their tasks and skills may vary (such as a primary health care team with a social worker, doctor, and health visitor concerned with different aspects of patient care); their task and skills may be similar (such as an emergency team of social workers dealing with any out-of-hours problem) or their skills may be the same and their tasks different (such as an area mental health specialist team of qualified social workers dealing with hospital and divisional work). Until the ASWs are actually *in situ* it is difficult to predict which type of team will operate most effectively. There are obvious advantages to the specialist mental health team where energies and resources can be concentrated on one client group but this also has the disadvantage of creating a feeling of élitism and a lack of concern and awareness by other teams to the problems of mental disorder.

What are some of the advantages and disadvantages of a team approach? While the virtues of teams are extolled by social workers, the reality is often confusing, frustrating, and time wasting. Some of the obvious advantages include the opportunity to pool skills and share work by using the specialist knowledge of team members, gaining wider professional awareness of problems of the client group, exploring a variety of potential solutions to problems, understanding the role of other professionals, thus breaking down stereotypes, and the giving and receiving of support, stimulation, and feedback.

The disadvantages of teamwork include having to work closely with people you may dislike and not agree with, spending time in lengthy meetings where efforts may be directed towards group maintenance rather than towards the task, individual initiatives may be hindered by pressure towards group conformity, and less contact with clients because of team demands.

What factors should be considered in deciding whether or not to assign a task to an individual or a team? Hooyman (1979: 466) suggests the following: (1) nature of the task; (2) characteristics of individual team members (that is, expertise, commitment to the outcome, and dependence on each other's support of the outcome); (3) importance of producing a high-quality product; (4) importance of a high degree of commitment to the solution – the necessity of accepting the product or decision; and (5) operating effectiveness of the team. Thus the main focus of teamwork is on the nature of the task to be achieved but many of the difficulties of teamwork arise from poor leadership, strain in personal relationships, or lack of conflict resolution.

Pincus and Minahan (1973: 82) argue that collaboration is always an achievement, not a gift. The achievement of collaboration involves identifying areas of conflict, exploring ways of resolving these conflicts, and developing strategies for building a cohesive and effective team. There will be opposing points of view wherever any group of people work together, and the management of these differences is the responsibility of both the team leader and the team members. Handy (1976: 214) usefully distinguishes between types of disagreement as argument, competition, and conflict. The first, argument, can be a more fruitful medium for learning, sharing, testing of ideas, progressing towards a better solution than could be reached by an individual alone. For this to occur it is necessary to have confidence and trust in other team members, to have a challenging task, and to make full use of knowledge and skills of colleagues. Otherwise argument can degenerate into non-productive conflict. The second source of disagreement, competition, can be useful in setting standards (by seeing what others are doing and thus improving your own methods), by stimulating members to try new ways, by focusing on achieving specific objectives, and by sorting out good methods from bad. It is unhelpful when competition is aimed at achieving power and influence for personal gain at the expense of the team. Team members then enter into the arena of the win–lose syndrome where the person who has lost resolves never to do so again and blocks any initiative, regardless of its quality, by the person who defeated him.

The current cut-back in resources and the resultant focus on efficiency through evaluation studies within social service agencies has meant areas of competition and conflict have been heightened. Mental health workers wanting resources to develop community schemes will find themselves in direct competition with workers focusing on other client groups. Symptoms of conflict may emerge as poor communication with both team members and management, as jealousy and hostility between teams ('if it wasn't for the mental health team having the director's ear and getting more staff we would have our new team member'), as minor problems becoming major issues (lack of a coffee room developing into a feeling of being exploited by management), with relations between team members becoming formalized (written memos being sent to a colleague in the next office), as a proliferation of myths, rules, and regulations ('someone told me we're not allowed to do that'), or as low morale within the team ('we may want to use the mentally handicapped day centre as a centre for the mentally disordered but we'll never be able to achieve it').

Occasionally conflict may be resolved by neglecting or appearing to ignore it, for example if it has arisen because of particular pressures that one team member is experiencing; it may also be resolved by separating the main protagonists in the conflict, but this works only if their tasks are functionally independent. In most cases the conflict must be confronted and a resolution attempted. Some useful steps in resolving conflict are the following:

1 Identify the problem(s)
    (a) through individual consultation/frank discussion/supervision;
    (b) through meetings with groups of staff and/or the entire team;
    (c) through self appraisal by team members and analysis of leadership style by the team leader.
2 Look for common goals and clearly identify them.
3 Clarify team members' expectations of the resolutions to the difficulties and establish boundaries on areas that cannot be resolved.
4 Establish team commitment to the consistent application of agreed rules and resolutions.
5 Develop a climate of trust in the team in which conflict can be purposefully expressed and tackled at an early stage.
6 Reappraise the individual and team goals as a move in facilitating positive team development.
7 Reach team agreement on future action.

The above steps assume a willingness on the part of team members to manage conflict and, in so doing, resolve it. This implies a commitment to working together as a team. Yet social workers are ill-prepared for this task. Generally, social work training focuses on the acquisition of case work skills and this individual ethos is reinforced in agencies where allocation of work is done on an individual basis. One would not expect a long-distance runner to become a member of a relay team without practice and preparation, nor would a football team go onto the pitch for a Saturday match without team practice. Yet social workers with no prior preparation are put into teams and expected to function effectively as a group for forty hours a week. This naïve assumption by many organizations and teams denies the wealth of information now available on group formation. Brill (1976: 48) identifies five stages in the evolution of a team: orientation, accommodation, negotiation, operation, and dissolution.

ORIENTATION

This is concerned with introducing team members to the areas of work with which they will be involved and in providing both structure for support and freedom for experimentation. This recognizes the common feelings of stress, anxiety, and dependency experienced by team members in this stage. For the mental health worker who is part of a generic team this could mean sharing with colleagues the type of work they would expect to carry, the particular knowledge this entails and the help they would be able to offer other team members either through shared work or consultation on mental health problems.

ACCOMMODATION

This stage is characterized by an adaptation to individual differences, and the development of some shared team goals. The generic team might, with the encouragement of the mental health worker, begin to share information on community mental health resources and identify gaps in the service while recognizing that not all team members would wish to become actively involved in this exercise.

NEGOTIATION

This implies the team members have reached agreement on tasks to be carried out and role differences.

In practice this could be the recognition that some of the mental health worker's time would be spent working in a day centre with the mentally disordered, and that clients attending the day centre would be part of the mental health worker's case load.

OPERATION

This is the stage at which the team, having worked out its own internal structure, puts energy into achieving the goals it has set itself. In the example above this could mean that, having identified gaps in community resources, some of the team members, with the help of the mental health worker, decide to recruit, select, and train volunteers to work in a day centre.

DISSOLUTION

This final stage arrives when the agreed objectives have been attempted, the team evaluates the experience and refocuses on other areas of work. This could mean the team would find that volunteers were not recruited and the reasons for the failure of their objectives would be assessed. It could also mean that a volunteer programme was established, that the mental health worker took responsibility for its continuation and the other team members put their energies into their individual work loads – until another common team objective was identified.

The developing role of the newly approved mental health social worker is one that should be carefully thought out in these early stages. Roles can calcify once they are well established whereas an emerging role can be creatively exploited to meet new challenges. The ASWs can provide specialist knowledge to teams and should be seen as a valuable resource. Some of the areas in which they may make a contribution include the following:

WORK WITH ETHNIC MINORITIES

The mental health worker will have an educational role in the team by providing information on the ethnic demography of the area, the types of disorder and handicap experienced by particular ethnic groups (which will help social workers in the early identification of unusual behaviour), and the resources existing within cultural communities which could provide support for clients. This worker could also provide advice on the appropriateness of setting up special facilities, such as a group for depressed and isolated Asian women who might need to meet as a group but, because of language and cultural differences, separate from the local community.

WORK WITH GENERIC TEAMS

The mental health worker will have a role with intermediate treatment workers in examining links between persistent delinquency and mental disorder in adolescents. This might involve giving advice on the difference between truancy and school refusal or on recognizing signs of adolescent depression which could lead to suicide attempts.

The role could also include picking up early indications of disturbed or unusual behaviour in children from information provided by family workers. If other team members see the mental health worker as a resource to be tapped, then this expertise can be used for the benefit of the entire team.

COMMUNITY WORK

As part of the approved mental health social worker's role is to develop community resources for the mentally disordered, this worker will need to liaise with existing statutory and voluntary resources, identify gaps in the service, and work towards alleviating these needs. The help of the team will be needed in sharing knowledge of contacts, creating space and time for these contacts to be followed up and developed, and joint working on ordering existing work so that specialist skills can be used effectively. In some areas group homes are supervised by different workers, each working autonomously. A team might decide that the mental health worker would have oversight of all group homes in their area. This could mean more flexibility in placing people in homes suitable to their needs at a particular time and also more control on the types of referrals made to group homes because of the contacts with consultants and other specialists in the mental health field.

As the role of the ASW within a team develops, the opportunity is present for new and innovative ways of using this resource. We can plunge ahead without thought – as A. A. Milne in *Winnie-the-Pooh* puts it:

> 'Here is Edward Bear, coming downstairs now, bump, bump, bump, on the back of his head, behind Christopher Robin. It is, as far as he knows, the only way of coming downstairs, but sometimes he feels that there really is another way, if only he could stop bumping for a moment and think of it. And then he feels that perhaps there isn't.'

Or we can stop at the top of the stairs and look at different ways of achieving our objectives.

This chapter has attempted to demystify teamwork as something that either happens or does not, regardless of our interventions. It has: identified the characteristics of teams versus networks; discussed the disadvantages, as well as the advantages, of teams; suggested some of the varieties of teams to which a mental health worker might be attached; highlighted symptoms of conflict within a team and suggested ways of dealing with this conflict; traced the evolution of a team through its developmental stages; and concluded by looking at some of the specialist skills that a mental health worker can bring to a team. The opportunity is right for creative teamwork and it is hoped that the field will respond to the challenge.

# 15
# Working with other professions

## Ann Davis

In Chapter 14 Muir has highlighted the importance of developing an organization and practice of social work based on effective teamwork. It is equally important for social workers to consider their relationships with other professions. Social workers can make full use of their knowledge and skills in helping mentally disordered people and their families only if they are able to work productively with other professions. A comprehensive and effective mental health service depends on multi-disciplinary working.

A great deal is claimed for multi-disciplinary working or teamwork in policy documents and the professional literature. It is promoted as a method of working which can have a positive impact in three main areas. First, it is held to be essential to good professional practice; second, it is seen as a way of compensating for a lack of organizational and administrative coherence in the mental health services; and finally, a multi-disciplinary approach to planning and managing the services is considered the key to establishing a comprehensive and responsive local service.

The discussions about the value of a multi-disciplinary approach to practice have drawn heavily on the notion of 'multi-disciplinary teamwork'. As Muir points out in Chapter 14, this phrase needs to be treated with caution as it can encompass a wide range of working arrangements. However, whatever its form, multi-disciplinary teamwork is considered to enhance professional practice because the lone professional worker cannot be expected to possess all the knowledge and skills needed to help a mentally ill or handicapped individual. What is required,

> 'is a group of professionals who share in assessment, planning and treatment, co-operating to provide a comprehensive and well-coordinated service. Each member contributes according to his skills and the client's or family's needs, and the contribution of each will vary from case to case. The recipients of the service do not feel confused or embarrassed at the variety of professionals intervening in their lives, but reassured that a group of people will help them in a variety of ways.'
>
> (Hudson 1982: 8)

In other words, the contribution of each professional is augmented by joint working and the needs of the client are served in the best way possible by this approach.

The second reason given for the importance of multi-disciplinary work is that it is the main way of overcoming the problems raised by the absence of a coherent administrative base to services for mentally ill and mentally handicapped people. The success of any community-based local service for these client groups depends on a co-ordinated input of resources and skills from a range of statutory and voluntary agencies. As Better Services for the Mentally Ill claims, in its discussion of how its vision of district-based services is to become reality, 'A number of different elements make up the comprehensive network of services envisaged in the new pattern. It is however the building up of teamwork and close relationships between professional staffs and lay groups that turns facilities into a working and comprehensive network of services' (DHSS 1975: 20).

It is not just at a practice and service level that multi-disciplinary teamwork brings rewards. Many DHSS documents exhort those responsible for managing and planning mental health services to utilize this approach. This appears to mean that each service should draw on the expertise of multi-disciplinary groups when planning for change and deciding on priorities. It also means that managers should work across the boundaries of their employing organizations in order to ensure that change takes place in any local service on the basis of an agreed and co-ordinated strategy.

Debate about the strengths and limitations of a multi-disciplinary approach remains largely academic. For in reality most social workers work in a world in which there are considerable problems communicating with other professions and engaging in joint practice.

Obviously the form these problems take will vary according to the location of the social worker. The community-based social worker is most likely to be working alone with individuals and their families. Contact with other professions will generally be limited and focused around crises where joint assessment and management may be required. In contrast social workers based in such facilities as health centres, day care units, child guidance centres, and specialist hospital units, will find that they have to negotiate sustained contact with other professions. Research into multi-disciplinary settings has confirmed that they are often situations in which there is a 'lack of mutual respect, power struggles, poor co-ordination, and some members – especially social workers, but often also nurses and psychologists feeling under-valued and under-used' (Hudson 1982).

This chapter examines some of the realities of working with other professions that social workers face. It does this by discussing three common problem areas: the inappropriate referral, establishing joint working, and sharing information. It also considers some of the strategies that might be employed in tackling each one.

## The inappropriate referral

The first contact between social workers and members of other professions is often by means of a referral, a request for social work help for a named individual. Social workers commonly complain that many of the referrals they receive from doctors, nurses, health visitors, and others are in-appropriate. They call for intervention which is not part of the social work task. Some workers view this recurring experience as a failure on the part of other professions to understand the role of the social worker and social services departments in relation to mentally ill and mentally handicapped people. Other workers take the view that inappropriate referrals are the result of social workers being unable to clarify what they have to contribute to the support and care of mentally ill and handicapped people.

Whatever form the explanation takes it points to a failure of communication between social workers and other professions. If this is the case then it suggests that social workers could improve the way they work with other professions by communicating more with them about the social work task.

There is a range of strategies that can be used here. However, before using them individual social workers and social work teams need to review their own understanding of their role and responsibilities in relation to work with mentally ill and handicapped people. This review should take into account a number of factors, including the statutory duties and responsibilities carried, the prime concern of social work with the social factors that contribute to individual and family problems, and the local authority resources which social workers can make available. It should also include a realistic appraisal of what each individual social worker brings to his work. Social workers vary considerably in their interests and skills, as well as in their knowledge of mental illness and mental handicap. It is this blend of individual knowledge and skills within a framework of statutory duties and responsibilities that makes up the social work contribution to services for mentally ill and mentally handicapped people. Individuals and teams who are actively considering this kind of review might find the BASW discussion paper on this topic a useful starting-point (BASW 1974).

Having established what social workers can contribute to the care of mentally disordered people, many more opportunities have to be taken to convey this to others. There is evidence that such opportunities are increased if a social worker or group of social workers share common territory with other professions. Corney and Briscoe's (1977) account of the work of social workers in the primary health care services compares two schemes. The first, an 'attachment scheme', involved regular social work input to a health centre. This centre made a room available for social workers from an area team who attended four mornings a week on a rotating basis. The second scheme, a 'liaison' scheme, covered five GP practices. No facilities were made available at these practices but referrals were made by phone, with social workers visiting fortnightly to discuss patients.

Both schemes resulted, as GP attachments do, in a much higher rate of referrals of psychiatric problems than the social workers usually encountered in their area team. However, comparisons showed interesting differences between the source and type of referral made in each scheme. Social workers found that on the attachment scheme there were more practical and relationship problems referred than in the liaison scheme. Many of these referrals came from health visitors rather than from the GPs. In fact a third of all referrals to social workers on the attachment scheme came from health visitors compared with 5 per cent in the liaison scheme. The reason for these differences seemed to be that on the attachment scheme 'the different professions operating in the health centre learned about each others' work and roles. The social workers felt this resulted in increasingly appropriate referrals as the scheme progressed and preconceptions as to what type of cases were appropriate for referral were often changed and extended' (Corney and Briscoe 1977).

However, shared territory does not always improve professional co-operation. At times social workers may need to engage in intense, short-term work with colleagues, focused on the problem of referrals, in order to bring about change. For example, a social worker attached to a hospital day unit for mentally handicapped people, felt she was being under-used by the nursing staff who ran the unit. The social worker was concerned that although the unit covered a deprived inner-city catchment area with a high percentage of one-parent households and poor housing, she received very few referrals. Over a period of one month she arranged to visit the unit daily to talk to nursing staff about their clients. The onus was on the nursing staff to share their views about each user. This period of regular discussion resulted in an increase in referrals from nursing staff and more regular appropriate use of the social worker.

Social workers can also have an impact if they contribute to the training programmes of other professions. Target groups need to be identified and schemes devised where students are exchanged and joint teaching on particular topics becomes part of the curriculum.

The problem of inappropriate referrals is not just a problem of a lack of understanding and communication between social workers and other professions. Some referrals are labelled 'inappropriate' because they are requests for resources which are so scarce they are virtually unobtainable. When social workers and local authority social services departments cannot meet the legitimate requests of other professions there is a tendency to reach for the label 'inappropriate referral' rather than acknowledge the scarcity of their existing resources. This response is not of course unique to social workers. In a situation of scarce resources social workers find their own referrals to the health services refused as inappropriate. A great deal of the underlying frustration and poor working between professions operating in the mental health services stems from a chronic lack of resources. There are of course no short-term answers to this problem, but it is crucial that social workers separate the inappropriate referral from the unmet referral. A record of those referrals that fall within the remit of the social worker but that could not be met because of a lack of personnel or other services, is essential evidence in arguing for increased provision. Sharing this information with other professions is, in the long run, more productive than treating their requests for social work help as if they have failed to understand what social work can offer.

## Establishing joint working

Trying to establish good joint working arrangements with other professions can be a time-consuming task, which generally has low priority on social workers' schedules. Yet where joint work becomes part of a local service many benefits accrue to those involved. Working with anxiety, stress, and breakdown, the 'wear and tear' of recurring difficulties, and long-standing disability all take their toll on professionals, as well as clients and their families. Sharing the uncertainties of working in this area can lift some of the pressures felt by the lone practitioner. It can also expand the options open to the client who receives the service.

The problems that community-based social workers face in establishing joint work, centre on improving the contacts they have with primary health care workers and specialist workers around two main areas of work. The first is the crisis or emergency, when joint assessment and discussion is essential if sound decisions are to be reached about the management of a client's situation. The second is the area of recurring work with clients who have complex or long-standing difficulties. Here good working relations with other professions can result in arrangements that give focused attention to the client, without overlapping and perhaps conflicting efforts being made by a number of professionals involved.

With these two areas of work in mind it is important that community-based area teams give some regular attention to their relationships with local GPs and other workers attached to their practices. This can take the form of lunchtime meetings or office open-days, when information can be exchanged and difficulties discussed. It is sometimes the case that such events fail to attract GPs and where this is the problem other strategies may have to be employed. One option worth considering is that tried by an inner-city team of social workers who were particularly concerned about the lack of joint working with local GPs in situations where elderly mentally confused people were being managed at home. Over a period of some nine months members of the team had been involved in a dozen or more cases where careful monitoring was required to support relatives and prevent rapid deterioration. On a number of occasions social workers had been unable to reach agreements about management with the relevant GPs who said they were too busy to discuss these cases.

The team invited local GPs to a lunchtime discussion on the confused elderly, but with no response. They decided therefore to circulate the GPs with four short anonymous case histories which highlighted the importance of joint work and management of the elderly. These were attached to an invitation to join the team for a discussion. The response was immediate with several GPs attending the discussion because they were concerned that the cases cited were their patients. On the basis of this joint interest a useful exchange took place which resulted in the long term in some very productive joint work with three or four of the GPs.

Where areas of common interest and involvement are identified with other professions, opportunities should be taken to set up projects which allow for combined work in particular areas. The Lozells Open Door Advisory Service (LODAS) in Birmingham is one example here. This is a service available one afternoon a week to parents who are having difficulties with their children. An educational psychologist and a social worker (employed by the education service) are available in each session and work towards a joint recommendation which is offered to the parents. These recommendations usually include some form of positive action that the parent can take with an invitation to return if there are further difficulties. The workers involved find these sessions stimulate fresh ideas about an area of work which they commonly tackle alone.

### Sharing information

If members of different professions are to work together to provide individuals with a coherent and co-ordinated programme of care, then information has to be shared. This will range from information about a client's background and current circumstances, to information on the contribution being made by others to the client's treatment and management.

Situations in which social workers find themselves excluded from sharing such information most typically occur in relation to specialist teams. In some instances these teams are consultant-led, that is they do not operate as a group of professionals with an equal, but different, contribution to make to assessment and care. Rather they operate as a group of professionals who supplement, when requested, the work of the consultant member. With this style of leadership some consultants make independent decisions about who should know what, which may result in other team members being excluded from sharing basic information. In other teams the nursing discipline may be dominant and it may prove difficult for 'outsiders' like social workers or psychologists to gain access to information which they can use to form a view about their potential contribution.

Where this kind of problem occurs it is usually difficult to resolve at a team level, unless the social worker is able to gain support from other team members. This may prove possible for social workers permanently attached to a team but is less likely for workers who have sporadic contact. The issue at stake is the professional autonomy of the social worker in deciding on the available information what contribution he can make to individual care. Where social workers have been attached to specialist units or where a social work team is based in a specialist health facility, it is on the assumption that their skills will be used in a multi-disciplinary setting. Without access to basic information a social worker cannot contribute as a team member and this is the issue that needs to be raised in a number of forums, outside the team meeting.

Social work managers and team leaders have a role to play here in reaching agreements with their health counterparts about policy regarding access to information. If a health specialist unit is using a social work service then there must be a clear policy about the basis on which the service is provided and this should include use of patient's case notes, etc.

For social workers (including ASWs) working from a community-base the problem of shared information commonly takes another form. Here, notification of a client leaving hospital or information about decisions reached in ward rounds may not be shared. Such a lack of sharing undermines attempts to provide continuity of care between community and institution. This failure to share may be the result of a failure to use the liaison potential of the specialist social worker based in hospital. If this is the case then the strategies to be adopted will mirror those used in enhancing joint work with other professionals. Except that in this case social workers, working from different agencies, will need to educate each other. If there is no liaison social worker then attention has to be given to alerting the specialist team to the needs of those involved in after-care, follow-up, or ongoing work, and establishing procedures to ensure that relevant information reaches the community-based social worker who can use it. In the absence of such arrangements assumptions are made on both sides that there is a lack of interest in sharing client care.

## Conclusions

The strategies discussed here for tackling some of the common problems that social workers face in working with other professions, call for some time to be given to working with professional networks. Work with such networks, by individual practitioners, teams, and social service managers, is as vital to good social work practice as work undertaken to strengthen clients' own social networks. The purpose of such work must always be informed by a concern to improve the help made available to our clients. If it is successful it will do a great deal to overcome some of the fragmented and confusing help that clients currently receive.

# PART FIVE
# SOCIAL WORK METHOD
# AND PROCESSES

# Introduction

## M. Rolf Olsen

Elsewhere (Olsen 1978: 1–2) I have reported that in 1973 my colleagues at Birmingham University introduced the unitary model into the graduate social work courses. Not as a 'course' or an 'option', but into the total syllabus so that all courses were taught within this unifying framework. The aim was to educate and train social workers within the philosophy of the unitary model and with the knowledge and skills that it implies. The basis for this initiative was rooted in the recognition of the adverse consequences of a social work practice based primarily upon the agency and its organization and methods, rather than the presenting problems of the client and the systems to which he belongs. In relation to the mentally disordered, research (Olsen 1976b, 1978) shows that this group suffer from multiple handicaps consequent upon mental illness, long-institutionalization, and loss of family and community contacts. All of which points to the need to develop services based upon the needs of the patient in terms of his membership of a community rather than just a living group.

This requires all social workers to have sufficient knowledge and skills in order to conceptualize and practise in a holistic and integrated way; to be able to take account of all systems which affect the individual or group; to identify unmet material need, poor service delivery, and inadequate resources; to promote the application of the rich variety of techniques available to social work on a teamwork and intra- and inter-organizational

188 SOCIAL WORK AND MENTAL HEALTH

basis; and to contribute to the improvement and further development of social policy. It is only by this effort that social work can hope effectively to ameliorate the profound level of disadvantage experienced by the mentally disordered.

Previous papers in this volume and those to follow under the title of 'social work method and processes' examine and develop this philosophy within the framework offered by Pincus and Minahan (1973) and Howard Goldstein (1973). The model they advocate implies an extensive view of what should constitute social work practice, demands that social work considers all systems which infringe upon clients, and implies the ability to apply a variety of techniques and strategies to all the appropriate systems contributing to the clients' difficulties. Their framework is one which accommodates and allows the development of a wide spectrum of theoretical ideas and practice techniques. It also offers a structure for analysing and defining problems; establishing the need for change; determining goals; agreeing strategies for achieving stated goals; and undertaking assessment of the outcome to agreed strategies. In addition the model promotes the importance of establishing agreement with clients about all aspects of their difficulties and the remedies to resolve them.

# 16
## Interviewing

*Lynne Muir*

Interviewing is one of social work's most important activities. An interview may be defined as a conversation with a purpose which is mutually accepted by all participants, a somewhat formal structure, a clearly defined allocation of roles, and as a set of norms regulating the process of interaction. This means that all parties involved should know why they have met, the meeting should normally take an agreed amount of time, and all parties should be clear as to who is the social worker and who is to be helped. There are unwritten rules determining the interview structure. Unfortunately this poses particular problems for the mentally disordered person who may find it difficult to focus on an interview and may not have had previous interview experience on which to build.

In Chapter 2 Olsen summarizes the Mental Health Act 1983 and highlights the obligation placed on the ASW by Section 13(2) to interview the patient in a suitable manner. This raises a number of questions. In particular:

1 Should the ASW interview patients individually or in their living groups?
2 What can the social worker do if the patient refuses, or is unable, to respond?
3 How can non-English-speaking clients be interviewed?

4  What happens to those patients who cannot be interviewed because of a handicap such as deafness?

It is impossible to make suggestions to cover every eventuality but the aims of this chapter are to look at the phenomenon of communication in terms of what enhances and what impedes it; to review those factors found to be helpful in working with people; to discuss the main interviewing skills; and to outline the stages of an interview, taking into account the various types of interview in which the mental health worker will be engaged.

### The process of communication

Interviewing is a process of communication and as such relies heavily on our perceptions and assumptions about a situation. An example of how perceptions vary can be shown in the illustration below. Look at the diagram for a few seconds and then write down how many squares you see.

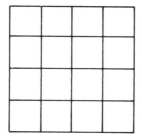

When people do this exercise the number of squares seen varies from 16 to 25 and initially most would maintain that their answer was correct. The point is that we all have the same information (the illustration) but we perceive it differently and therefore make different assumptions about the data. (There are, in fact, 30 squares in the diagram.) This means that we respond or react to what we *think* we hear or see, not necessarily to what has actually been said or seen.

Satir (1967) writes of communication operating on two levels: the denotative level or the literal content and the metacommunicative level which comments on both the literal content and the nature of the relationship between the people involved. Most communication is at the second level and includes literal and emotional components. The statement, 'I'm telling you I'm upset but you don't seem to believe it' combines these two aspects, as do most of our messages. Discrepancies arise when the verbal metacommunication does not complement the non-verbal metacommunication. For example a client might say, 'I feel you can help me sort out my problems, and I really am ready to do something about them', while standing by the door with his coat on. These difficulties are exacerbated for the mentally disordered person who often is not able accurately to assess either his own or others' messages for their meaning nor able to weigh attitudes, intentions, or feelings accurately.

Some of the factors that mitigate against effective communication between worker and client include the following:

1 Stereotyping can occur when a person's individuality is not allowed to transcend the group of which he is a member – such as a worker labelling a client as a 'typical' paranoid schizophrenic or a client seeing the worker as part of a hospital conspiracy to keep him confined.
2 Physical condition is a factor in that if a client arrives at the end of a long and tiring day a worker may be less enthusiastic about giving him time than if he comes early in the day; equally, if a worker visits a family in the midst of putting a number of active children to bed, concentration on an interview will be limited.
3 Social, educational, and class differences between a client and a worker can block communication. This can emerge as different expectations of service, as shown in this example:

'The social worker wanted to know all about our background when we were young and all that, and I said to my husband, "Well, to my opinion, that's nothing to do with it." The social worker just talked about us most of the time, instead of trying to get to the bottom of the problem.'

(Mayer and Timms 1970: 71)

4 Language, particularly the use of jargon or words that mean different things to different people, can be a barrier. Cormican (1979) in discussing language differences, includes working with the non-English-speaking client, varying dialects such as professional jargon or differences in geographic areas, various ethnic backgrounds, and age differences.
5 Feelings that are held by the worker and client and brought to the interview can also affect communication. The worker may bring hopes of helping, fears of harming, or antipathy to conflict, while the client may come with hopeful expectations of help, the need to be accepted, and the fear of being blamed.
6 Inattentiveness by either party is perhaps the greatest block to communication. Either the mind wanders (with the worker thinking of other things but with his 'listening' face on) or one anticipates what the other is going to say and therefore does not listen to what is actually being said.

While the hazards listed above can hinder effective communication, there are other factors that facilitate it. The most important of these are:

1 Listening with complete attention and with what is often referred to as the 'third ear', which means listening for the meaning behind the words.
2 Clarity of expression so that people with whom one is communicating know exactly what is meant.
3 Awareness of non-verbal messages such as body posture and facial expressions which are being given by both client and worker and responding to these signals at an appropriate moment.
4 A strong self-concept in that if a person feels secure and confident, then he is able to receive and give messages with fewer distortions.
5 Genuineness and authenticity of approach by indicating that the worker is willing to share his own thoughts and feelings as a human being (when they are appropriate to the situation) and that he is not going to hide behind a professional façade of distance and detachment.
6 Empathy is the ability to enter imaginatively into the inner life of someone else and be able to communicate to him an appreciation of his feelings.
7 Confidentiality means making clear to the client what the boundaries are (details of criminal activities will need to be passed on, or some information will need to be shared with other professionals).
8 Feedback, which is checking back with the client to ensure accurate understanding on both sides.

## Core conditions

While all of these factors are important in conducting a successful interview, extensive research undertaken by Truax and Carkhuff (1967) indicates that there are three core conditions that are of primary importance. These are *empathy*, *non-possessive warmth*, and *genuineness*. They believe a worker can develop skill in these areas. A programme for interview training is outlined in detail by Fischer (1978).

Empathy, as defined above, is the ability to feel 'with' someone, not just feel 'for' them (which is sympathy). There is an American Indian saying 'never judge a man until you have walked a moon in his moccasins' which succinctly summarizes empathy. It is emotional sensitivity to the experience of others.

Non-possessive warmth, the second core condition, is a generic term for the demonstration by the worker that the interview is underpinned by certain social work values. Biestek (1967) identifies these qualities as: (a) the ability to see each person as a unique human being, different to all other human beings; (b) the recognition by the worker that clients need to be able honestly to express negative, as well as positive, feelings; (c) clients should sense in a worker a controlled level of emotional commitment based upon a realistic appraisal of the client's position, problems, and needs; (d) workers need to be able to communicate their concern and acceptance of the client's reality, without approving necessarily of his behaviour or attitudes, but not passing judgement on that behaviour; (e) the worker believes, and communicates that belief to the client, that asking for help does not mean giving up the right to determine one's own destiny. This point can be a difficult area for the mental health worker who may have to decide whether or not a potential suicide is in a state of mind to be self-determining.

The final core condition, genuineness, is the ability of a worker to be himself, free of phoniness and defensiveness, and as spontaneous as he feels appropriate at the moment.

## Interviewing skills

Interviewing skills improve with practice and many workers use tape recorders or closed-circuit television as a way of evaluating, criticizing, and improving their techniques. A useful framework has been devised by Ivey (1971) for breaking down an interview into its component parts. The related groups are: skills useful in beginning interviews, listening skills, skills of self-expression, and interpretation.

### BEGINNING INTERVIEWS

1   Attending behaviour includes a relaxed, attentive posture, eye contact, verbal following, and thoughtful listening.
2   Open invitation to talk is the ability to ask open-ended questions that encourage the other person verbally to explore his thoughts or feelings. Questions that require only a 'yes' or 'no' answer or double questions ('are you coping better with your job now and are things easier at home?' ) are not helpful.
3   Minimal encouragers to talk are head nods, repetition of one or two words, or non-verbal gestures such as a smile, and should directly follow from what the client has said. Many interviewers talk too much and should practise controlling this tendency.

### LISTENING SKILLS

1   Reflection is the process of being able to communicate to the client understanding of his *feelings* as he experiences them.
2   Summarization of feeling is the ability to summarize the emotional aspects of the interview in a clear form showing the diverse and

complex feelings of the client so that he may respond, 'that's right, but I hadn't recognized that I felt that way before.'

3   Paraphrasing is a restatement of the *content* that helps the client move on.

4   Summative paraphrasing is concerned with reviewing the essential content of the session by clarifying confusions, or highlighting specific areas which help the client focus on decisions or issues.

### SKILLS OF SELF-EXPRESSION

1   Expression of feeling relates to the discussion earlier in this chapter on good communication being fostered by openness and genuine expression of feelings experienced by the interviewer at the moment.

2   Expression of content has been described as the ability clearly and succinctly, without the use of jargon, to present facts or information.

3   Direct, mutual communication is the development of an open relationship where both client and worker can express their feelings and experiences.

### INTERPRETATION

This is a complex skill which is influenced by the theoretical perspective of the worker. A behaviourist will see situations in ways which differ from that of a dynamically orientated worker. Interpretation is useful only when the client can use the material presented and when the worker understands the client's view of his situation. Interpretation involves presenting to the client an alternative frame of reference of his situation, with the goal of helping the client better understand his feelings and behaviour.

## Stages of an interview

The mental health worker will be involved in interviews with a variety of people ranging from meetings with doctors and other professionals, families, community contacts, and individual clients. The purpose of these interviews may be to select clients suitable for using community resources, assess the home environment of a hospitalized client, gather relevant information from doctors and others on the mental state of a client, decide whether or not to recommend a Section, or counsel individuals. Each type of interview will have features specific to that contact.

In interviewing GPs or other professionals, it is important that the worker recognizes their contribution as well as the social work contribution, is not defensive and apologetic for taking time, knows the relevant sections of the Mental Health Act (and can refer to them if necessary), and has marshalled his own evidence so that the material can be clearly and concisely stated. Families often find it easier to be interviewed in their own home although the social worker may find coping with animals, television, and children more threatening in this setting. Haley (1976) suggests that in the beginning it is better to see together everyone who lives in a household so that the worker can gain an understanding of the problem and the social environment that maintains it.

There are some general principles that apply to most situations. Kadushin (1972) outlines a process through which a typical interview moves and Priestley and McGuire (1983) have refined this process into exercises designed to help the interviewer plan the various stages.

Before starting an interview it is helpful to remember some advice given by Brandon (1981) who suggests beginning the interview with a serene mind. Although the instruction comes from a Japanese motor-cycle manual, it applies even more to helping people. To be able to give undivided attention in the interview, a worker needs to cultivate a serene mind, leaving personal concerns, work problems, and telephone calls outside the interview setting. The meeting should start and end at a mutually agreed time as beginnings and endings are very important. The former contributes to the purposeful tone of the interview and the latter sets the scene for future contacts. While the worker may have set goals for himself, it is important to move at the client's pace and not rush through the interview so that nothing long term is achieved.

Usually the interview begins with conversation designed to set a relaxed atmosphere and is followed by open-ended questions about the agreed purpose of meeting ('Well, Mr Harris, the time for leaving hospital is getting close, what are your thoughts about that?'). These questions may be followed by more specific and detailed questions ('is there help that you need in sorting out your welfare benefits?'). This phase leads into a concentration on accomplishing the mutually agreed purpose and dis-cussion may focus upon one area in depth. The choice of an area is somewhat arbitrary and may focus on feelings ('I imagine it may be difficult for you to talk about the feelings you have when your wife says she isn't sure she wants you home'), or on practical concerns ('shall we make a list of the things that need to be done before you go home?'). The final phase of development and termination in the interview process involves a recapitulation of what has been covered, what decisions have been reached, and what remains to be done. For our imaginary Mr Harris, this might sound something like, 'We have covered a lot of ground today, Mr Harris. We have talked about some of the practical difficulties that may arise and your feelings of concern about going home, as well as your pleasure in being able to return to your dog and garden. We have decided that I will visit Mrs Harris this week to discuss our proposals for your twice-a-week involvement in a day centre. When you and I meet next week we will begin to finalize your plans for leaving. Is this how things seem to you?'

## Interview problems

An interview does not always go smoothly. Through trial and error, difficulties can be overcome if the interviewer experiments with new ways and is creative in their application. Three areas in which many interviewers experience discomfort are working with reluctant clients, dealing with silence, and interviewing ethnic clients. Keith-Lucas (1972) stresses the importance of remembering that most people do not want to be helped in any significant way and that even those who do ask for help are often afraid of the help offered. Engaging reluctant clients is a pertinent problem for mental health workers who may be seen as people who will deprive the client of his freedom. Munro, Manthei, and Small (1979: 46), suggest giving the client time to feel comfortable and develop trust as well as trying out a wide variety of invitations to talk or participate.

Most interviewers find silence difficult and so attempt to fill the gaps. A worker must differentiate between various kinds of silence and react in a variety of ways. Some of the types of silence are the following:

1   A client needs time to sort out his thoughts and feelings and the worker should respect this.
2   Something tragic, shocking, or frightening has been raised and the client needs time to absorb it.
3   The client is confused and does not understand what is being talked about (this silence should be broken quickly or more confusion will result).
4   The client sees the worker as an authority figure to be resisted but the worker needs not to respond as if it is a personal rejection.
5   The client is silent because he does not know what is expected of him, in which case the worker needs to give some hints on how to proceed.

Another area of difficulty for interviewers is across racial or language lines. While it is clear that any interview with non-English-speaking clients will be more effective if the worker is familiar with the client's language, this is not always possible. Kadushin (1979) suggests that in an interview of this type, the worker should carefully observe formalities that indicate respect, be aware of personal racial bias, and familiarize himself with the cultural background of the client. If an interpreter is used other difficulties arise, and some suggestions for working through these are discussed by Ahmed (1982).

## Conclusion

This chapter has outlined some of the elements affecting the process of communication, examining the difficulties as well as the enhancing factors. It has identified the core conditions of empathy, acceptance, and congruency as necessary demonstrable qualities for the effective interviewer. The particular interviewing skills of attending behaviour, open invitation, and minimal encouragers to talk, reflection and summarization of feeling, paraphrasing and summative paraphrasing, and interpretation have been described, and the stages of an interview identified including the specific problems of silence, the reluctant client, and ethnic differences.

Successful interviewing is a learned skill. To improve this skill we need to be prepared to look at our ways of relating and communicating with others, examine our interview technique, modify our approach if necessary, and be aware of the interview process so that we control the interview rather than it controlling us.

# 17
# Groupwork practice

## *Lynne Muir*

The proliferation of the use of groups by social workers more accustomed to work with individuals has led to confusion as to what theories, strategies, and knowledge comprise a legitimate background for entering the new, and often threatening, world of groups. Use of groups with the mentally disordered is not a new concept in Britain. Therapeutic group work was developed by Bion (1961), working with shell-shocked victims in the immediate post-war period when he focused on the behaviour of the group as a whole, not on individuals; by Foulkes and Anthony (1965) who experimented with the idea of the leader interpreting themes arising from free association conversation; by Maxwell-Jones (Walton 1971) who worked in communities based on the concept of sharing authority between staff and patients. A wider use of group work with the mentally disordered developed during the 1960s and 1970s when large psychiatric hospitals began to place residents in small group homes in the community, day centres were opened by social services departments, voluntary organizations such as MIND and special mental health projects were started.

This chapter provides the worker, particularly one with limited experience of group work, with a beginning understanding of the principles and processes underlying practice. Included is group dynamic theory relevant to any type of small group, the steps involved in starting a group and various strategies of intervention.

## What is a group?

Imagine yourself in a room of people who do not know one another. Each is looking at the other and feeling nervous, detached, anxious, isolated, or fantasizing about the abilities, thoughts, and feelings of the others. At this point the gathering of people is not a group in our terms. For this collection of people to become a group there must be interaction between members, which may be verbal or non-verbal; feelings between members, which may be negative or positive; and a common purpose or goal. If these three factors are present, you have a group. People at a bus stop waiting for a bus could not, by this definition, be called a group. Yet if something happened, such as someone pushing into the queue, then the people waiting might begin to complain to one another, feel angry at the queue jumper, and unite in the common goal of getting the person to the back of the line. Should there be feelings, interactions, and a goal, they would comprise a group until the bus arrived. Using this definition, a group can exist for a very short time or for a period of years.

The processes that go on within a group have been written about extensively (Argyle 1969; Cartwright and Zander 1968; Glasser, Sarri, and Vinter 1974). The five areas to be covered here are: group norms, patterns of influence, group structure, communication processes, and roles within groups.

### GROUP NORMS

The first characteristic of a group is that it develops its own norms or rules of behaviour. When a group is new, or a new member has joined, they will be hesitant about behaving in any definitive way because the norms are either not yet established or are unknown. Norms tend to be established by consensus with members encouraged to adhere to the rules and deviants being punished in various ways. In a new group a smoker will often wait to see if others smoke before lighting a cigarette or wait until someone asks if there are objections to smoking, at which time, if permission has been granted, a number of people will light cigarettes. This is a testing of rules acceptable to the group and the person who smokes without gaining permission may find he is criticized or excluded. Other common group norms are such things as time of arrival, actual starting and finishing time, particular chairs that people sit on, and patterns and modes of talking (members may share information on medication at each meeting). Norms can be identified in any group and are often the factors that give each group its own individuality.

INFLUENCE

The second characteristic of a group is the pattern of influence. An experience common to many people is that of sitting in a group and making, what seems to you, a valid suggestion. No notice is taken of your comment however, and the group continues its deliberations. Later in the session another member makes exactly the same suggestion but this time the group members respond enthusiastically. Your inclination may be to speak out and say, 'I suggested that earlier', in which case the group members may think you are trying to take credit for another person's idea (as they may not have consciously registered your contribution), or you may withdraw from the group and sulk (which lowers your influence rate even more). A more profitable use of time would be to recognize that a high influencer at one point in the meeting may be a low influencer at another point. Influence is based on:

1  The ability to reward others (the group member who has free passes to a local bingo house may be able to affect decisions on a group outing which otherwise would cost the members more).
2  Legitimate authority (the approved mental health worker represents the organization and usually controls many of the resources such as venue and transport).
3  Expert knowledge (a mental health group will listen to a member knowledgeable about resources).
4  Charismatic influence (someone with personal attractiveness for the other group members is often given attention).
5  Status and reputation (a delinquent group may defer to a member who is held in high repute because of his success in criminal activities).
6  Information control (the workers are powerful in groups because they decide, by withholding or sharing, what information is received by members).
7  Relationship networks (members often have established friendships outside the group and these affect relationships within the group).

The worker needs to be aware of the patterns of influence operating within the group as they affect the dynamics of the group and its consequent success or failure.


GROUP STRUCTURE

The third area for discussion is group structure or the developmental stages through which a group goes. Tuckman (1965: 384–99) divides this process into four easily remembered stages: forming, storming, norming, and performing. The first stage, forming, is characterized by anxiety and dependency on the worker with most comments being directed towards the worker as well as members testing to ascertain the group norms. Storming, the second stage, includes conflict between sub-groups, disagreements between members, resistance to group control, and rebellion against the worker. The next stage, norming, shows the development of group norms and cohesion, the resolution of conflicts and mutual support. Performing, which is the final stage, is indicated by flexible and functional roles within the group, the resolution of interpersonal problems, and the use of the group resources for the achievement of the task. These four phases are cyclical, not linear, which means that a group may be at the performing stage when the entrance of a new member to the group throws the whole group back to the forming stage.

An example of this cyclical process was illustrated in a support group for depressed single-parent women. The members, who had been meeting for some weeks, had formed supportive networks within the group. A worker, with the permission of the members, introduced a new woman into the group. In a discussion the new member paired with one established member against another established member. As this interference in the existing supportive relationships threatened the usual membership, the member who was being disagreed with by the pair, burst into tears and left the room. The worker later persuaded her to return to the meeting but she remained silent for the remainder of the session. The workers feared that none of the women would attend again, but, on looking at the process, realized that the group had reverted to the forming stage with the introduction of the new member, and had then progressed to the storming stage during the progress of the meeting. This, in fact, is what had happened and subsequent sessions saw the group working through, once more, to the performing stage, this time with the inclusion of the new member

Some writers include a fifth stage, mourning, in the process. This ending phase of a group is characterized by reactions such as denial that the group is finishing, regression to former behaviour patterns, rejection of the group and worker, or the desire for a ritual ending such as a party. Northen (1969) provides an excellent description of group termination.

## COMMUNICATION

Communication is the fourth major area to consider in observing a group. The adage that we should believe half of what we see and a quarter of what we hear is a way of saying we should respond as much, if not more, to non-verbal messages as to verbal messages.

In a verbal transaction we respond to what we think we hear or what we expect to hear, rather than to the actual message that is given. So it is not the actual words to which we respond, but to our interpretation of those words. Factors that affect our interpretation of verbal messages include our feelings about ourselves and the person giving the message; whether we feel we have a position to uphold such as status, reputation, or a place in the hierarchy; language barriers that can be either jargon, accents, technical terms, or actual language differences; the physical condition of feeling tired at the end of the day and therefore not receptive to messages; and finally, a feeling of never being adequately understood. All these factors will affect our perception, interpretation, and response to a verbal message.

Added to the above are all the interpretations made on the non-verbal signals which everyone gives in a transaction. Whereas we may ask for clarification of a verbal communication, this is often less true with non-verbal messages. We usually do not ask, if a person's voice has a hint of irritation in it, if they are feeling tired or are angry at us. Instead we make an interpretation as to what that voice tone means and then respond on the basis of that interpretation. Voice tone is only one of a number of non-verbal methods of communication. Other physical methods include body posture, eye contact, smell, and facial gestures (tongue in cheek or a wink). Non-verbal messages are also passed through music (soft music tends to calm while loud music tends to excite), and dancing (often favoured by courting couples), as well as through gestures (thumbs up or a V sign), and symbols (religious habits or wedding rings). A difficulty arising from non-verbal messages is our lack of awareness of their affect on us. In any transaction a worker needs to be conscious of both the verbal and non-verbal messages, as mental disorder may affect the perception of messages.

## ROLES

The roles that group members carry complete the list of group character-istics to be discussed in this section.

A useful typology was developed by Bales (1950) in which he stated that every verbal or non-verbal contribution by a member could be categorized as either contributing to the achievement of the group task or concerned with group feelings and maintenance. The behaviour that is linked to task achievement includes defining the task, asking or giving opinions, asking or giving information/suggestions, and testing the feasibility of the decisions. Behaviour that is concerned with group feeling can be helpful or unhelpful, verbal or non-verbal. This covers humorous or tension-releasing actions, encouraging, supporting nods or comments, as well as disparaging remarks, withdrawing from group involvement, and self-aggrandizing statements or behaviour.

Group roles usually are shared among the members and can be easily identified by an observant worker. The worker needs to be aware of these roles in order to modify unhelpful behaviour and to provide opportunities for members to experiment with various ways of behaving.

## Starting groups

A group is more than the sum of its parts but is also defined by the individual characteristics of its members. By adding or subtracting members the character of a group can be changed totally. What factors need to be considered before starting a group?

The intention to form a group raises certain questions for the worker: When is a group appropriate for an individual? What kind of goals are possible to evaluate? What size should the group be and how should members be selected? What is the role of the worker(s)?


### WHEN IS A GROUP APPROPRIATE?

Deciding whether or not to suggest to a client that he joins a group is affected by several factors:

1 Can the person relate to other people? Members (very shy and with-drawn or very aggressive and confronting people) whose behaviour differs widely from others in the group may find themselves in an intolerable situation. Also, much of the benefit of a group comes from shared interaction, so the ability to gain from this is crucial.
2 Can the person relate to the worker? This is particularly important in adolescent groups, such as Intermediate Treatment programmes, where the influence of delinquent members may be stronger and more effective than the influence of the worker.
3 Can the member participate in shared decision-making? Much of the activity in groups is about co-operation, sharing, relating to one another, and jointly deciding on issues. The ability to be able to partici-pate in joint decision-making, at a minimal level of functioning at least, is an important skill.
4 Can the member learn from the 'here and now' focus of a group as contrasted to the 'there and then' focus of a one-to-one situation? In a one-to-one interview a member may give an anecdotal account of past examples about others not listening to him whereas in a group, if a similar thing occurs, then the member may have immediate feedback as to why this is happening. People who are very defensive or very disturbed are likely to find this type of feedback too threatening which will limit the learning they can gain from such a group.

While a field mental health worker should consider the above factors before recommending a group for a client, they are not always feasible considerations for a residential worker. He is faced with the fact of existing and ongoing groups in hostels and hospitals and must decide how to cope with the problems of communication, relationships, and co-operative living.

EVALUATING GOALS

Goal formulation (Glasser, Sarri, and Vinter 1974: 126–48) is crucial in effective groupwork practice. A person may refer himself, be referred by another agency or worker, or be sought out by the worker. Whichever way he comes, he will have some idea as to what he hopes to gain from a group. Equally, the worker will have certain purposes in mind which will be a composite of agency, personal, and professional goals and these may correspond to, or conflict with, the goals of the client. The purposes of both the worker and clients should be clarified early in the life of the group.

Three mental health workers formed a group for clients suffering from a variety of mental disorders who all had experienced a recent bereavement. The aim of the workers was to help the members develop practical coping skills. The members came to participate in a social afternoon, and to get attention and help from the workers. The specific objectives of the group were clarified jointly in the following manner.

GIVEN
A group of six people and three workers to meet for two hours weekly for fourteen weeks at a day centre.

BEHAVIOUR
1  Each member will learn one new practical skill such as changing a fuse or cooking a meal.
2  Each member will meet with one other member, at least once, outside the group.
3  Each member will share an interest of his/hers with the rest of the group.
4  Each member will know the welfare benefits to which he/she is entitled.
5  Each member will speak at least once to the group about his/her loss.
6  Each meeting will end with a shared meal prepared by all.

CRITERIA
In evaluating the above goals at the end of fourteen weeks, the workers and members will discuss each point and jointly decide which ones have been achieved (with specific examples), and for which members.

The point about this exercise was that the goals or objectives were made very specific, related to the stated aims of both workers and members, and could be evaluated by tangible behaviour. Too often in groups aims are stated so vaguely that there is no way of knowing at the end of the group whether or not anything has been achieved. Bloom (1975: 177) refers to this as driving with your eyes closed – you are going places but do not know for certain where you are or what you did that got you there.

## SIZE OF GROUP

The size of the group is determined by the nature of the interaction desired. The smaller the group the greater the potential and demand for close relationships; the higher the rate of membership participation, the stronger the group pressures on each member and the greater the flexibility of the group to modify its goals to meet changing needs. Too small a group, however, means you may have no group if members are absent or drop out. When a group is larger than about eight, a formal structure begins to develop, sub-groups appear, communications are directed towards the worker, the number of interactions possible increases, and the group tends to find difficulty in making decisions.

In deciding upon the size of a group and in selecting members for a group, a worker needs to consider the needs of the clients, their prior group experiences, their personalities, and whether or not they want to join a particular group. Effective groups have members who want to be there so the decision on whether or not to join should be a critical attribute.

In selecting members for a group it is generally better to have a group with a variety of personalities and behaviour, and similar descriptive characteristics such as age and similar type of illness (all mentally disordered). Bertcher and Maple (1977) have devised a method for rating potential members on a chart which lists behavioural characteristics. The items, depending upon the purpose of the group, may range from social skills to the ability to communicate. From this rating of each possible member, a balanced group can then be composed. This method implies a pool of potential members which may mean delaying the start of a group until a pool from which to choose can be built up.

An exception to this general rule is suggested by Rose (1977) who says it is possible to have a group from very different backgrounds for the behavioural treatment of a range of phobias, as the emphasis is on the problem, not on the interaction with others.

## ROLE OF THE WORKER

Whereas in casework the context of treatment is a one-to-one relationship with the client demanding, and receiving, the undivided attention of the worker and the relationship between them being the main tool of the helping process, the situation in group work is somewhat different. Social group work recognizes the influence of the group processes and the worker tries to mobilize these forces for the benefit of the group and each member. The group, then, is both the context and the means of achieving the task. The influence of the worker is also of central importance. In working with a group the worker recognizes himself as a central figure trying to balance the needs of individuals with the needs of the group as a whole. Often it is the worker who has formed the group, knows all the members and, through the agency, maintains a continuous, albeit tenuous, link with all the members. The role of the worker as a central figure will vary according to the needs, setting, maturity, and stage of development of the group. It is important to recognize that the worker is a central person by virtue of the professional situation and setting and by the use of the skills he possesses in working with people.

Wilson and Ryland (1949: 68), in a classic formulation, illustrated the decreasing activity of the worker in relation to the increasing ability of the members to use the group (*Figure 17.1*).

The degree of activity of the worker will vary not only from group to group but also within a given group over a period of time.

Part of the skill of the worker lies in knowing when to be active and when to sit back. In most groups composed of social work clients the emphasis of the worker is upon behavioural and attitudinal change. For example, a typical group might be composed of hospital outpatients who meet weekly to talk about how they are coping with life pressures. This might involve behavioural training on how to carry on a conversation in a shop or catch a bus on their own, as well as including discussions with other group members on their attitudes to their daily life. In these groups the worker will take an active role in selecting members, forming and modifying the group, establishing the purpose and contract of the groups, and acting as a central person in fostering co-operative relationships in the group, in trying to help group members to transfer the learning to outside situations at the termination of the group, and in evaluating the success or failure of the group. As the members become more competent in dealing with the group processes, the role of the worker modifies to one of offering help when needed or requested.

STRATEGIES OF INTERVENTION

How does a worker decide between the various models of intervening in a group? While theories are written as though they were discrete, in practice the edges of one theory blend into another. The four models outlined in *Table 17.1* are ones that are used most frequently in work with the mentally disordered. For clarity they are separately identified but, within a group, workers might use one or more models during the course of a meeting.

A group for depressed and isolated women described in *Community Care* (Nelson and Wigglesworth 1983) illustrates the initial use of the remedial model where the workers set up a structured group with a planned programme involving some factual teaching which later became experimental learning with the women setting tasks for themselves to achieve.

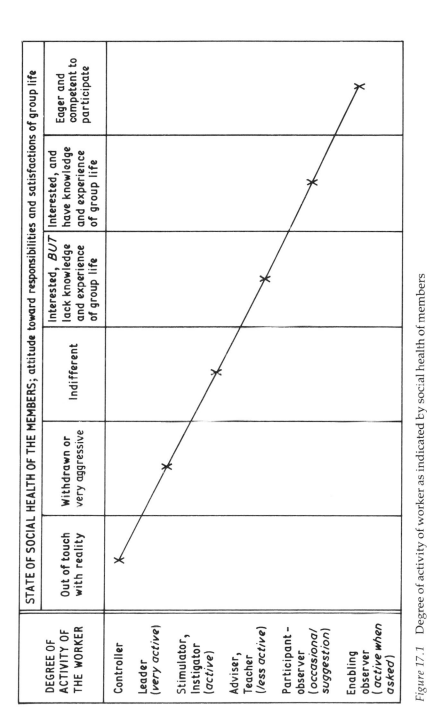

*Figure 17.1* Degree of activity of worker as indicated by social health of members

*Table 17.1*   Group models used in work with the mentally disordered

|  | *therapeutic* | *remedial* | *self-actualizing* | *behaviour modification* |
|---|---|---|---|---|
| purpose of group | To gain insight into individual and group behaviour | To remedy social dysfunctioning by specific and planned change | To develop unrealized personal resources | To modify and change existing learned behaviour |
| setting | Hospitals and day centres | Social services depts | Day centres and social services depts | Hospitals, residential settings, and social services depts |
| client group | Mentally disordered | Mentally disordered and mentally handicapped | Mentally disordered | Mentally disordered and mentally handicapped |
| role of worker | Interpretative | Planner and organizer | Instigator and resource | Role model and teacher |
| programme/ activity | Talking in group with no fixed programme | Planned programme geared to needs of group members | Creativity exercises, art, drama, feedback | Social skill training, role-plays |

An example of the use of the self-actualizing model is a psychiatric day centre that offers members the opportunity to develop their latent potential through activities such as yoga, cooking, gestalt, relaxation, keep fit, discussion, and music. Whiteley and Gordon (1979) describe the use of the therapeutic model in different types of institutions such as hospitals, hostels, and day centres. They emphasize the importance of workers being clear which strategies are being used at any one point.

It has been the intention of this chapter to alert the mental health worker to some of the dynamics operating within small groups so that this understanding may influence the methods of intervention and choice of strategies the worker may choose. The wider use of groups with the mentally disordered is a growing area of practice. Their effective use can be enhanced through clearly defined and evaluated objectives, carefully formed and selected membership, and awareness of tested theories.

# 18

# Behavioural approaches with psychiatric patients

*Brian Sheldon*

In Chapter 7 evidence from psychological, genetic, and psychiatric research led me to propose that our approach to preventive and after-care work with psychotic patients should be concerned with enlisting the help of relatives and others to provide a stable living environment, and with offering more specialized advice on the management of particular problems. In the case of clients suffering from neurotic disorders – where their problems seem to stem predominantly from learned maladaptive responses to otherwise tolerable environments – then I suggested that we have a broader therapeutic role. Such a conclusion needs to be qualified only by a sense of caution over the reliability of psychiatric diagnoses (which by and large social workers already possess) and by the facts that the need to develop good, honest working relationships and to help where possible with practical difficulties, apply to all our work. This being so, there is a set of techniques available to social workers, with a potential for producing therapeutic gains in both fields of mental disorder:

1 *Behaviour modification approaches* or *stimulus-control* techniques seek to alter maladaptive behaviour and strengthen useful responses by paying attention to factors in the environment in which they occur. These detailed behaviour–management programmes are often used with the help of *mediators* – people who know and regularly come into contact with the client.

2 *Behaviour therapy* or *response-control* techniques are concerned more
with the 'unlearning' of unreasonable fears and anxieties, and with the
direct teaching of new responses aimed at remedying deficits in the
client's behavioural repertoire.

In fact the distinctions between these two types of work have become
blurred over the years as successful combinations of approaches have
been developed, such as techniques to teach new social skills and
approaches to remove positive consequences from avoidance behaviour.

As to why social workers should make use of these techniques rather
than others, there is now a very large literature testifying to their effectiveness in psychiatric and related settings. Behaviour modification is not
the only game in town, but rarely does anything else come close to the
results it can produce. In a complicated and much-haggled-over field, an
authoritative research review by Kazdin and Wilson (1978) came to the
following conclusions on this point:

(i) Comparison studies of behavioural methods and other approaches
show the former achieving consistently better results. Not a single
study showed behaviour therapy to be inferior to other psychotherapeutic methods.
(ii) No evidence of sympton-substitution following behavioural
therapy was obtained, even in studies explicitly designed to un-
cover negative side-effects.
(iii) Behaviour therapy was found to be more broadly applicable to the
full range of psychological disorders than traditional psychotherapeutic approaches.
(iv) Behavioural therapy is capable of producing broadly based treatment effects on specific target behaviours and related measures of
general psychological functioning.
(see Rachman and Wilson 1980: 120)

To these findings should be added recent results from social work research
showing a long-awaited reversal of the negative trends of earlier years
now that behavioural and other well-focused approaches are beginning to
make an impact on practice (see Reid and Hanrahan 1980). The case for the
application of behavioural and cognitive-behavioural principles to those
parts of social work where applied psychology is relevant, is now over-
whelming. The same can be said of the sub-field of psychiatric social work
(see Hudson 1982). The application of behavioural approaches to
problems arising from mental handicap is well known, but in addition the
methods have been used successfully as an aid to the treatment of schizophrenic, depressed, phobic, and obsessive-compulsive patients, as well
as to counter secondary problems arising from present patterns of care: for

example, institutionalization (Ayllon and Azrin 1965). Their use in preventive work and in training programmes to equip patients with the skills they will need to survive in the community is patchier, but arguably, this work is down to us. There are some results from these less-well-controlled settings, however, and they are very encouraging (Sheldon 1982; Stern 1978; Stuart 1977; Tharp and Wetzel 1969).

## General principles

A grasp of the general principles of behavioural psychology which underlie therapeutic work of the type being discussed here, is essential if such approaches are not to be mis-applied or used in an unhelpfully rigid and stereotyped manner. Here are some basic assumptions of the approach:

1 The greater portion of the behavioural repertoire with which individuals are equipped, is the product of *learning*. This vast range of possible responses is acquired through a lengthy interaction with an ambivalent physical and social environment. People adapt to, and are active in, their environment for the satisfaction of their own physical needs, and for the satisfaction of a much broader range of appetites which, with the development of society and culture, have become associated with these. The original goals of behaviour were connected with the drive for physical homocostasis in the face of 'heartless, witless nature'. But the position is now infinitely more complicated. Suffice it to say that men and women dying for love, practising celibacy, or fostering a mentally handicapped adult, do not threaten this view. All these examples are examples of learned, goal-directed behaviour.

2 Genetic and physiological factors also influence behaviour in more general ways, and there is an interaction between these and environment.

3 Two broad processes of associative learning account for the acquisition and maintenance of motor, verbal, and emotional responses. These are: *classical* or *respondent conditioning*, revealed to us by the great Russian physiologist I. P. Pavlov (the fact that most readers will now have an image in their heads of a dog, salivating to the sound of a bell, is a good example of this form of learning); and *operant* or *instrumental conditioning*, investigated by the American psychologists E. L. Thorndike and B. F. Skinner (1953). This latter form of learning assumes that feedback from the environment in the form of patterns of positive and negative consequences influences how we are likely to behave in similar circumstances in future.

4 Outside physical pathology, behaviours that we judge to be maladaptive or abnormal are learned in exactly the same way as behaviours that

we are disposed to call adaptive or normal. Any apparent differences between the two, apart from questions of degree, are a property of the evaluative and attributive judgements that observers make about behaviour, rather than of the behaviour itself or its origins.

5 It is possible for human beings to acquire whole sequences of behaviour 'at a distance'. Observational learning or *modelling* followed by subsequent rehearsal, accounts for much of the complex social behaviour with which we are equipped (Bandura 1969). Nor should we forget the 'quantum leap' in acquiring the potential for new behaviours made possible by language.

6 It is not the case that behaviourists are uninterested in thoughts and feelings. Psychologists of this persuasion have contributed much to our understanding of both these sets of phenomena. However, while it is possible for each of us to have access to the contents of our own consciousness, it is very difficult to do this in a reliable way with other people. Therefore the methodological position of behaviourism is to limit inference to internal goings-on as much as possible by concentrating on overt performances and factors in the environment with which they appear to co-vary. There is, however, a more relaxed attitude to such questions within the discipline these days. The arrival of cognitive-behaviour modification (see Meichenbaum 1977) represents a fusion of behavioural and cognitive approaches. In these approaches it is acknowledged that thoughts – or, more particularly, images and patterns of 'self-talk' – may do much to 'cue', maintain, or reinforce our overt behaviour. Cognitive-behavioural approaches attempt to change the patterns of dialogue we have with ourselves (for example the tendency of nervous people to talk themselves into failure) to see whether this has a direct effect on behaviour. Such approaches have been used with profit in the treatment of depression, chronic shyness, and types of social inadequacy in clients. However, although new information or a different way of thinking about behaviour and future intentions might affect our *view* of life and our problems, the ultimate test has to be whether behavioural change appears as a result of these cognitive manipulations. There is much in the literature of behavioural psychology and the psychology of attitude change to caution us against over-reliance on attempts at cognitive realignment. The extra ingredient of graded rehearsal of new performances seems to this author, and to many others, a wise precaution (Eysenck 1984).

7 Assessment procedures should concentrate as far as possible on tangible behaviour and events in the here and now. It is important to distinguish between the congeniality of therapeutic encounters and the degree of useful change achieved in respect of pre-negotiated goals. This insistence on evaluating in terms of specific target behaviours, together with the routine application of experimental principles to work

with single cases, accounts for the greater replicability of findings in this field.

I think that the best way to explain the main approaches referred to above is to provide an example of each.

### Example of a behaviour modification scheme to reduce delusional expressions

The programme used in this case (Sheldon 1982) was part of a broader social work approach and was designed to lift from the shoulders of a basically caring family the pressure created by their daughter's delusional preoccupations. Katherine was in her parents' words 'obsessed' with ideas of electronic surveillance and men watching the house. The ex-patriate Hungarian family had had a bad time in Budapest during the uprising of 1956, and talk of this kind was particularly upsetting to them.

Although she was only 24, Katherine's condition had been chronic over a number of years. She had had several informal admissions to psychiatric hospital. Social workers were under the impression that these were due more to social crises within the family than to any sudden worsening of Katherine's condition. Katherine's dislike of hospital was the motivation for her to take part in a short series of discussions about how family life could be improved. The hypothesis that her parents' desire through lengthy discussion to challenge and so banish her unreasonable belief might actually be reinforcing the problem, was openly talked about. It was suggested that in future, delusional references should be completely ignored, except for one brief reassurance per day. Normal conversations, however, would be responded to with appropriate enthusiasm. Should Katherine feel any urgent desire to discuss her beliefs, then these could be taken up in private with the social worker during a scheduled visit. While Katherine was not able to accept that her ideas were false (attempts to place them in the context of the family's history achieved little) she rather diffidently agreed to give the scheme a try.

The approach used in this case was *differential reinforcement*. Delusional talk was placed on *extinction* (was not reinforced with attention), but all other forms of conversation were reinforced. Following a short period of rather stilted interaction, her parents reported that they could manage this without undue self-consciousness. After the first thirty-three days of operation, episodes of delusional talk never again rose above 2 per day – compared with an average of between 5 and 6 items per day prior to intervention. The programme lasted ninety-two days in all, with twice-weekly visits to get it established, weekly visits to check its stability, and a fortnightly 'drop-in' session thereafter. Follow-up at six months revealed a maintained level of improvement of roughly the order described (see also p. 237).

It is possible with the benefit of new knowledge to see this case as one involving the over-stimulation of a schizophrenic client by well-meaning relatives (Vaughn and Leff 1976). In-depth discussions of delusions in an attempt to dispel them tended to end in criticisms of Katherine, and occasionally in rows leading to further florid episodes. Katherine learned through this scheme that parental interest and affection were readily available to her, *except* in a form which threatened family stability. Her parents got a much broader message: that many of their problems were, after all, under their own control.

Katherine may well have continued to harbour delusional *thoughts* as before, but it was her expression of these which caused trouble. It should also be noted that there is some evidence that topics that receive no conversational reinforcement are less often thought about (Homme 1965).

## An example of modelling procedures

Paulette (26) had spent five years in hospitals and psychiatric clinics of various kinds. She was diagnosed as schizophrenic and presented as a shy, withdrawn, self-preoccupied young woman of rather bizarre behaviour. She would avoid the centre of rooms for example, as if they had been mined; constantly hung her head; shuffled around the house all day and neglected her dress and personal hygiene. Her case was referred to social services for after-care following discharge from a psychiatric unit and the failure of a course of rehabilitation therapy.

First, the view was put to Paulette that people could only think her mad if her behaviour put this idea into their heads. This was in reaction to her expressed feelings of over-conspicuousness and inadequacy when confronted with new people or situations. She also had worries that if she got into conversation with people they would quickly find out about her psychiatric history. It was decided not to delve further into the historical background of this problem, but to identify one or two clear behavioural deficits, and try to remedy them. Two basic items of behaviour, capable of being built on later, were selected: walking confidently into a room and introducing herself; and giving non-verbal reinforcement to other people during a conversation, as a means of conveying interest and understanding (and thereby counteracting Paulette's usually rather vacant expression).

These two classes of behaviour were broken down into their component parts – such as opening conversations, nodding while listening, closing down conversations – and repeatedly modelled by two students. The students played counter-roles and also offered constructive criticism on each other's performance. The sessions became increasingly friendly and light-hearted, and always ended with a more relaxed period of general conversation on topics known to interest the client. After seven half-hour sessions, the client had mastered walking confidently into the room and her mother and younger brother were introduced into the programme to look for, and reinforce, behaviours of a similar kind throughout the rest of the day.

Believable, non-verbal signals of understanding were harder to establish. Paulette's performance approximated to that of the modellers' only vaguely and mechanically, and the initial programme had to be slowed down and re-thought. Maintaining eye contact was discovered to be a primary problem and this was cued and selectively reinforced with approval wherever it occurred. When low levels of eye contact had been established, Paulette's other non-verbal behaviour improved substantially.

By the end of the students' placement, Paulette had two new pieces of social behaviour which she did not possess before and her family showed increasing tolerance towards her, and an increasing interest in what else she might be capable of. For further information on the application of skill training techniques with psychiatric patients see Trower, Bryant, and Argyle (1977).

## The origins and treatment of a phobia

Mrs Wood, aged 40, was referred to the social services department for 'support' by her exasperated family doctor. In his view Mrs Wood suffered from agoraphobia (profound fear of going out of doors), a 'dependent personality', and a number of unspecified 'psychiatric difficulties'. The following case history emerged:

— Mrs Wood had a lifelong fear of hospitals, stemming from her mother's confinement with her younger sister, when her mother had nearly died in childbirth.
— Mrs Wood became pregnant 'by accident', comparatively late in life. In order to persuade her to have the baby in hospital, the doctor had played up the dangers of a home confinement, raising her already high level of anxiety about the birth.
— One hot summer's day, when she was seven months pregnant, Mrs Wood had fainted while crossing a footbridge spanning a small river near to her home. 'I was sure I was going to fall in, and when I came round, people said an ambulance was on the way. I panicked. People were trying to hold me down. I knew I had to get away, I got very upset, and eventually I persuaded someone to take me home. When I got in I was shaking all over. I shut and bolted the doors, back and front . . . I was sure that the ambulance was going to call at the house . . . I hid out

of sight of the windows . . . and eventually (it took about an hour) I calmed down, and sat waiting for my husband to come home from work.'

— Mrs Wood had her baby at home, against medical advice. It was a painful birth but without serious complications. She tried to go out several times after that but never got further than the front garden or, if at night, as far as the front gate.

— She reported the following feelings at each attempt: 'Shivering; awful feelings in the pit of my stomach; pounding heart; light-headedness . . . In the daytime everywhere seems very bright and stark. I feel conspicuous out in the open, almost as if I might be struck down any minute . . . My breathing is loud in my ears all the time and my biggest fear is that I shall collapse . . . I have thought at times that I should die.'

— Mrs Wood eventually gave up these attempts and remained indoors for the next four years. For the first two of these she reported that she did not really miss going out: 'the family were very good, they took the baby out, got the shopping, they are marvellous; so are the neighbours.' Later, however, Mrs Wood began to experience feelings of dissatisfaction and frustration with her confined existence.

If we examine this case in the light of classical conditioning theory, the following pattern emerges.

— Against a background of heightened anxiety about pregnancy, dreading the thought of having to go into hospital, Mrs Wood experiences a traumatic incident which arouses in her a very powerful fear reaction.

— This incident, when paired with the previously neutral stimulus of the footbridge and other stimuli associated with being out of doors (for example seeing other people), produces eventually a conditioned response to these stimuli. Even after the incident itself passed, and the pregnancy was over and although she was perfectly well, and the crowd no longer in sight (the eliciting stimuli), she still experienced a powerful fear reaction to the original context.

— Mrs Wood reports that her panic state was made worse by the attempts of would-be helpers to restrain her until the ambulance came. Escape-behaviour was prevented, which always intensifies fear.

— This conditioned fear response quickly generalizes to virtually all outdoor circumstances, even though, objectively, they barely resemble the circumstances of her collapse. Furthermore, every time Mrs Wood tries to go out of doors at this stage she is punished for the attempt by her strong anxiety reaction, even though she sees these feelings as irrational and illogical.

— Every time Mrs Wood manages to escape from the circumstances that

elicit the conditioned fear response, her strongly adversive fears are terminated: this strengthens her avoidance behaviour, and makes future experiments less likely.
— Mrs Wood's family and friends reward her long-term maladaptation to her phobia by relieving her of many of her day-to-day responsibilities.
— There is a strong possibility that people such as Mrs Wood who liked to describe herself as being 'of a nervous disposition' are especially prone to acquire fear reactions and associations of this kind.

This client was treated by *in vivo desensitization*. This approach (which now requires re-thinking in the light of research (Cooke 1968; Marks 1971)) contains the following elements:

1 An elaborate hierarchy of fear-provoking stimuli, for example: standing in porch – standing in garden – at front gate – on pavement – across the road – near the shops – at the edge of town, *until* – stand alone on footbridge for 10 minutes.
2 These accompanied assignments are backed up by deep relaxation and breathing exercises which the client is taught at home, and practises regularly.
3 The idea is that the client will *slide* through the items of the hierarchy over a longish period, feeling no sudden upsurge of anxiety.

This was always an effective method, as it was in the case of Mrs Wood. But it is not particularly efficient. Research now strongly suggests that the only really essential elements in the removal of unreasonable fears are: (a) getting the client into the fear-provoking circumstances as quickly as possible; (b) aiding the client to stay there though in a state of considerable anxiety – helped by previously rehearsed coping strategies and plenty of reassurance from the therapist – until the anxiety subsides. This approach is called *rapid exposure* and it is remarkably effective with clients who can be persuaded to confront their fears and stay facing them for long enough. For those clients who are resolutely unwilling to do this, or whom the therapist believes would be likely to panic and leave the scene (thus intensifying their fears), *slow exposure* is indicated. The principles are the same but a few graded assignments are used before the final confrontation. Relaxation therapy may help some clients in its own right, but it does not seem to be an essential accompaniment of exposure techniques.

Rapid exposure techniques necessarily create anxiety in clients (the fact that no one stays anxious forever is their active ingredient) and so, without being too dramatic about it, some simple precautions are necessary before social workers make use of them. People with heart ailments or respiratory difficulties should not attempt resolutions of this type. The routine safety measure of involving the GP or psychiatrist in such cases at an early stage is only common sense.

## Conclusions

A chapter of this length, on a topic of this size, can only aim to whet the appetite of the reader. However, my impression is that many social workers avoid the main course (see cited references) as a result of (generally) rather vaguely held ethical objections. There is for example that almost Pavlovian association of behaviourism with aversion therapy and brainwashing. The fact that such practices are far removed from the day-to-day business of social work does not seem to help. It might be a useful challenge to those who are not well disposed to behavioural methods, and therefore unlikely to read more extended discussions of their ethical implications (see Sheldon 1982: Chapter 8), to consider just two points:

1 Though phrases like 'useful responses' and 'maladaptive behaviour' (both used in this chapter) contain value judgements: what does not? At least in this style of work they are clearly visible since what is being aimed for is couched in concrete, behavioural terms, and is therefore pretty-well unmistakable. The same cannot be said of many widely accepted approaches in social work.
2 *Not* intervening, or at least not using techniques with a proven record of effectiveness assessed by scientific standards, is *also* an ethical decision. It represents a pattern of behaviour that we would all deplore in, say, garage mechanics, or medical practitioners.

Consumer research has shown consistently that clients expect advice and an active approach to their problems, not just conversational reviews of their possible origins (Mayer and Timms 1970; Rees 1978; Rees and Wallace 1982). Perhaps the problem is ours?

# 19

## The management of
## crisis in the
## psychiatric emergency

## M. Rolf Olsen

The utilization of the crisis in the mental health emergency as the optimum moment for intervention is a concept, if not a technique, which has been known for more than twenty-five years. Yet in spite of its long pedigree, the notion has received scant attention and there has been little evaluation of its application or its effectiveness in practice in the UK. In contrast the American medical and social work literature continually reports on the successful application of the strategy. Here the evidence indicates that the use of this strategy in mental health emergencies does reduce the need for hospitalization, is as successful in restoring the patient with respect to both social adaptation and ability to cope with life's crises, and is cost effective in comparison with the costs of hospitalization.

### Theoretical considerations

Essentially the word crisis means that a point has been reached when a situation must change. Traditionally it refers to a physical state in which the stage has been reached in a disease or illness which indicates death or recovery. However the term 'crisis' is increasingly recognized as a crucial stage in a personal or social conflict situation and 'crisis intervention' as the process with the dual aims of lessening the impact of the stressful event and utilizing the crisis situation to promote positive change. In their final Report on Mental Illness and Health the American Joint Commission claimed that 'Generally speaking the word crisis means that a decisive point has been reached or a point in time when a situation must change' (Action for Mental Health 1961). Crisis is associated with stress. This is defined as a state of psychological upset or disequilibrium in an individual. In crisis this disequilibrium is of relatively brief duration and is generally self-limiting. It is a reaction to a specific event which is commonly perceived by those who experience it as an unexpected threat or loss. Examples of such events are death, retirement, serious illness, birth, loss of job, loss of income, or surgical operation. Caplan (1961, 1964) defines crisis as a state 'provoked when a person faces an obstacle to important life goals that is for a time insurmountable through the utilization of customary methods of problem solving'. He says a period of disorganization ensues which signifies both danger and opportunity, danger of descent into mental disorder or opportunity for successful treatment.

One of the earliest theoretical definitions of psychiatric crisis appeared in Erich Lindemann's classic paper Symptomatology and Management of Acute Grief which appeared in 1944. In it he showed that whilst grief is a normal reaction to a distressing situation, it may also be a psychogenic factor in psychosomatic disorder. In his paper Lindemann made the following points.

1 Acute grief is a definite syndrome with psychological and somatic symptomatology including preoccupation with the image of the deceased, guilt, hostile reactions and irritability towards others, loss of normal patterns of conduct, restlessness, and adoption of the traits of the deceased.
2 This syndrome may appear immediately after a crisis; it may be delayed; it may be exaggerated or apparently absent.
3 In place of the typical syndrome there may appear distorted pictures, each of which represents one special aspect of the grief syndrome.
4 By use of appropriate techniques these distorted pictures can be successfully transformed into a normal grief reaction with resolution.

Since Lindemann, a number of published papers have considered the application of crisis theory to a variety of fields. This range is clearly demonstrated by the selected papers which appear in Parad's edited work *Crisis Intervention: Selected Readings* which appeared in 1965. For example the paper by Donald Klein and Ann Ross demonstrates the value of using social perspectives in understanding the stresses of school entry. They view this transition as an experience not only for the child but the whole family and added new insights to the understanding of school phobia which up till then had been treated largely as a problem of mother–child pathology.

Stanley Cath (Parad 1965) looks at the crisis of growing old and concludes that for many living sufficiently long in itself brings inevitable personal loss, psychic and body depletion, and disease. He considers that it is during the degenerative phase of life that the greatest stress is presented to the individual. In the sixties and seventies, when a person can no longer realistically look forward to new starts, more positive identifications, or readily changing his ways, the number of depressive mood swings tends to increase, and there is a shift in frequency along the mood spectrum, from days of enlightened well-being to those of mildly depressive preoccupation, during which he searches for tokens of past affection and responses from memories. But to live in the company of his memories may serve little purpose if it awakens regrets as well as pleasures. This condition, of course, may not be accepted lightly, and rebellion may be manifested by temper outbursts.

David Kaplan and Edward Mason (Parad 1965) studied the maternal reactions to a premature birth in 60 cases. They conclude that there is a typical psychological experience for the mother of the premature baby which can be distinguished from the experience following full-term delivery, and they contrast the maternal stress accompanying premature birth with that of normal full-term delivery.

At term the woman is impatient both to see the baby and to discharge her burden. Whether she comes to the delivery anxious or calm, the atmosphere encourages her to feel that she will produce a normal child. The setting is geared to her needs and she manages the discomforts of labour because they are seen as temporary. When the events follow the expected pattern, the mother more readily feels a pride in her achievement and she receives rewards and recognition from the doctor, hospital staff, husband, family, and friends. Whereas a mother of a premature baby has a heightened concern after delivery about whether the baby is alive and will live, and later whether there is any abnormality. She sees the baby briefly before it is hurried into an incubator and taken off to a separate nursery or even a different hospital. Her most vivid recollections are about the baby's small size; its unusual colour and unattractive appearance add further to the shock. Usually the physician talks to the mother in guarded words, or else avoids contact with her for a few days. In general there seems to be no prompt and frank discussion about the prognosis or cause of prematurity, and a state of suspense is encouraged. The hospital staff finds it difficult to know how to respond; the mother needs support, but it is hard to give it without confirming her feeling of failure or futilely raising her hopes. A mother expecting to hear at any moment that her baby has died is apprehensive and prone to pick up the anxieties of other mothers or of the staff.

The nursery for the prematures frustrates most mothers in their desire to see the baby. Often it is on a different floor. The incubator obscures a good view, and frequently must remain on the other side of the room from the window in order to have oxygen immediately available. When a mother does visit, her baby's appearance is frightening. She may avoid visiting the nursery altogether or else be drawn to look at the baby in spite of the baby's reminding her of her failure.

In her paper, Children at Risk, Betty Irvine (Parad 1965) emphasizes the need to make preventative services promptly available to children who are 'at risk' because their parents have been hospitalized for mental illness. Such children are likely to be particularly vulnerable on account of previous disturbed relationships within the family, especially if the onset of the illness has been insidious. They are now exposed to the sudden loss of a parent, in circumstances that are likely to tinge the natural grief and distress with a heavy colouring of anxiety and guilt.

Physical illness can often be labelled and explained, and the length of absence can often be predicted; this is helpful to all but the youngest children. Mental illness can usually not be named or explained, and questions are apt to evoke uneasy equivocation, which creates an atmosphere of shameful and embarrassing mystery. Older children may suspect madness, and will feel ashamed of this as they would not be of a physical complaint. Guilt may well have been stimulated during the period of onset by repeated urging to be good, to keep quiet, for fear of giving mother a headache, because daddy is not well. They may have been more overtly accused of 'getting on mother's nerves', or of 'driving daddy round the bend'. When mother or father eventually 'goes round the bend' this will seem to be the fulfilment of a prophecy, the result of all those unheeded warnings.

There may have been scenes of violence, and the children may have been not only very frightened, but also quite confused about who was the victim and who was the aggressor. This is especially so if the child has been attached to a paranoid parent, who maybe for months or years has been accusing neighbours, relatives, or the other parent of conspiring to 'put him away'. Now he has been 'put away', so he was right all along; or perhaps the child feels he has been sent away as a punishment for difficult behaviour. Such children are apt to be both frightened and angry with those who 'put away' the missing parent for obscure reasons which they are usually too embarrassed to explain. The children therefore 'play up' in ways that set up a new round of anger and anxiety in relatives, since they seem to confirm all the natural fears about heredity.

## Intervening in psychiatric crisis

From the quoted papers it will be seen the concept of crisis is a broad one and that it embraces a variety of life experiences and presented problems in medicine, psychiatry, and social work. The concept, which has mainly grown out of ego-psychology, goes on to argue that in times of crisis individual defences are lowered and in such a state people are more willing to change. The technique is to focus on the presented situation with the aims of resolving the difficulties and restoring the individual to his previous level of equilibrium. There is more than one way to achieve this. For example, in working with a person who has unresolved grief, the aim is to achieve a resolution by enabling the client to grieve and express his sorrow and sense of loss. Klein and Ross in arguing that difficulties in starting school are more likely to be due to problems in role transition rather than phobia, advocate preventive intervention through group meetings prior to the child starting school as the way in which difficulties in transition can be most successfully dealt with. Social workers can best help mothers and families of premature babies by providing information about the risks and management of a premature child, acting as a liaison between hospital and community resources, and by helping the family to face and cope with their feelings. Irvine argues that policy and practice in the treatment and care of the mentally ill should always take the interests of the children explicitly into account in order to harmonize or balance them with those of the patient. There is as yet little evidence that this is systematically done. A very few hospitals are experimentally admitting pre-school children with their mentally ill mothers. This practice is usually advocated on the grounds of benefit to the mother, but it is believed to be of value to the children too, both as avoiding separation and as affording an opportunity for the child to enjoy skilled support in dealing with the problems with which his mother's illness confronts him. Where no such arrangements exist, the children are automatically separated from the parent who goes into hospital.

When a parent goes in to psychiatric hospital, the mere fact of separation, the pain of missing the absent person, is bound to be complicated more or less by the child's anxiety about the illness and the outcome, and by guilt for past unkindness, demandingness, or thoughtlessness. When these feelings are strong the child will need opportunity to talk them out; this some families or foster-parents can provide, but others may find it too hard to tolerate the expression of such feelings, and may smother it with reassurance or cheerful chatter in a way that relieves themselves more than the child.

In spite of this understanding the current management of the psychiatric crisis remains primitive. With one or two notable exceptions our solution to the emergency situation that cannot be contained within the living group is to remove the person defined as the patient to hospital, no matter whether the cause is thought to lie within the person himself, the nature of his relationships, his social environment, or in disease processes. This cannot be regarded as satisfactory, and we must ask ourselves whether it is possible to intervene more thoughtfully and with greater efficacy. From several points of view the personal, social, and economic gains to be made by interventive strategies which do not rely solely on hospitalization appear to be considerable.

In contrast to this situation, the American social work and medical literature continually reports on the successful application of the strategy. Parad, widely considered to be one of the major crisis theorists, in a published paper considered that in the USA crisis intervention with the mentally ill has now reached the situation where it is 'no longer an experimental fad but is now a generally accepted mode of social work practice in a wide variety of settings' (Parad 1976: 41). Parad goes on to report that the results of these theoretical and practice developments are reflected in a number of legislative changes. These include the provision in the Federal Community Mental Health Centres Act of 1963 mandating 24-hour emergency services. Second, some states, such as California, have passed legislation giving preference to the development of emergency services over hospitalization, residential care, and other forms of traditional outpatient care.

As indicated, the evidence that supports the use of this strategy in mental health emergencies is included in a number of papers. Parad considers that perhaps

'the most important and rigorous investigation into the effectiveness of family crisis intervention as a means of avoiding hospitalisation has been conducted by Dr Donald Langsley and his former colleagues at the University of Colorado, Department of Psychiatry, Denver (Langsley and Kaplan 1968; Langsley, Machotka, and Flomenhaft 1971). In this landmark study, 300 patients, all diagnosed by psychiatrists as requiring immediate hospitalisation, were randomly assigned to either a family crisis intervention treatment approach (experimental group) or to immediate psychiatric hospitalisation (control group). Follow-up interviews, after treatment, indicated that patients treated with a family crisis intervention approach were significantly less likely to be re-hospitalised than those who were initially hospitalised. Further follow-up studies at six and 18-month intervals indicated that the crisis intervention patients in the experimental group were faring as well as the hospitalised subjects, with respect to both social adaptation and ability to cope with life's crises. Moreover, those who were treated through outpatient family crisis intervention – when needing re-hospitalisation – were hospitalised for a significantly shorter period of time. Thus, the costs of mounting programmes for family crisis intervention are, in this era of cost-benefit consciousness, much reduced by family crisis intervention activities as compared with the expenses of hospitalising the patient. In addition, we cannot overlook the substantial social and other human costs in terms of the social stigma still associated, even during our current era of enlightenment, with the experience of hospitalisation.'

(Parad 1976: 46–7)

## The techniques and skills of psychiatric crisis intervention

Given this kind of evidence it becomes abundantly clear that we need radically to change the emphasis in our legislative framework as well as our methods of coping with the psychiatric emergency. *In toto*, the situation demands that we promote systems which stress 'growth and development' rather than 'illness and treatment'. To achieve this aspiration we need:

1 To enable the 'patient' and his living group to interpret their understanding of the meaning of the crisis and to mobilize their own resources for coping with the event.
2 To achieve this first aim we need to concentrate resources upon the individual and his living group rather than upon hospital-based services. Given the present economic situation, this will require greater political commitment than has so far been shown, and a substantial redirection of the scarce resources at present allocated to hospital services.
3 We must also develop services that aim at relieving the stress within the situation, rather than concentrating upon removing the individual to hospital. If removal from the living group is necessary, then we must recognize that this may be achieved in a number of ways and by removal to institutions other than hospital.

These principles will require the provision of a 24-hour crisis or resource service. This could be provided in a number of ways, and the local solution should reflect the particular circumstances. I think, however, that a great deal could be achieved through the establishment of the proposed 'crisis centres', inter-professionally manned, conveniently located, and through which all psychiatric emergencies would pass for screening, evaluation, management, and/or appropriate referral.

Crine (1981) reports on a number of schemes which variously interpret this philosophy:

'The Napsbury Hospital Crisis service breaks down their work into three parts. The first is assessment of the medical, psychological, social and personal aspects of the crisis by a psychiatrist and a social worker, thus disentangling illness from practical problems. The second is the provision of help, services and therapy during difficult periods to the family and friends of a sick individual, thus enabling them to cope without resorting to hospital. The third part of their work is actual intervention by a multi-disciplinary team of psychiatrist, social worker and nurse in the critical period of the onset of breakdown. The latter part of the work forms less than a third of the total calls to which their comprehensive service responds.

When Napsbury's workers do intervene in a crisis, they try to support and understand the family, assess their resources for coping, and then form a contract with them for short-term intervention. In this way, the family should not come to depend on the crisis team in the long term. Their practice is to encourage the healing potential in people rather than presenting themselves as the healers.

A report by the World Health Organisation's Regional Office for Europe (1979) recommends a similar practice to that used at Napsbury and stresses the importance of active participation by the patient in daily routines and decisions. It also argues that detailed analysis of the past should be avoided and that contracts should ideally last days rather than weeks.'                                                                                    (Crine 1981)

Research into the Napsbury Hospital Crisis Service suggests that it can improve the quality of psychiatric community care, prevent suicide and deliberate self-harm, and significantly reduce the rate of hospitalization and the number of needless admissions. The service maintains an urban population of 156,000 (1979) with a single admission ward of 126 beds; that is, 0.2 beds/1000 population, well below the DHSS minimum standard of 0.5 beds/1000 for traditional hospital-based psychiatric services. As a result, they claim to save £500,000 per year (at 1979 prices). The attempted suicide rate has stabilized in the team's area while it has increased in every other part of Greater London.

Crisis theory provides a framework within which the ASW could consider both emergency and long-term work. The important features of the theory are two-fold. First, it views the emergency situation as potentially therapeutic. It claims that, if expert help is given quickly, the client or family may, instead of becoming ill, function more adequately. Second, the concept of the utilizing of the crisis as the optimal moment for therapeutic intervention is, although underpinned by analytical concepts and dynamic theory of human development, essentially concerned with the here and now and the client's present situation. Its focus is on a current rather than on a retrospective analysis of the client's life pattern and as such it represents a rejection of the school that views the understanding of the 'present problem' as secondary to the unearthing of the 'real problem'. As such it questions the traditional pattern of history making and the period taken to obtain a history and suggests that in this process the worker may sacrifice an important opportunity to relate to the client's felt need.

If the concept were systematically adopted and evaluated the challenge presented to our knowledge base, current practice, the application of statutory powers, the organization of our services, and to our professed commitment to the mentally ill and the persons with whom they live, will be immense. However, it is only by this effort that we will begin to understand the differential nature and meaning of the psychiatric crisis, and determine which strategies and intervention are effective in resolving the situation.

# 20

# Evaluation of outcome to intervention

## *Brian Sheldon*

**Goal-setting and evaluation in psychiatric social work**

Most people consider the question of how best to evaluate their work when they are close to finishing it. By then it is too late. In any programme seeking to assess an outcome, there has to be some kind of 'before and after' comparison and it is essential that this comparison takes place within the same terms. This raises a number of questions about prior assessment, and unless these are dealt with satisfactorily, then the 'garbage in, garbage out' effect familiar to the users of computers, will be the most likely result obtained.

Evaluation can proceed on a qualitative or quantitative basis (that is, what *kind* of change, and what *degree* of change); ideally both considerations should be brought into the analysis. Here are the stages through which rigorous evaluation of single cases ought to proceed:

STAGES IN ASSESSMENT WITH A VIEW TO EVALUATION

1 Obtain a general description of the problem from as many different points of view as time and circumstances permit.
2 Find out who these problems affect and how, and in what way problem-elements interact. That is, what kinds of events appear to spark off what other kinds of events.

3  On the basis of these discussions, produce a brief account of their *aetiology* (the history and pattern of their development) and then reassess this in the light of comments from interested parties. Consumer research provides plenty of evidence that social workers often fail to share their working assumptions with clients – often with disastrous results (Mayer and Timms 1970; Rees and Wallace 1982).

4  Try to reduce this compendium version of problems to its component parts. Thus, Katherine's 'persecution complex' and 'mania' might map out as: 'Katherine spends about two hours of every day trying to interest her mother in her conviction that the house is being watched by secret policemen and that listening devices have been hidden in the room. When mother and other relatives try to discuss the implausibility of this with Katherine, she often gets very excited, and engages in animated and sometimes senseless conversations which usually end in her moving hurriedly out of the room, locking herself in her bedroom, and playing loud music.'

5  Assess existing motivation: have those directly concerned made attempts to overcome any of their problems? The question of how *motivatable* clients are, is answered more by experience. This, of course, can be a particularly difficult problem in mental health work.

6  Obtain an impression of the *assets* available. What potential difficulties have been avoided; what previous problems overcome? It is an easy matter in social work to concentrate on the psychopathology and overlook what people *can* do.

7  Try to arrive at a comprehensive *formulation* of the problems under review. This should contain (a) a clear aetiological account; and (b) hypotheses about how problems might be reduced. For example: 'Katherine's parents have a view of her schizophrenic illness which suggests to them that if they can only get to the bottom of what is worrying her, then their logical counter-arguments will change her view of the world, and hence her behaviour.' They also harbour the view that getting Katherine to express her worries will 'get them off her chest' or alternatively, that her feelings will be 'less bottled up'. Therefore, on occasion, they deliberately engage in conversation about the content of her delusions in the hope that such episodes of florid expression that occur will then be followed by a period of relative calm. However, when Katherine's delusional references become too florid, or when the family's everyday worries intrude, they lose patience and seek the help of their co-operative GP, who arranges a short period in hospital.

Therefore:

(a)  There is some evidence that Katherine's relatives over-stimulate her and make too many emotional demands (Vaughn and Leff 1976).

(b)  Also, they may well be encouraging the very behaviour of which they complain by selective attention. This leads to the family pressuring for admission to hospital.

(c) It may be that Katherine's behaviour is predictable in both content and amount and that family crises occur either when parents feel defeated in their attempts to unravel its origins or when outside pressures reduce their level of tolerance.

(d) A scheme designed to discourage references to television and other kinds of surveillance and to encourage conversation on other topics, ought to result in a reduction of delusional references, and remove the episodic pressure on their GP for compulsory admission to hospital.

Now of course, none of the above need be true. Nor need the schemes referred to produce any gains at all. The point is that the project is *testable*. If the relatives agree to withdraw their attention from delusional talk and to encourage other kinds of conversation, but this results in *no* reduction in the problematic behaviour, then this part of the scheme has *failed* and something else must be tried. Similarly, if delusional references reduce well below the previous average, but this does little to improve the family's ability to cope with Katherine, then this part of the scheme too has failed.

We see therefore that a statement about possible future happenings deserves to be called an hypothesis when it is potentially refutable (Popper 1963). That is, when it is possible to imagine pre-set conditions under which the prediction contained in it can be seen clearly not to have been fulfilled. If the goals we set ourselves do not conform to this pattern then *any* outcome can be massaged into the shape of a half success. When this is the case, we can learn little from our mistakes because we do not make them clearly enough or early enough.

It is obvious that in the case described above, it is perfectly possible that things might improve *qualitatively* in the short term, without any shift in the quantitative variables (less delusional talk; fewer requests for admission to hospital) occurring. There might be fewer but more florid delusional episodes, for example. It makes as little sense to overlook qualitative factors of this sort, as it does to ignore reports of changed feelings that are then not represented by how people subsequently behave. However, the advantage of hypotheses containing a prediction about *amounts* of change is that they serve to anchor discussions about *kinds* of change too. Thus, having noted the surprising fact of continued dissatisfaction with the behaviour of Katherine in the face of objectively fewer delusional references, it would be a relatively straightforward business to change focus, or to isolate the key ingredients of a really florid delusional episode (threats of physical retaliation, or the accompanying level of excitement, might be two such factors), clearly distinguish these with all concerned, and then proceed again with a quantitative assessment. In the case of a range of significant variations occurring, a simple scale might be appropriate (see Hersen and Bellack 1976).

8   In the examples given, *indicators* have been chosen to monitor the presence and level of the problem. These are usually key items of behaviour, or occurrences which reliably 'stand for' and appear to co-vary with, the appearance of, or the magnitude of, the problem under review. For example, we might try to anchor impressions of 'the level of integration with the local community' achieved by the staff of the psychiatric hospital by the extent to which the clients of the hostel use the range of regular facilities available in the community, rather than congregating in particular 'ghetto' establishments; or we might look at the attendance figures for local people at open days and open meetings; or at the number of complaints received. Indicators must validly represent the nature of the problem under review. To some extent their selection is arbitrary. For *some* depressive patients it is appropriate to observe attention to dress and personal hygiene as possible indicators for recovery. Other patients will cry into their washbasins, and pay meticulous attention to their dress as if they were about to attend their own funeral. The point here is that some conclusion about what would represent an improvement in *this* particular situation, has to be arrived at towards the end of the main assessment period.

Having dismantled the chief problem into its component parts and found reliable indicators of these, the next stage is to assess the incidence of one or two of these *prior* to intervention – by which I mean prior to deliberate, active, or specific intervention, because sometimes just discussing or assessing a problem helps to reduce its effects.

Assessing incidence assumes two things: that certain distinctly identifiable key items of behaviour, or problem-related indicators, are available for counting; and that the means and opportunity exist to carry out this task. For the first, there may well be problems which stubbornly refuse to be reduced to component parts in this way; the only way to find out is to try. For the second requirement, a list of available data-gathering methods follows. In the event that none of these can be used, then this approach to evaluation cannot be proceeded with.

APPROACHES TO DATA COLLECTION

*Direct observation*   This method is applicable where the problem-related behaviours occur at a high frequency and so relatively short periods of observation give a good idea of current rates.

*Time sampling*  This method is used where it is impracticable or undesirable for an observer to spend long periods of time with the client. Instead, say, ten 5-minute observations can be made at representative intervals throughout the day – perhaps by a mediator. This method is particularly useful in residential, day care and hospital settings, but it can deal only with behaviours of relatively high frequency.

*Participant observation*  This approach is useful where the presence of an outsider is less intrusive if he joins in whatever is going on. For example, family meetings, hostel work, groups, group discussions and so forth. The behaviour under review has to be somewhat independent of observer effects, or a few dummy runs can be made so that the activities of the observer merge into the background.

*Mechanical, electrical, and other aids to observation*  Tape recorders, video equipment, one-way screens, and other such aids are increasingly available in psychiatric clinics and child guidance centres. Clients quickly become familiar with such devices, though it is over-optimistic to suggest that they ever completely forget their presence.

*Observation by mediators*  This method is very common in behaviour therapy. Parents, relatives, hostel staff, nurses, and all who regularly come into contact with clients, can be enlisted to record, usually quite openly, the incidence of target behaviours.

*Self-observation*  The success of self-recording methods depends on: (a) a basically co-operative and mentally intact client; (b) a well-organized scheme; (c) a clear definition of what is to be counted, so that the client is in no doubt; (d) whether the behaviours under review are of a character to make deliberate distortion likely – it is a brave client who will report objectively on his own anti-social activities; a brave social worker who will offer an amnesty on such behaviour for recording purposes. One alternative is to monitor the occurrence of positive (generally acceptable) behaviours which are incompatible with the problem-related behaviours under review.

*Reliability checks*  It is possible to use the different methods discussed above in combination, thus adding greatly to their reliability. Where self-reports and reports of mediators agree substantially with each other, or with a short period of direct observation, then greater confidence can be placed on their assessment.

On the question of client attitudes to focused assessment and recording it is my experience that clients and relatives respond favourably to the following:

1 The clearly demonstrated assumption on the social worker's part that effective helping requires careful assessment (clients accept this from their GPs and community psychiatric nurses with little difficulty).
2 A sympathetic, but matter-of-fact, approach and time spent explaining how best to keep a record and what problems might arise.
3 Social reinforcement for recordkeeping.
4 Simple, well-produced proforma with clear instructions written on them.
5 The social worker actually using the records in front of clients and relatives, and going over the data with them.
6 Occasional rehearsal to iron out potential difficulties.

INTERPRETATION OF BASELINE DATA

All scientific data require interpretation; only rarely will a self-evident conclusion jump off the page. This is especially true of the kind of data gathered in natural settings, which almost always represent a compromise between rigour and relevance.

The first point of consideration is the length and stability of the pre-intervention (baseline) measure. The aim in baseline recording is to obtain a typical sample of behaviour, and so recording must continue long enough for odd fluctuations and recurring patterns to be seen in context. It may be that a pattern of aggressive behaviour will emerge on Mondays, or maybe in the presence of a particular group of people. It may be that the last two days may have been particularly difficult or particularly good, giving an artificial impression. Over a longer period such influences will show up and can give much valuable information. The ideal length for a baseline measure depends upon several different factors:

1 Some behaviours, for instance obsessional rituals or periods of rumination in depression, are likely to occur at high rate, and so observation over a period of two or three hours will give some idea of the stable frequency.
2 Where behaviours occur at low frequency, for example periods of conversation in a withdrawn schizophrenic patient, then baseline data must be collected over a longer period.
3 In all cases the ideal to aim for is a *stable* measure where there are no great swings in the rate of performance. This is not to say that there will be no fluctuations, just that these ought roughly to cancel each other out.
4 Ideally the more recorded observations of behaviours being monitored, the better. In practice this usually means the longer the baseline period the better. However, a balance is usually struck between therapeutic considerations and the need for careful assessment. Clients and relatives will sometimes suffer problems for months or years, but the arrival of professional help can make further delay difficult to bear.

## Types of single-case experimental design (SCED)

### AB DESIGNS

Examples of the simplest kinds of SCEDs are the AB designs which make straightforward 'before and after' comparisons (see *Figures 20.1* and *20.2*). The recording of the target behaviour (or some reliable indicator of it) is continued after the start of the program designed to alter its frequency. AB designs are a considerable advance on impressionistic case studies and are likely to be the most widely used method in social work. However they are

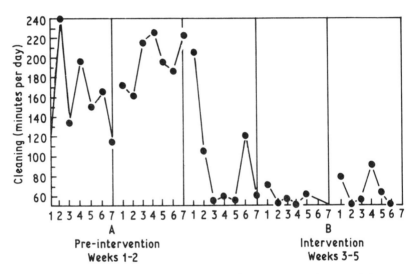

*Figure 20.1*  A case involving (amongst other things) intense bursts of obsessional house-cleaning on the part of a psychiatric outpatient. Intervention took the form of a comprehensive cognitive behaviour modification scheme

*Source:* Oliver (1981). Reproduced by permission.

*quasi*-experimental rather than fully experimental. That is, they offer good correlational evidence in the outcome, but when using them we cannot be quite sure which of the many new variables introduced into a case by the actions of the social worker is the potent one, nor can we be absolutely sure that we have not just intervened at a fortuitous moment when the problem was in decline anyway. However, certain precautions can be taken to minimize this possibility. The first among these concerns the length and stability of the baseline. If we are able to obtain evidence of this steady trend in problematic behaviour over a week or two, and all those concerned with the problem (such as relatives) consider that a fairly typical level, then it is a considerable coincidence if this level turns steadily downwards as soon as the therapeutic influence designed to combat the problem is introduced. Further measures that we can take to guard against distortions present in data from AB designs are as follows:

1 We can get to know something about the research in the area of the problem we are trying to deal with. If the literature suggests that a particular problem is generally resistant to treatment and yet we are managing quite respectable gains, then there is some justification in believing that these gains are not serendipitous.
2 We can monitor the problem over a longer period. That is, extend the baseline period and watch for trends of this kind which are seemingly independent of the thing we are trying to do.
3 We can arrange for follow-up visits. This procedure is relatively inexpensive, can be greatly reassuring to clients and their relatives, and need not be carried out by the worker who handled the case originally.
4 We can apply a more sophisticated evaluation design (see *Figures 20.3* and *20.4*).

Another example of an AB design is with a mildly agoraphobic day patient in a psychiatric hostel (*Figure 20.2*). This shows that simply

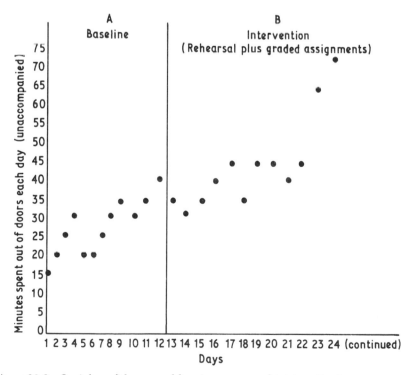

*Figure 20.2*   Social confidence problem in an ex-psychiatric patient

recording the incidence of trips out of doors increased their level. Such a result is fine from a therapeutic point of view, but frustrating from the standpoint of outcome evaluation!

ABA DESIGNS

The ABA design is an advance on the simple AB approach, since it includes a return-to-baseline phase at the end. Like the AB design, it offers a useful means of checking whether learning has taken place as a result of the programme. The example in *Figure 20.3* comes from a child guidance setting. Here the item of behaviour being measured (night-time interruption) is an *indicator* since the social worker dealing with the case thought that the problem might really be a psychiatric one – the child reported (rather unconvincingly in my view) a series of nightmares which it was said caused him to come into his parents' room. The social worker also entertained the hypothesis that the problem might really be a sexual one, and that mother and son were in some kind of unconscious collusion to head off the unwelcome attentions of father. The couple were eventually referred for sexual counselling, but though this was successful, the problem with the child remained. A scheme directly to discourage night-time interruptions was introduced and after twenty-two days was proving fairly successful. Then all but brief monitoring visits were suspended to check whether the results were due to the attentions of the social worker. The incidence of problematic behaviour began to increase, but was brought under control later. This somewhat messy case (the GP, though he knew of the social worker's involvement, was prescribing night-time hypnotics in the second A phase) is typical of work done in field settings.

ABAB DESIGNS

These are undoubtedly the most satisfactory evaluation procedures from an experimental point of view, although their scope is limited to situations where the social worker has a fair amount of control (perhaps through working with a co-operative group of relatives or hostel staff) over the day-to-day circumstances in which problems occur.

In this approach, problematic behaviour, new behaviour, or particular skills are recorded prior to intervention in the usual way (see *Figure 20.4* (A)). Then the main treatment programme is started (B). When a stable positive effect emerges, the scheme is withdrawn for a period (A). A comparison between the two phases is then made, and following this the treatment programme is restarted (B) and further comparisons are made.

This graph features an attempt to get relatives to respond to ordinary conversations and pointedly to ignore delusional references in the hope of reducing them since they were found to be very distressing to the family

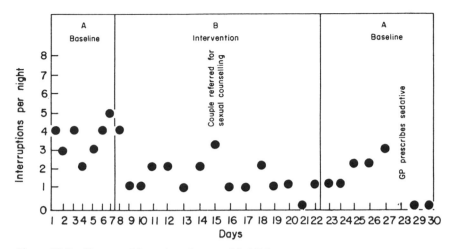

*Figure 20.3*   Sleep problems in a 4-year-old child
Reinforcement used: model farm animals, stories, sweets, and a star chart. Play
therapy and family counselling approaches were also employed.
*Source:* Sheldon (1982).

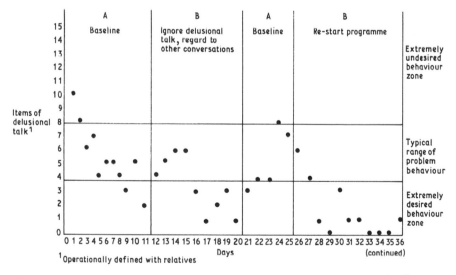

*Figure 20.4*   Contingency management scheme for reducing delusional talk in a
psychiatric patient living at home with relatives

*Notes:* [1]Operationally defined with relatives.

and produced pressure for hospitalization. The patient was fully involved in the scheme and understood its purpose (see pp. 213–14).

The idea of halting a successful programme just as it is getting into gear is often viewed with misgiving and obviously there are cases where it would be dangerous or unethical to suspend treatment to make an independent check on the efficacy of the procedures in use. But, safety considerations aside, if a particular pattern of behaviour can be seen to vary with the approaches used, then this is well worth knowing. Treatment procedures can almost always be re-established, to roughly the same effect, and there is a very positive demonstration effect to be gained. When relatives see that their problems go away if they stop attending to particular anti-social behaviour and concentrate their attention elsewhere, but reappear if they suspend this practice, then a very powerful lesson has been learned.

BAB DESIGNS

BAB designs are ideal for evaluating work where for various reasons it would be unwise to delay intervention while a baseline is established. *Figure 20.5* is an example of a group BAB design, which features a token

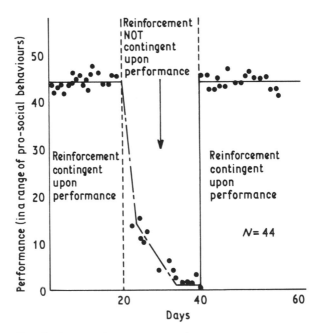

*Figure 20.5*   Results from a token economy scheme

*Source:* Ayllon and Azrin (1965). Reproduced by permission.

economy scheme to increase the rate of pro-social behaviours (such as making choices, asking questions of staff, initiating conversations, attending rehabilitation classes, etc.) among a group of chronic psychiatric inpatients.

## MULTIPLE BASELINE DESIGNS

Multiple baseline designs use each defined element of a problem as a control for the others. There are two distinct advantages with this approach: first, it does away with the need for a suspension or reversal phase; and second, the worker can try out one method at a time in a complex case. The procedure here is as follows: the pre-intervention rate of each different target behaviour is recorded. When a stable rate appears in one behaviour, the treatment programme is applied first to that behaviour. During the next stage, two things need to be noted: (a) the difference that intervention is making (if any) to the first target behaviour; and (b) whether the base rates of the other behaviours to which the treatment variable has *not* yet been applied are changing substantially (co-varying) with the target behaviour. If *not* then the programme is applied to the next behaviour and after a suitable interval the procedures outlined above are applied again. This process continues until the scheme is in operation for all the target behaviours.

## MULTIPLE BASELINES ACROSS SETTINGS

Another multiple measurement approach is the 'baseline across settings' design. With this approach problems in different *settings* are baselined and the treatment variable is applied to each in sequence, according to the principles outlined above.

A wide range of single-case evaluation procedures is available and the main approaches likely to be applicable to social work have been outlined here. For further details of the different types of design available, consult Hersen and Barlow's excellent handbook (1976).

## Qualitative approaches

I have already argued that qualitative factors form an important part of the evaluation of any therapeutic programme. However, the point will bear repetition given the present polarization in the profession between behaviourists, who sometimes give the impression that they would rather not handle this type of data, and those, for example caseworkers and family therapists, whose work could perhaps benefit from the introduction of a little quantitative rigour.

The ideal situation is where data of each kind are available; each to act as a supplement to the other. After all, there is little point to qualitative data that suggest that Mary is more confident about going outside the hostel these days, if there is no notable increase in the number of occasions she does so; still less is there any virtue in carefully compiled graphs that show a 25 per cent increase in this behaviour, but do not record that Mary still dreads the experience and is likely to avoid it at the first opportunity afforded her.

The most essential components in rigorous, qualitative evaluation are the ideas of *hypothesis* and *falsification* (see Popper 1963; Lakatos 1970). Social workers are not, by and large, used to making their predictions public, or to showing their 'working out' in the margin, as it were. Records are written up in the passive and express few opinions as to what might have led to what. A range of ambiguous phrases (my favourite is 'come to terms with') occupy the space where a clear admission of failure, or a well-defended claim of success, ought to appear. The normal excuse for this is that social problems do not yield such clear-cut results. Partly this is true, but then with intractable cases surely one looks for much smaller, but still discernible, gains; or for a clear judgement that for example, despite one or two positive trends, Mr Jones is still so chronically dependent and institutionalized as to make his survival outside the hospital unlikely.

We can only evaluate our work to good effect if the possibility of success and failure is established, and the end-states which would typify one or the other of these results are mapped out in advance. In my experience clients respond well to an approach within which they are asked to say what would constitute success for them in their present circumstances and to exemplify their views ('I'd be out of hospital, living on my own in a quiet place with someone looking in from time to time'); or failure ('I'd still be in here, bored and not able to sleep'). This hypothetical patient may, of course, change his mind in six months' time, and then these definitions would have to change too. Similarly, some desirable end-states are beyond our powers to deliver; or we may disagree as to their desirability. In these cases open negotiation must take place. All this can occur only if our definitions and targets are phrased in such a way that reality has the opportunity to shout back 'No'. And therefore it follows that we must learn to make provisional yet public predictions about what we can do (and not do), and to reassess these (but not *merge* or make over-subtle interpretations of them) when circumstances have not gone our way. It is my firm view that a willingness to share and to negotiate our aspirations with clients and their relatives in this way will produce sufficient goodwill to overcome all but the very worst communication difficulties inherent in work with the mentally disordered.

## SPECIMEN EXAMINATION PAPER 2
*Ann Davis*


### SOCIAL WORK ASSESSMENT: THE APPLICATION OF LEGAL AND CLINICAL KNOWLEDGE
*(Notes in Appendix 3)*


YOU MUST ATTEMPT EACH QUESTION RELATED TO CASE ILLUSTRATIONS 1 AND 2 AND TO *EITHER* 3 *OR* 4. BRIEF ANSWERS WILL SUFFICE. IT IS IMPORTANT TO IDENTIFY THE MAIN POINTS WHICH APPROVED SOCIAL WORKERS SHOULD KNOW AND NEED TO TAKE INTO ACCOUNT WHEN MAKING JUDGEMENTS.


### ALL QUESTIONS WILL CARRY EQUAL MARKS.    TIME ALLOWED – 1½ HOURS


1    *Agitated man*

You are on duty and receive a telephone call at 9 a.m. from the local police station. They report that in the early hours of the morning a man of about 30 years was found sleeping rough in the park. When questioned the man appeared excited and agitated, refused to give his name and address, and answered questions with rhymes and jingles. He was taken to the police station and searched in order to establish his identity. During the course of the search he began screaming and hitting out, and was held down and handcuffed by several officers.

The police surgeon has been called out as the police consider the man needs to be compulsorily detained in a psychiatric hospital.

*Question 1*
(a)  What steps would you take to assess this situation?
(b)  If you decide that compulsory admission is appropriate, outline the procedure you would adopt as an Approved Social Worker.

2  *Mrs P*

Mrs P is 70 years of age. She has been a widow for nine months and now lives alone. Her son has contacted the local social services department as he is very worried about his mother's safety. He says that his mother has been 'strange' for several years, but was cared for by his father. Since his death Mrs P has had difficulty in remembering to feed and wash herself and clean the house. When he has visited he has found her on several occasions eating raw meat, or apparently unaware that she had left the gas on. Recently she has become confused about time, and thinks day is night and night is day. As a consequence she has been wandering the streets at night, trying to buy food, and sleeping during the day.

*Question 2*
(a)  Outline the possible explanations of Mrs P's behaviour and the risks she faces; *and*
(b)  What do you consider is the most appropriate course of action for an Approved Social Worker to pursue?

3  *Mrs K*

You have received a call from a local GP. His patient Mrs K, a woman of Asian origin who is 43 years old, has taken to her bed, refuses to eat, and occasionally speaks to her family about wanting to die. Over the past ten years Mrs K has been admitted to psychiatric hospital on four occasions, including several admissions under Section 26 of the 1959 Mental Health Act.

The doctor thinks that she needs treatment urgently, but he has been unable to persuade her to take her medication or to go to hospital voluntarily. He has therefore left his recommendation for compulsory admission at his surgery for you to pick up, and he has asked the consultant from the local hospital to call at Mrs K's home as soon as possible.

*Question 3*
(a)  What course of action would you take as an Approved Social Worker in this case?
(b)  What would you take into account in deciding whether compulsory admission was necessary?

4   *Mr T*

You are on night duty and are contacted by the police. They have been called to a local board-and-lodging house at the request of the landlady. One of her boarders, Mr T, a 30-year-old man, who was discharged from a mental handicap hospital two months ago, has attacked her. This attack followed a period of two days in which he became increasingly restless and agitated and verbally abusive towards her and other boarders. He also began to tear at his clothes and hair. Earlier that evening he had refused to go to bed and when the landlady had insisted he had punched her. The landlady wants Mr T removed from her premises immediately and the police consider he needs to be taken back to hospital.

*Question 4*
(a) What would your immediate course of action be as an Approved Social Worker?
(b) What should you take into account when making a decision as to whether Mr T should be admitted to hospital on a compulsory order?

## SPECIMEN EXAMINATION PAPER 3
### Brian Sheldon

### ANALYSIS OF CASE MATERIAL RELEVANT TO THE ROLE AND RESPONSIBILITIES OF APPROVED SOCIAL WORKERS
### TIME ALLOWED – 2 HOURS
*(Notes in Appendix 3)*

### YOU MUST ANSWER ALL FOUR QUESTIONS WHICH RELATE TO THE CASE REPORT (OVERLEAF)

### YOU MAY CONSULT A COPY OF THE MENTAL HEALTH ACT 1983

### YOU ARE ENCOURAGED TO ILLUSTRATE YOUR ANSWERS WITH REFERENCE TO YOUR OWN EXPERIENCE OF CURRENT PRACTICE

Question 1   List the factors that you consider would be of importance in making a thorough assessment of this case, justifying each inclusion as you proceed.

Question 2   What alternative courses of action are open to the Approved Social Worker in this case? Discuss briefly the advantages and disadvantages of each as you see them.

Question 3   What therapeutic opportunities might be present in a case such as this? Explain how you would approach this question with the client and her family, mentioning what approaches you would consider using and why.

Question 4   What implications do cases such as this have for the organization and delivery of mental health services in your area?

*Case Report on Katherine Androvski (29)*

At the weekly case allocation meeting you are handed a file relating to the above client. Clipped to the front are (a) a letter from her mother complaining of lack of support from the department and of the disruptive effect of her daughter's constant talk of surveillance by planted electronic devices and by strange men watching the house from the street; (b) a note of a conversation between the duty officer and the GP to the effect that the family is at risk of breaking up unless something is done soon, together with an observation that given the patient's history of agreeing to informal admission but then discharging herself prematurely, the local psychiatric hospital will want a compulsory treatment order to be made next time.

The case record contains the following information:

1   The Androvski family comprises Mr Androvski aged 49 (father), Mrs Androvski, 48 (mother), Klaus Androvski, 52 (uncle), and Katherine, 29. They fled from Budapest to Germany in 1956, and from there came to Britain where they had distant relatives. Katherine's brother Peter (now 21) was born in England.

2   They now occupy a rambling, somewhat ramshackle house on the edge of town. Mr Androvski, Senior, is a sheet-metal worker but his job is precarious. Mrs Androvski has always worked in the home – lately because of Katherine's need for constant care. Uncle Klaus has never worked and brother Peter is a student at a local polytechnic reading Engineering Sciences. Katherine has done shop work and has some secretarial qualifications, but she has never held a job for longer than four months. Much of her life she has been unemployed.

3   Katherine has been admitted informally to hospital on four occasions, and has been in either a deluded or withdrawn state each time. When confronted with the necessity for treatment, she has always acquiesced but has subsequently discharged herself before this has got underway. On one occasion she simply walked out of the hospital without telling anyone.

4   The family are described in spasmodic after-care reports as 'intelligent', 'supportive', and 'intense'. They do their best to talk Katherine out of her 'moods' and try hard to reason away her fears that she is being watched. These protracted confrontations of the problem (on one occasion this involved the local priest)

sometimes work temporarily, but equally they often increase the floridity of Katherine's delusions and lead to odd behaviour such as the playing of loud music with the curtains drawn and the doors locked.

5   A letter from the psychiatrist to the family doctor implies that Katherine's condition is chronic but stable most of the time. Requests for admission to hospital are apparently as much related to the family's capacity to cope with Katherine and with their financial and other problems, as with any rapid deterioration in the patient's mental state.

6   Katherine has been prescribed various psychotropic drugs and when she takes her tablets as ordered the family report that they do inhibit her more extreme behaviour. However, she frequently refuses medication from her mother, and any insistence tends to add a 'poisoning' dimension to her symptoms.

7   Four different social workers have handled this case in the past, each for a short period. The after-care seems to have been on a routine basis following Katherine's return home from a period in hospital. The file contains no social history, only reports of lengthy encounters with the family. One previous social worker found them 'oppressive', another 'caring and very supportive', but opinion from social workers and the GP is unanimous over the fact that they are 'demanding'.

8   The present referral is three days old.

# Appendix 1
## Drugs acting on the Central Nervous System

**British National Formulary (No. 6 (1983))**
HEADINGS AND SUBSECTIONS

4.1 *Hypnotics, sedatives, and anxiolytics*
   1 Hypnotics and sedatives
   2 Anxiolytics
   3 Barbiturates and similar hypnotics and sedatives

4.2 *Drugs used in psychoses and related disorders*
   1 Antipsychotic drugs
   2 Antipsychotic depot preparations
   3 Lithium salts

4.3 *Antidepressant drugs*
   1 Tricyclic and related antidepressant drugs
   2 Monoamine – oxidase inhibitors
   3 Compound antidepressant preparations

4.4 *Central nervous stimulants*
   1 Weak central nervous stimulants
   2 Amphetamines and cocaine

4.5 *Appetite suppressants*
   1 Bulk-forming drugs
   2 Centrally-acting appetite suppressants

4.6  *Drugs used in nausea and vertigo*

4.7  *Analgesics*
    1  Analgesic used for mild to moderate pain
    2  Narcotic and other analgesics used for severe pain
    3  Trigeminal neuralgia
    4  Antimigraine drugs

4.8  *Antiepileptics*
    1  Control of epilepsy
    2  Drugs used in status epilepticus

4.9  *Drugs used in parkinsonism and related disorders*
    1  Dopaminergic drugs used in parkinsonism
    2  Anticholinergic drugs used in parkinsonism
    3  Drugs used in chorea, tics, and related disorders

# Appendix 2
## Checklist of key mental health statutory and voluntary agencies

### Mental Health Act Commission offices

*Central Policy Committee and*
*Southern and South Western*
*Regional Committee*
Floors 1 and 2
Hepburn House
Marsham Street
London SW1P 4HW
01 211 8061

*West Midlands and North*
*Western Regional Committee*
Cressington House
249 St Mary's Road
Garston
Liverpool L19 0NF
051 427 2061

*East Midlands and North*
*Eastern Regional Committee*
Spur A Block 5
Government Buildings
Chalfont Drive
Western Boulevard
Nottingham NG8 3RZ
0602 293409

### Government departments

*The Under-Secretary of State*
Department of Health and
    Social Security
Mental Health Division
Alexander Fleming House
Elephant and Castle
London SE1 6BY
01 407 5522

*The Under-Secretary of State*
The Home Office
C3 Division
Queen Anne's Gate
London SW1
01 213 2000

## The Court of Protection

*The Court of Protection*
Staffordshire House
25 Store Street
London WC2
01 636 6877

## Mental Health Review Tribunals (MHRT)

*Clerk to the Nottingham
Tribunal Office*
Spur A Block 5
Government Buildings
Chalfont Drive
Western Boulevard
Nottingham NG8 3RZ
0602 294222/3

*Clerk to the Mersey
Tribunal Office*
3rd Floor
Cressington House
249 St Mary's Road
Garston
Liverpool L19 0NF
051 494 0095

*Clerk to the London
Tribunal Office*
Hepburn House
Marsham Street
London SW1 4HW
01 211 7325/7356

*Clerk to the Welsh
Tribunal Office*
2nd Floor
New Crown Building
Cathays Park
Cardiff CN1 3NQ
0222 825798

## Law Society and Legal Aid offices

*London South*
The Law Society
No. 1 Legal Aid Area
Area Headquarters
29/37 Red Lion Street
London WC1R 4PP
01 405 6991

*South-eastern*
The Law Society
No. 2 Legal Aid Area
Area Headquarters
9–12 Middle Street
Brighton BN1 1AS
0273 27003

*Southern*
The Law Society
No. 3 Legal Aid Area
Area Headquarters
Crown House
10 Crown Street
Reading RG1 2SJ
0734 589696

*South-western*
The Law Society
No. 4 Legal Aid Area
Area Headquarters
Whitefriars (Block C)
Lewins Mead
Bristol BS1 2LR
0272 214801

*South Wales*
The Law Society
No. 5 Legal Aid Area
Area Headquarters
Marland House
Central Square
Cardiff CF1 1PF
0222 388971/7

*West Midland*
The Law Society
No. 6 Legal Aid Area
Area Headquarters
Podium
Centre City House
5 Hill Street
Birmingham B5 4UD
021 632 6541

*North-western*
The Law Society
No. 7 Legal Aid Area
Area Headquarters
Pall Mall Court
67 King Street
Manchester M60 9AX
061 832 7112

*Northern*
The Law Society
No. 8 Legal Aid Area
Area Headquarters
18 Newgate Shopping Centre
Newcastle-upon-Tyne NE1 5RU
0632 23461/4

*North-eastern*
The Law Society
No. 9 Legal Aid Area
Area Headquarters
City House
New Station Street
Leeds LS1 4JS
0532 442851/6

*East Midland*
The Law Society
No. 10 Legal Aid Area
Area Headquarters
5 Friar Lane
Nottingham NG1 6BW
0602 42341/4

*Eastern*
The Law Society
No. 11 Legal Aid Area
Area Headquarters
Kett House
Station Road
Cambridge CB1 2JT
0223 66511/7

*Chester and District*
The Law Society
No. 12 Legal Aid Area
Area Headquarters
North West House
City Road
Chester CH1 2AL
0244 23591

*London East*
The Law Society
No. 13 Legal Aid Area
Area Headquarters
29/37 Red Lion Street
London WC1R 4PP
01 405 6991

*London West*
The Law Society
No. 14 Legal Aid Area
Area Headquarters
29/37 Red Lion Street
London WC1R 4PP
01 405 6991

*Merseyside*
The Law Society
No. 15 Legal Aid Area
Area Headquarters
Moor House
James Street
Liverpool L2 7SA
051 236 8371

## Voluntary organizations and services

*Age Concern*
Bernard Sunley House
60 Pitcairn Road
Mitcham
Surrey
01 640 5431

*Alcoholics Anonymous*
PO Box 514
11 Redcliffe Road
London SW10

*British Association of
Behavioural Psychotherapy*
Sec. W. W. Lomas
Social Services Dept
Craig House
Bank Street
Bury BL9 0BA

*British Institute of
Mental Handicap (BIMH)*
Wolverhampton Road
Kidderminster
Worcs DY10 3PP
0562 850251

*Campaign for Mentally
Handicapped People (CMH)*
16 Fitzroy Square
London W1P 5HQ
01 387 9571

*Children's Legal Centre*
20 Compton Place
London N1 2UN
01 359 6251/2

*Community Health Council
Information Service*
362 Euston Road
London NW1
01 388 4943/4

*King's Fund Centre*
126 Albert Street
London NW1
01 267 6111

*MENCAP*
123 Golden Lane
London EC1Y 0RT
01 253 9433

*Mental Health Foundation*
8 Hallam Street
London W1N 6DH
01 580 0145

*MIND*
22 Harley Street
London W1N 2ED
01 637 0741

*National Council for Civil
Liberties (NCCL)*
21 Tabard Street
London SE1 4LA
01 403 3888

*National Schizophrenia
Fellowship*
79 Victoria Road
Surbiton
Surrey KT6 4NS
01 390 3561/2/3

*Northern Schizophrenia
Fellowship*
38 Collingwood Buildings
Collingwood Street
Newcastle-upon-Tyne
0632 614343

*North West Schizophrenia
Fellowship*
10/12 Beaumont Street
Warrington
Cheshire WA1 1UW
0925 571680

*Phobics Society*
4 Cheltenham Road
Manchester M21
061 881 1937

*Richmond Fellowship for Mental
Welfare and Rehabilitation*
8 Addison Road
London W14 8DL
01 603 6373

*Samaritans*
17 Uxbridge Road
Slough
Berks
0753 32713

*The Patients' Association*
11 Dartmouth Street
London SW1H 9BN
01 222 4992

*The Good Practices in*
*Mental Health Project*
The International Hospital Federation
67 Kentish Town Road
London NW1 8NY

## Professional bodies

*British Association of*
*Social Workers (BASW)*
16 Kent Street
Birmingham B5 6RD
021 622 3911

*Central Council for Education*
*and Training in Social Work (CCETSW)*
Derbyshire House
St Chad's Street
London WC1H 8AD
01 278 2455

*Royal College of Nursing*
*of the UK*
20 Cavendish Square
London W1M 0AB
01 409 3333

*The Royal College of*
*Psychiatrists*
17 Belgrave Square
London SW1 8PG
01 235 2351

# Appendix 3
## Model answers and notes to specimen examination papers 1–3
## Answers to specimen examination paper 1

*M. Rolf Olsen*

| Question | | Answers |
|---|---|---|
| 1 | | (d)(e)(g)(h) |
| 2 | | (b)(f) |
| 3 | | (a)(c)(d)(e)(g) |
| 4 | Section 2(2) | (b)(d) |
| | Section 3(2) | (e)(f)(h) |
| | Section 4(1–2) | (b)(d)(g) |
| | Section 7(1–2) | (i)(j)(k) |
| 5 | | (b)(d)(e) |
| 6 | | (b) |
| 7 | | (e) |
| 8 | Section 2(2) | 28 days |
| | Section 3(2) | 6 months |
| | Section 4(1–2) | 72 hours |
| | Section 7(1–2) | 6 months |
| 9 | Section 2(2) | 14 days |
| | Section 3(2) | 14 days |
| | Section 4(1–2) | 24 hours |
| | Section 7(1–2) | 14 days |
| 10 | | (d) |
| 11 | | (f) |
| 12 | | The managers of the hospital to which admission is sought. |

| | |
|---|---|
| 13 | (c)(f)(g) |
| 14 | No |
| 15 | 72 hours |
| 16 | 28 days |
| 17 | Yes |
| 18 | (d) |
| 19 | The correct sequence of numbers is: 3, 1, 4, 2, 6, 5, 8, 7. |
| 20 | 6 months |
| 21 | 5 years |
| 22 | (c) |
| 23 | (e) |
| 24 | (d) |
| 25 | (b) |

26
(a) Which is immediately necessary to save the patient's life; or
(b) which (not being irreversible or hazardous) is immediately necessary to prevent serious deterioration of condition; or
(c) which (not being irreversible or hazardous) is immediately necessary to alleviate serious suffering by the patient; or
(d) which (not being irreversible or hazardous) is immediately necessary and represents the minimum interference necessary to prevent the patient from behaving violently or being a danger to himself or others.

27
(a) Within 14 days.
(b) Within first 6 months, within second 6 months, and during each subsequent 12-month period.
(c) As (b).

28
doctors
nurses
social workers
lawyers
lay
psychologists

29
(a) Appointing doctors to provide second opinions relating to consent to treatment.
(b) Visiting and interviewing patients detained under the Act.
(c) Investigating complaints laid by patients.
(d) Investigating complaints laid by non-patients.
(e) Investigating complaints laid by MPs.
(f) Receiving reports from RMOs on the treatment of patients where Section 57 or 58 safeguards have been necessary.
(g) Reviewing any decision to withhold a postal packet.
(h) Preparing a Code of Practice.
(i) Preparing a bi-annual report to be laid before Parliament.

| | |
|---|---|
| 30 | (c) |
| 31 | 1 person |

# Notes to specimen examination paper 2

## *Ann Davis*

It is impossible with this section of the Examination Paper to provide one 'right' answer against which candidates can assess their performance. The manner in which each candidate answers these questions will vary.

In order to assess the merit of your own answers to the paper a summary of the main points which should have been covered is provided. Candidates should check that their answers cover these points in a systematic way, and that their own views are substantiated with appropriate arguments.

Finally, it might be of considerable value for those preparing for the ASW examinations to share their answers to these questions with others in their group. This will demonstrate alternative approaches as well as providing help to those who are experiencing difficulties putting their thoughts into written form.

*Question 1*

(a) Candidates should indicate what information they would need to obtain in order to reach a judgement about this man's condition and from whom they might obtain it. They should outline the possible social, psychological, and clinical explanations of his condition. Particular attention should be given to the arrangements that should be made to interview this man in a suitable manner and the purpose of the interview.

(b) In the light of the answer given in (a) candidates should outline under what circumstances a compulsory admission might be deemed appropriate. Consideration should be given to whether this is an emergency situation, warranting use of a Section 4 or whether a Section 2 would in the circumstances be more appropriate. Candidates should indicate that they understand what the role of the Approved Social Worker is in relation to the chosen section in respect to the client, the nearest relative if he is known, and the hospital managers.

## Question 2

(a) Candidates should demonstrate that they have knowledge of the possible clinical and social explanations of Mrs P's behaviour, making particular reference to the often complex relationship between physical and mental deterioration in someone of her years. In outlining the risks that Mrs P faces candidates should establish whether she is a danger to the health and safety of herself and others.

(b) Candidates should indicate how they would assess this situation, bearing in mind the source of referral.

Candidates should cover the options available for Mrs P's treatment or support both at home and in hospital or other residential provision. They should also make reference to relevant local facilities. If suggesting domiciliary care candidates should specify how they would satisfy themselves that an adequate alternative to hospital care was being provided. If suggesting hospital care they should indicate on what basis it might be provided.

## Question 3

(a) Candidates should indicate what background information they might gather and from what sources. They should outline what response they would make to the GP's request to pick up a compulsory admission form, and give reasons for their response. They should describe how they would arrange to interview Mrs K in a suitable manner and what the purpose of their interview would be. Attention should be given to how candidates would use their knowledge of clinical, psychological, and social explanation of Mrs K's behaviour and how they would take into account her cultural background. Finally, candidates should indicate what their role would be in relation to other family members and the visiting consultant.

(b) Candidates in outlining the reasons why compulsory admission might be necessary should indicate that they have a knowledge of the treatments available, and the circumstances in which they might be given. They should also examine all possible alternatives to hospital admission.

## Question 4

(a) Candidates should indicate how they would reach a fuller understanding of why this incident occurred, taking into account the presence of the police and the agitation of the landlady and Mr T. They should review the possible social, clinical, and psychological reasons for Mr T's behaviour and outline the contact they would seek to establish with him and the landlady.

(b) Candidates should demonstrate their understanding of the distinctions made in the Act between mental illness, mental disorder, mental impairment, and severe mental impairment and discuss how these distinctions might be relevant in considering Mr T's admission to hospital. They should also consider the issue of treatability. Candidates should outline alternatives to hospital admission in this situation and their feasibility.

# Notes to specimen examination paper 3

## Brian Sheldon

This part of the examination is designed to assess a candidate's familiarity with the clinical and social implications of mental disorder. Examiners will be assessing the judgement of candidates, their ability to think logically and to analyse complex situations, their ability to set down a clear plan of action, their familiarity with local provision and, of course, their knowledge of their duties under the Mental Health Act 1983.

As with specimen examination paper 2 (pp. 241–43) it is not possible to suggest 'right and wrong' answers to this part of the examination. However, idiosyncratic views of mental disorder and associated problems; obvious lack of sensitivity to the issues involved; or suggestions for procedures that are illegal under the new legislation, must attract penalties.

The following observations are therefore of a general character and are based on experience of marking a large number of mock assessment papers from ASW training courses:

1 Many answers contain vague references to factors such as 'cultural implications' or 'background family dynamics'. It is very difficult for examiners to give credit for the inclusion of such broad references. Better to put forward a definite point of view and defend it.
2 Many answers contain little or no discussion of the implications of particular forms of mental disorder, their nature, or likely prognosis. It is not straying into medical territory to consider the kinds of behaviour often associated with particular diagnoses and their possible effects on relatives.

3 Many candidates fail to go beyond the case material itself and look at its implications. Often, two or three possible outcomes, or two or three sets of influences, might have a bearing on a case. Where specific information is not given candidates can afford to speculate a little about what is *likely* to happen or *likely* to be important in the case.

4 Answers are often couched in terms of 'counsels of perfection'. That is, they are highly idealized accounts of the provision of perfect services in an authority with an unbelievable level of provision. Markers are likely to give credit for a discussion of the day-to-day problems of providing care in particular local circumstances.

5 Some candidates leave themselves out of the picture completely. That is, they appear only as the organizers of services on behalf of the client. It should be remembered that social workers also have a therapeutic role of their own, that they *themselves* may have something to offer clients and relatives.

6 Although other parts of the examination assess detailed knowledge of the Mental Health Act 1983, discussion of the duties and powers it confers on ASWs is often appropriate in this section too. This is because it is the framework within which all services are provided and the client's civil liberties protected.

# References

ACE (1982) Working Towards Integration. Conference Report Spastics Society, London.
—— (1983) Special Education Handbook – The New Law on Children with Special Needs. London: Advisory Centre for Education.
Action for Mental Health (1961) *Final Report of the Joint Commission on Mental Illness and Health*. New York: Basic Books.
Ahmed, S. (1982) Translation is at Best An Echo. *Community Care* 22 April.
Argyle, M. (1969) *Social Interaction*. London: Tavistock Publications.
Ashurst, P. and Ward, D. (1980) The Leverhulme Counselling Project: A Problem of Design and Evaluation. In E. M. Goldberg and N. Connelly (eds) *Evaluative Research in Social Care*. London: Policy Studies Institute, Heinemann Educational Books.
Aves (1969) *The Voluntary Worker in the Social Services*. Report of a Committee jointly set up by the National Council of Social Service and the National Institute for Social Work Training. London: Allen & Unwin.
Ayllon, T. and Azrin, N. H. (1965) The Measurement and Reinforcement of the Behaviour of Psychotics. *Journal of the Experimental Analyses of Behaviour* 8: 357–83.
Baker, A. A. (1956) Factory in a Hospital. *Lancet* i: 278–79.
Bales, R. (1950) *Interaction Process Analysis*. New York: Addison.
Bandura, A. (1969) *Principles of Behavior Modification*. New York: Holt Rinehart & Winston.
Bank-Mikkelson, N. (1969) A Metropolitan Area in Denmark, Copenhagen. In R. Kugel and W. Wolfensberger *Changing Patterns in Residential Services for the Mentally Retarded*. Washington DC: President's Committee on Mental Retardation.

Barton, R. (1976) *Institutional Neurosis*, 3rd edn. Bristol: John Wright.

Barton, W. E. (1953) Out-patient Psychiatry and Family Care. *American Journal of Psychiatry* 110: 533.

BASW (1974) *Aspects of the Social Care of the Mentally Ill: A Discussion Paper.* Birmingham: BASW.

—— (1977) *Mental Health Crisis Services – A New Philosophy.* Birmingham: BASW.

—— (1983) *The Mental Health Act 1983: A Guide for Social Workers.* Birmingham: BASW.

Bayley, M. (1973) The Community Can Care. *New Society* October.

Bender, M. (1975) *Amino Acid Metabolism.* London: Academic Press.

—— (1983) For What and For Whom? *Community Care* 13 January.

Bennett, D. (1981) *What Direction for Psychiatric Day Services?* In MIND. *Mental Health Year Book.* London: MIND.

Beresford, P. and Tuckwell, P. (1978) Schools for All. London: CMH.

Bertcher, H. and Maple, F. (1977) *Creating Groups* vol. 2. Beverly Hills, Calif.: Sage Publications.

Betts, T. (1982) Psychiatry and Epilepsy. In J. Laidlaw and A. Richens (eds) *Textbook of Epilepsy.* Edinburgh: Churchill Livingstone.

Biestek, F. (1967) *The Casework Relationship.* London: Allen & Unwin.

Bion, W. (1961) *Experience in Groups.* London: Tavistock Publications.

Birch, A. (1983) *What Chance Have We Got?* Manchester: MIND.

Bloom, M. (1975) *The Paradox of Helping.* Chichester: John Wiley.

Blunden, R. (1980) Individual Plans for Mentally Handicapped People: A Draft Procedural Guide. Mental Handicap in Wales, Applied Research Unit.

Brandon, D. (1981) *Day Care in the North West.* In MIND, *Mental Health Year Book.* London: MIND.

—— (1982) *The Trick of Being Ordinary: Notes for Volunteers and Students.* London: MIND.

Breuning, S. E. and Poling, A. D. (1982) *Drugs and Mental Retardation.* Springfield, Illinois: Charles C. Thomas.

Brewer, C. and Lait, J. (1980) *Can Social Work Survive?* London: Temple Smith.

Brill, N. (1976) *Teamwork: Working Together in the Human Services.* Philadelphia, PA: Lippincott.

Brown, G. W. (1959) Experiences of Discharged Chronic Schizophrenic Patients in Various Types of Living Group. *Milbank Memorial Fund Quarterly* 37: 105.

Brown, G. W. and Birley, J. L. T. (1968) Crises and Life Changes and the Onset of Schizophrenia. *Journal of Health and Social Behaviour* 9: 203–14.

Brown, G. W., Birley, J. L. T., and Wing, J. K. (1972) Influence of Family Life on the Course of Schizophrenic Disorders: A Replication. *British Journal of Psychiatry* 121: 241–58.

Brown, G. W., Carstairs, G. M., and Topping, G. (1958) Post-mental Hospital Adjustment of Chronic Mental Patients. *Lancet* ii: 685–89.

Brown, G. W. and Harris, T. (1978) *Social Origins of Depression: A Study of Psychiatric Disorder in Women.* London: Tavistock Publications.

Brown, G. W., Monck, E. M., Carstairs, G. M., and Wing, J. K. (1962) Influence of Family Life on the Course of Schizophrenic Illness. *British Journal of Preventive and Social Medicine* 16: 55.

Caplan, G. (1961) *An Approach to Community Mental Health*. London: Tavistock Publications.

—— (1964) *Principles of Preventive Psychiatry*. London: Tavistock Publications.

Carlyle, T. (1843) *Past and Present* Bk 1, Ch. 4.

Carstairs, G. M., O'Connor, N., and Rawnsley, K. (1956) Organisation of a Hospital Workshop for Chronic Psychotic Patients. *British Journal of Preventive and Social Medicine* 10: 136–40.

Carter, J. (1981) *Day Care Services for Adults*. London: Allen & Unwin.

Cartwright, D. and Zander, A. (1968) *Group Dynamics, Research and Theory* 3rd edn. New York: Harper & Row.

CCETSW (1983) Co-operation in Training. Part II – Inservice Training. London: CCETSW.

CCETSW(GNC) (1982) Co-operation in Training. Part I – Qualifying Training. London: GNC/CCETSW.

Central Birmingham Community Health Council (1979) *Good Practices in Mental Health*. 45 Bull Street, Birmingham 4.

Chaadayev, P. J. (1972) *Memoires of a Madman*. Oxford: Mouette Press.

Chien, C. P. and Cole, J. O. (1973) Landlord-Supervised Cooperative Apartments: A New Modality for Community Based Treatment. *American Journal of Psychiatry* 130: 156–69.

Clare, A. (1976) *Psychiatry in Dissent*. London: Tavistock Publications.

Clarke, J. (1971) An Analysis of Crisis Management by Mental Welfare Officers. *British Journal of Social Work* 1 (1): 27–39.

CMH (1972) Even Better Services for the Mentally Handicapped. London: CMH.

—— (1973) The Action Now. London: CMH.

Cohen, L. (1955) Vocational Planning and Mental Illness. *Personnel and Guidance Journal* 28 September.

Community Care (1983) *The Coventry Crisis Team. Community Care* 23 June.

Cooke, G. (1968) Evaluation of the Ethicacy of the Components of Reciprocal Inhibition Psychotherapy. *Journal of Abnormal Psychology* 73.

Cooper, J. E. (1979) *Crisis Admission Units and Emergency Psychiatric Services*, Public Health in Europe 2. Copenhagen: World Health Organisation Regional Office for Europe.

Cormican, J. (1979) Linguistic Issues in Interviewing. In B. Compton and B. Galaway (eds) *Social Work Processes*. Homewood, Illinois: Dorsey.

Corney, R. H. and Briscoe, M. E. (1977) Investigation into Different Types of Attachment Schemes. *Social Work Today* 9 (15): 10–14.

Crine, A. (1981) How Crisis Intervention Can Help Change People's Lives. *Mind Out* 48, April.

Cunningham, C. (1983) Early Support and Intervention: the HARC Infant Project. In P. Mittler and H. McConachie (eds) *Parent, Professionals and Mentally Handicapped*. London: Croom Helm.

Darley, P. J. and Kenny, W. J. (1971) Community Care and the 'Queequeg Syndrome' – a Phenomenological Evaluation of Methods of Rehabilitation for Psychotic Patients. *American Journal of Psychiatry* 127: 1333–338.

Davis, A. (1981) *The Residential Solution*. London: Tavistock Publications.

Davis, A. and Davis, A. (1982) Care in the Community. *Community Care* 6 May.

Davis, A. and Hayton, C. (forthcoming 1984) *Who Benefits? – the Rubery Hill Benefit Project*. London: King's Fund.

Day, K. A. (1983) A Hospital Based Psychiatric Unit for Mentally Handicapped Adults. *Mental Handicap* 2 (December), BIMH.

DES (1971) The 1970 Education Act. London: HMSO.

―― (1978) Special Education Needs. (The Warnock Report) Cmnd 7212. London: HMSO.

―― (1981) The Education Act 1981. London: HMSO.

―― (1981) The Education Act 1981 (Commencement No. 2) Order 1983, Statutory Instruments 1983 7 (C.1). London: HMSO.

―― (1981) Circul. 8/81. The Education Act 1981. London: DES.

―― (1983) Circular 1/82. Assessments and Statements of Special Educational Needs (Joint Circular with DHSS Health Circular HC(83)3 and Local Authority Circular LAC (83)2). London: DES.

―― (1983) The Education (Special Educational Needs) Regulations 1983, Statutory Instrument 1983 29. London: HMSO.

DHSS (1968) Report of the Committee on Local Authority and Allied Personal Social Services. (The Seebohm Committee) Cmnd 3703. London: HMSO.

―― (1969) Report of the Committee of Enquiry into Allegations of Ill-treatment and Other Irregularities at Ely Hospital, Cardiff. Cmnd 3785. London: HMSO.

―― (1971a) Better Services for the Mentally Handicapped. Cmnd 4683. London: HMSO.

―― (1971b) Report of the Farleigh Hospital Committee of Enquiry. Cmnd 4557. London: HMSO.

―― (1972) Report of the Committee of Inquiry into Whittingham Hospital. Cmnd 4871. London: HMSO.

―― (1975) Better Services for the Mentally Ill. Cmnd 6233. London: HMSO.

―― (1976) A Review of the Mental Health Act 1959. London: HMSO.

―― (1977) Joint Care Planning HC (77)17. London: HMSO.

―― (1978) Report of the Working Party on the Organisational and Management Problems of Mental Illness Hospitals. (The Nodder Report) London: HMSO.

―― (1980) Mental Handicap: Progress, Problems and Priorities. London: HMSO.

―― (1981a) Health Services Development Helping to get Children out of Hospital. £1 million for £1 million. Scheme HC(81)13 LAC(81)9. London: HMSO.

―― (1981b) *Care in the Community*. London: HMSO.

―― (1983a) Extension of Joint Finance to Education for Disabled and Housing. DHSS DA(83)39. London: HMSO.

―― (1983b) Care in the Community and Joint Finance HC(83)6. LAC (83)5. London: HMSO.

―― (1984) Helping Mentally Handicapped People with Special Problems. London: HMSO.

DHSS/Welsh Office (1974) *Social Work Support for the Health Service*. London: HMSO.

DOE (1977) The Housing (Homeless Persons) Act. Section 4. London: HMSO.

Dunn, S. and Moss, T. (1978) Group Work as a Vehicle to Self-help. *Social Work Today* 10 (14): 16–17.

Dunne, D. (1977) Looking at Mental Health Practice. *Social Work Today* 8 (40).

Durkheim, E. (1952) *Suicide*. London: Routledge & Kegan Paul.

Early, D. (1960) The Industrial Therapy Organisation (Bristol), A Development of Work in Hospital. *Lancet* ii: 754–57.

Equal Opportunities Commission (1982) *Who Cares for the Carers?* Manchester: EOC.

Etherington, S. (1983) *Housing and Mental Health: A Guide for Housing Workers*. London: MIND and Circle 33 Housing Trust Ltd.

Evans, R. (1978) Unitary Models of Practice and the Social Work Team. In M. R. Olsen (ed.) *The Unitary Model: Its Implications for Social Work Theory and Practice*. Birmingham: BASW.

Eysenck, H. J. (1957) *Sense and Nonsense in Psychology*. Harmondsworth: Penguin.

—— (1961) *Fact and Fiction in Psychology*. Harmondsworth: Penguin.

—— (1976) *The Future of Psychiatry*. London: Methuen.

—— (1984) Is Behaviour Therapy on Course? *Behavioural Psychotherapy* 12 (1): 2–6.

Eysenck, H. J., vs Kamin, L. (1981) *Intelligence: The Battle for the Mind*. London: Pan.

Fairweather, G. W., Sanders, D. H., and Maynard, H. (1969) *Community Life for the Mentally Ill: An Alternative to Institutional Care*. Chicago: Aldine.

Felce, D. (1983) A Wessex Home from Home. *Nursing Times* Aug.

Firth, H. (1982) Mentally Handicapped People with Special Needs. London: King's Fund.

Fischer, J. (1978) *Effective Casework Practice, An Eclectic Approach*. New York. McGraw-Hill.

Fisher, M., Newton, C., and Sainsbury, E. (1984) *Mental Health Social Work Observed*. London: Allen & Unwin.

Foulkes, S. H. and Anthony, E. J. (1965) *Group Psychotherapy: Psychoanalytic Approach*. Harmondsworth: Penguin.

Friedman, I., Von Mering, O., and Hinko, E. N. (1966) Intermittent Patienthood. *Archives of Genetic Psychiatry*, 14: 386; 392.

Garber, H. and Heber, F. R. (1977) The Milwaukee Project. In P. Mittler *Research to Practice in Mental Retardation* vol. 1. Baltimore, Maryland: University Park Press.

Glasser, P., Sarri, R., and Vinter, R. (1974) *Individual Change in Small Groups*. New York: Free Press.

GNC (1982) Training Syllabus for Nurses Caring for People with Mental Handicap. London: RNB.

Goffman, E. (1961) *Asylums: Essays on the Social Situation of Mental Patients and Other Inmates*. Harmondsworth: Penguin.

Gold, M. (1972) Stimulus Factors in Skill Training of the Retarded on a Complex Assembly Task. *American Journal of Mental Deficiency*. 1975.

Goldberg, D. and Huxley, P. (1980) *Mental Illness in the Community*. London: Tavistock Publications.

Goldstein, H. (1973) *Social Work Practice: A Unitary Approach*. Columbia: University of South Carolina Press.

Goodwin, D. W. (1976) Adoption Studies of Alcoholism. *Journal of Open Psychiatry* 7: 54–63.

Gostin, L. (1983a) *A Practical Guide to Mental Health Law*. London: MIND.

—— (1983b) *The Court of Protection*. London: MIND.

Gunzburg, H. C. (1976) Progress Assessment Charts. Stratford Social Education Publications.

Haley, J. (1976) *Problem-Solving Therapy*. San Francisco, Calif.: Jossey-Bass.

Handy, C. (1976) *Understanding Organizations*. Harmondsworth: Penguin.

Heine, R. W. (1953) A Comparison of Patient Reports on Psycho-Analytic, Non-Directive and Adlerian Therapists. *American Journal of Psychotherapy* 7.

Hersen, M. and Barlow, D. (1976) *Single Case Experimental Designs*. Oxford: Pergamon Press.

Hersen, M. and Bellack, D. (1976) *Behavioural Assessment*. Oxford: Pergamon Press.

Hewitt, S. E. K. (1980) The Retarded and the Police. *Police Studies*. 3 Spring.

—— (1983) Interviewing Mentally Handicapped Persons. *Mental Handicap* 2 (March), BIMH.

Hey, A. (1979) Organising Teams – Alternative Patterns. In M. Marshall, M. Preston Shoot, and E. Wincott (eds) *Teamwork – For and Against*. Birmingham: BASW.

Hinshelwood, R. and Manning, N. (eds) (1979) *Therapeutic Communities*. London: Routledge & Kegan Paul.

HMSO (1957) Report of the Royal Commission on the Law Relating to Mental Illness and Mental Deficiency 1954–57. Cmnd 169. London: HMSO.

—— (1970) Chronically Sick and Disabled Persons Act. London: HMSO.

—— (1975) Report of the Committee on Mentally Abnormal Offenders (The Butler Committee). Cmnd 6244. London: HMSO.

—— (1979) Report of the Committee of Enquiry into Mental Handicap Nursing and Care vols. 1 and 2 (The Jay Committee). Cmnd 7468. London: HMSO.

Hollis, J. H. and Meyers, C. E. (1982) Life Threatening Behavior Analysis and Intervention. Monograph No. 5, Washington D.C.: American Association for Mental Deficiency.

Holme, A. and Maizels, J. (1978) *Social Workers and Volunteers*. Birmingham: BASW.

Homme, L. E. (1965) Control of Coverants, the Operants of the Mind. Perspectives in Psychology. *Psychological Record* 15.

Hooyman, G. (1979) Team Building in the Human Services. In B. Compton and B. Galaway (eds) *Social Work Processes*. Homewood, Illinois: Dorsey.

Houtts, P. S. and Scott, R. E. (1975) Goal Planning with Developmentally Disabled Persons. Dept. of Behavioral Sciences, Pennsylvania University.

Hudson, B. (1982) *Social Work with Psychiatric Patients*. London: Macmillan.

Independent Development Council (1981) Response to Care in the Community. IDC King's Fund Centre Conference.

—— (1982) Elements of a Comprehensive Local Service for People with Mental Handicap. London: IDC King's Fund Centre.

Ivey, A. E. (1971) *Microcounselling – Innovations in Interviewing Training*. Springfield, Illinois: Charles C. Thomas.

Jackson, G. (1967) Authority and the Mental Welfare Officer. *British Journal of Psychiatric Social Work* 9(1): 22–4.

Jansen, E. (ed.) (1980) *The Therapeutic Community*. London: Croom Helm.

Jenkins, P. (1980) Speech to MENCAP Conference, 10 December.

Johnstone, E. C., Deakin, J. F. W., Frith, C. D., Lawler, P., McPherson, K., Stevens, M., and Crow, T. J. (1980) The Northwick Park Electro-Convulsive Therapy Trial. *Lancet* 20/27 December.

Jones, K. (1977) Mental Health Administration: Reflections from the British Experience. *Administration in Mental Health* 4 (2).

Jones, M. C. (1983) Behaviour Problems in Handicapped Children. London: Souvenir Press.

Jowell, T. (1981) *The Brecknock Community and Mental Health Project*. In MIND, *Mental Health Year Book*. London: MIND.

Kadushin, A. (1972) *The Social Work Interview*. New York: Columbia University Press.

—— (1979) The Racial Factor in the Interview. In B. Compton and B. Galaway (eds) *Social Work Processes*. Homewood, Illinois: Dorsey.

Kazdin, A. E. and Wilson, G. T. (1978) *Evaluation of Behavior Therapy: Issues, Evidence and Research Strategies*. Cambridge, Mass.: Ballinger.

Keith-Lucas, A. (1972) *Giving and Taking Help*. Chapel Hill: University of North Carolina Press.

Kempton, W. (1973) Guidelines for Planning a Training Course on Human Sexuality and the Retarded. Philadelphia, PA: Planned Parenthood Association.

Kendell, R. E. (1973) Psychiatric Diagnoses: A Study of How They Are Made. *British Journal of Psychiatry* 122: 437–45.

Keskiner, A., Zalman, M. J., Ruppert, E. H., and Ulett, G. A. (1972) The Foster Community: A Partnership in Psychiatric Rehabilitation. *American Journal of Psychiatry* 129 (3): 283–88.

King, R. D., Raynes, N. V., and Tizard, J. (1971) *Patterns of Residential Care*. London: Routledge & Kegan Paul.

King's Fund (1980) An Ordinary Life Project Paper. London: King's Fund Centre.

—— (1981) Short Term Care for Mentally Handicapped Children. London: King's Fund Centre.

—— (1984) A Vocational Service for People with a Mental Handicap. London: King's Fund Centre.

Lakatos, L. (1970) Falsification and the Methodology of Scientific Research Programmes. In L. Lakatos and A. Musgrave (eds) *Criticism and the Growth of Knowledge*. Cambridge: Cambridge University Press.

Lamb, H. R. and Goertzel, V. (1971) Discharged Mental Patients – Are They Really in the Community? *Archives of Genetic Psychiatry* 24: 29–34.

Langsley, D. G., Machotka, P., and Flomenhaft, K. (1971) Avoiding Mental Hospital Admissions: A Follow-up Study. *American Journal of Psychiatry* 127: 1391–394.

Langsley, D. G. and Kaplan, D. (1968) *The Treatment of Families in Crisis*. New York: Grune and Stratton.

Lindemann, E. (1944) Symptomatology and Management of Acute Grief. *American Journal of Psychiatry* 101.

London Borough of Wandsworth (1976) *Project 74: A Research Study in which Mentally Handicapped People Speak for Themselves*. Social Services Department, Research & Planning Section.

McCormack, M. (1970) *Away from Home: The Mentally Handicapped in Residential Care*. London: Constable.

McLiesh, J. (1975) *Soviet Psychology*. London: Methuen.

Macrea, J. (1970) *Schizophrenia*. London: Methuen.

Mandelbrote, B. M. and Folkard, S. (1961) Some Factors Related to Outcome and Social Adjustment in Schizophrenia. *Acta Psychiatrica Scandinavica* 27: 223–35.

Marks, I. M. (1971) Flooding versus Desensitisation in the Treatment of Phobic Patients. *British Journal of Psychiatry* 118.

Matson, J. L. and Mulick, J. A. (1983) *Handbook of Mental Retardation*. New York: Pergamon Press.

Mayer, J. E. and Timms, N. (1970) *The Client Speaks*. London: Routledge & Kegan Paul.

Meichenbaum, D. (1977) *Cognitive Behavior Modification*. Morristown, N.J.: General Learning Press.

Mental Welfare Commission for Scotland (1970) *Boarding-out in Scotland*.

MIND (1974) Report 13. Co-ordination or Chaos – The Rundown of Psychiatric Hospitals. London: MIND.

—— (1978) Evidence on Mental Handicap. Birmingham: Apex. BIMH.

—— (1981) *Mental Health Year Book*. London: MIND.

—— (1983) *Common Concern: MIND's Manifesto for a New Mental Health Service*. London: MIND.

Ministry of Health (1962) A Hospital Plan for England and Wales. Cmnd 1604. London: HMSO.

Mittler, P. (1977) *Research to Practice in Mental Retardation*, vols 1 and 2. Baltimore, Maryland: University Park Press.

Monck, E. M. (1963) Employment Experiences of 127 Discharged Schizophrenic Men in London. *British Journal of Preventive and Social Medicine* 17: 101.

Morgan, R. and Cheadle, J. (1981) *Psychiatric Rehabilitation*. Surbiton: National Schizophrenia Fellowship.

Morris, P. (1969) *Put Away*. London: Routledge & Kegan Paul.

Muir, L. (1983) *The Use of Volunteers in Three Intermediate Treatment Projects, 1979–1983*. Leicester: NAYC.

Munro, E. A., Manthei, R. J., and Small, J. J. (1979) *Counselling. A Skills Approach* revised edn. London: Methuen.

National Development Group for the Mentally Handicapped (1977a) *Helping Mentally Handicapped School Leavers*. Pamphlet no. 3. London: NDG.

—— (1977b) *Day Services for Mentally Handicapped Adults*. Pamphlet no. 5. London: NDG.

Nelson, B. and Wigglesworth, S. (1983) A Problem Shared *Community Care* 26 May.

Nihira, K. (1974) The Adaptive Behavior Rating Scales. Washington DC: American Association for Mental Deficiency.

Nirje, B. (1969) The Normalization Principle. In R. Kugel and W. Wolfensberger *Changing Patterns in Residential Services for the Mentally Retarded*. Washington DC: President's Committee on Mental Retardation.

Northen, H. (1969) *Social Work with Groups*. New York: Columbia University Press.

North Western RHA (1982) Services for People who are Mentally Handicapped. A Model District Service. Manchester.

Oliver, J. (1981) The Behavioural Treatment of a Case of Obsessional House Cleaning in a Personality Disordered Client. *International Journal of Behavioural Social Work* 1 (1) 39–54.

Olsen, M. R. (1976a) Boarding-out The Long-stay Psychiatric Patient. In *Differential Approaches in Social Work with the Mentally Disordered*. Birmingham: BASW.

—— (1976b) The Personal and Social Consequences of the Discharge of the Long-stay Psychiatric Patient from the North Wales Hospital, Denbigh (1965–66). PhD thesis: University of Wales.

—— (ed.) (1978) *The Unitary Model: Its Implications for Social Work Theory and Practice*. Birmingham: BASW.

—— (1979a) Boarding-out and Substitute Family Care of the Psychiatric Patient. In *The Care of the Mentally Disordered: an Examination of Some Alternatives to Hospital Care*. Birmingham: BASW.

—— (1979b) Now Radical Reform is Needed. *Community Care* 8 February.

—— (1979c) Constraints on the Mentally Disordered. *Social Work Today* 7 October.

—— (1980) The Question of Social Work. Inaugural lecture, obtainable from Birmingham University.

—— (1981) Untrained and Unsafe. *Social Work Today* 10 November.

—— (1982) Approval Rating. *Social Work Today* 9 February.

—— (1983) A Critical Evaluation of the Proposals for Training Approved Social Workers. In *Approved Social Work: Principles and Practice*. London: MIND.

Oswin, M. (1973) *The Empty Hours: A Study of the Week-end Life of Handicapped Children in Institutions*. Harmondsworth: Penguin.

Parad, H. (1965) *Crisis Intervention: Selected Readings*. New York: Family Service Association of America.

—— (1976) Crisis Intervention in Mental Health Emergencies: Theory and Technique in Work with the Emotionally Disturbed and Mentally Disordered. In M. Rolf Olsen (ed.) *Differential Approaches in Social Work with the Mentally Disordered*. Birmingham: BASW.

Patmore, C. (1981) *Day Centres, Unemployment and the Future*. In MIND, *Mental Health Year Book*. London: MIND.

Payne, M. (1982) *Working in Teams*. Birmingham: BASW.

Peace, S. (1980) *Caring from Day to Day: Research on Day Hospitals for Elderly Mentally Infirm People*. London: MIND.

Penfold, M. (1980) Family Homes for the Handicapped: Northallerton. North Yorkshire Social Services Dept. Mimeo.

Pincus, A. and Minahan, A. (1973) *Social Work Practice: Model and Method*. Itasca, Illinois: F. E. Peacock.

Popper, K. (1963) *Conjectures and Refutations*. London: Routledge & Kegan Paul.

Preistley, P. and McGuire, J. (1983) *Learning to Help*. London: Tavistock Publications.

Race, D. G. and Race, D. M. (1979) *The Cherries Group Home: A Beginning*. London: HMSO.

Rachman, S. J. and Wilson, G. T. (1980) *The Effects of Psychological Therapy*. Oxford: Pergamon Press.

Raynes, N., Pratt, M., and Rose, S. (1979) *Organizational Structure and the Care of the Mentally Retarded*. London: Croom Helm.

Rees, S. (1978) *Social Work Face to Face*. London: Edward Arnold.

Rees, S. and Wallace, A. (1982) *Verdicts on Social Work*. London: Edward Arnold.

Reid, W. J. and Hanrahan, P. (1980) The Effectiveness of Social Work: Recent Evidence. In E. M. Goldberg and N. Connelly, *Evaluative Research in Social Care*. Policy Studies Institute, London: Heinemann Educational Books.

Reiner, B. S. and Kaufman, M. D. (1969) *Character Disorders in the Parents of Delinquents*. New York: FSAA.

Richardson, A. (1984) Working with Self-help Groups. Policy Studies Institute, London.

Rose, S. (1977) *Group Therapy. A Behavioral Approach*. Englewood Cliffs, N.J.: Prentice-Hall.

Royal College of Psychiatrists (1977) Memorandum on the Use of ECT. London: Royal College of Psychiatrists.

Rush, B. (1812) *Medical Inquiries and Observations upon the Diseases of the Mind*. New York: Hafner.

Ryan, J. and Thomas, F. (1980) *The Politics of Mental Handicap*. Harmondsworth: Penguin.

Sandall, H., Hawley, T. T., and Gordon, G. C. (1975) The St. Louis Community Homes Program: Graduated Support for Long-term Care. *American Journal of Psychiatry* June: 132–36.

Sandifer, M. G., Pettus, L., and Quale, D. (1964) A Study of Psychiatric Diagnosis. *Journal of Nervous and Mental Disease* 139.

Satir, V. (1967) *Conjoint Family Therapy* revised edn. Palo Alto, Calif.: Science and Behavior Books.

Schindler-Rainman, E. and Lippitt, A. (1977) *The Volunteer Community: Creative Use of Human Resources* 2nd edn. San Diego, Calif.: University Associates.

Shearer, A. (1981) Bringing Mentally Handicapped Children out of Hospital. No. 30. Project Paper. London: King's Fund.

Sheldon, B. (1982) *Behaviour Modification: Theory, Practice, and Philosophy*. London: Tavistock Publications.

Shields, J. and Slater, E. (1967) Genetic Aspects of Schizophrenia. *Hospital Medicine* April 579–84.

Skinner, B. F. (1953) *Science and Human Behaviour*. London: Macmillan.

Slater, E. and Cowie, V. (1971) *The Genetics of Mental Disorder*. London: Oxford University Press.

Slater, H. (1971) Community Care for the Mentally Frail *Social Work Today* 2 (6): 132–36.

—— (1979) Community Care for the Mentally Frail. In M. R. Olsen (ed.) *The Care of the Mentally Disordered: an Examination of Some Alternatives to Hospital Care*. Birmingham: BASW.

Smith, G. (1975) Institutional Dependence is Reversible *Social Work Today* 6 (14): 426–28.

—— (1979) Family Substitute Care in the Rehabilitation of the Discharged Psychiatric Patient. In M. R. Olsen (ed.) *The Care of the Mentally Disordered: an Examination of Some Alternatives to Hospital Care*. Birmingham: BASW.

Smith, J., Glossop, G., Hall, J., and Kushlick, A. (1977) Report of First Six Months of a Home Teaching Service. Winchester: Health Care Evaluation Team.

South West Thames RHA (1983) Future Pattern of Service for Mentally Handicapped People.

Stern, R. (1978) *Behavioural Techniques*. London: Academic Press.

Stringham, J. A. (1952) Rehabilitating Chronic Neuropsychiatric Patients. *American Journal of Psychiatry*. 108: 924–28.

Stuart, R. B. (ed.) (1977) *Behavioral Self Management: Strategies, Techniques and Outcome*. New York: Brunner/Mazell.

Szasz, T. (1971) *The Manufacture of Madness*. London: Routledge & Kegan Paul.

—— (1978) The Case against Compulsory Psychiatric Intervention. *Lancet* 13 May.

Temerlin, M. K. (1968) Suggestion Effects in Psychiatric Diagnosis. *Journal of Nervous and Mental Disease* 147 (4).

Tharp, R. G. and Wetzel, R. J. (1969) *Behaviour Modification in the Natural Environment*. London: Academic Press.

Thomas, A., Chess, S., and Birch, H. G. (1968) *Temperament and Behavior Disorder in Children*. New York: University Press.

Thomas, D., Firth, H., and Kendall, A. (1978) ENCOR – A Way Ahead. London: CMH.

Tizard, J., Sinclair, I., and Clarke, R. V. G. (eds) (1975) *Varieties of Residential Experience*. London: Routledge & Kegan Paul.

Towell, D. and Davis, A. (forthcoming 1984) *Moving Out from the Large Hospitals – Involving the People (Staff and Patients)*. MIND Annual Conference 1983, London.

Towell, D. and Harries, C. (1979) *Innovations in Patient Care*. London: Croom Helm.

Townsend, P. (1970) The Political Sociology of Mental Handicap: A Case Study of Policy Failure. In *The Social Minority*. London: Allen Lane.

Trower, P., Bryant, B., and Argyle, M. (1977) *Social Skills and Mental Health*. London: Methuen.

Truax, C. and Carkhuff, R. (1967) *Towards Effective Counselling and Psychotherapy: Training and Practice*. Chicago: Aldine.

Tsuang, M. and Vandermey, R. (1980) *Genes and the Mind*. London: Oxford University Press.

Tuckman, B. W. (1965) Development Sequence in Small Groups. *Psychological Bulletin* 63 (6): 384–99.

Tyne, A. (1977) *Residential Provision for Adults who are Mentally Handicapped*. Enquiry Paper no. 5. London: CMH.

Ullman, L. P. and Krasner, L. (1969) *A Psychological Approach to Abnormal Behavior*. Englewood Cliffs, N.J.: Prentice-Hall.

Utting, B. (1979) News. *Social Work Today* 10: 35.

Vaughn, C. E. and Leff, J. P. (1976) The Influence of Family and Social Factors on the Course of Psychotic Illness. *British Journal of Psychiatry* 129: 125–37.

Walker, M. (1981) What is the Makaton Vocabulary: Special Education. *Forward Trends* 8 (3).

Walton, H. (ed.) (1971) *Small Group Psychotherapy*. Harmondsworth: Penguin.

Ward, L. (1977) Clarifying the Residential Social Work Task. *Social Work Today* 9 (2): 25.

Webb, A. and Hobdell, M. (1980) Co-ordination and Teamwork in the Health and Personal Social Services. In T. Briggs (ed.) *Teamwork in the Personal Social Services and Health Care: British and American Perspectives*. London: Croom Helm.

Welsh Office (1982) Report of the All Wales Working Party on Services for Mentally Handicapped People. Cardiff: Welsh Office.

White, T. and Holden, A. (1979) Services for the Mentally Ill. In M. R. Olsen (ed.) *The Care of the Mentally Disordered*. Birmingham: BASW.

Whiteley, J. S. and Gordon, J. (1979) *Group Approaches in Psychiatry*. London: Routledge & Kegan Paul.

Williams, P. and Shoultz, B. (1982) *We Can Speak for Ourselves*. London: Souvenir Press.

Wilson, G. and Ryland, G. (1949) *Social Group Work Practice*. Chicago, Illinois: Riverside Press.

Wing, J. K. (1957) Family Care Systems in Norway and Holland. *Lancet* 2: 884–86.
—— (1978) *Reasoning about Madness*. Oxford: Oxford University Press.
Wing, J. K. and Brown, L. W. (1970) *Institutionalism and Schizophrenia: A Comparative Study of Three Hospitals*. Cambridge: Cambridge University Press.
Wing, J. K. and Freudenberg, R. K. (1961) The Response of Severely Ill and Chronic Schizophrenic Patients to Social Stimulation. *American Journal of Psychiatry* 118: 311–22.
Wing, J. K. and Giddens, R. G. T. (1959) Industrial Rehabilitation of Male Chronic Schizophrenic Patients. *Lancet* ii: 505–7.
Wing, J. K. and Olsen, M. R. (1979) *Community Care of the Mentally Disabled*. Oxford: Oxford University Press.
Winokur, G. (1970) Genetic Findings and Methodological Considerations in Manic Depressive Disease. *British Journal of Psychiatry* 117: 267–74.
Wittkower, E. D. and Tendresse, J. E. (1955) Rehabilitation of Chronic Schizophrenics by a New Method of Occupational Therapy. *British Journal of Medical Psychology* 1 (28): 42–7.
Wolfensberger, W. (1972) The Principle of Normalisation in Human Services. Toronto: National Institute of Mental Retardation.
—— (1980) The definition of Normalization. In R. J. Flynn and K. E. Nirsch *Normalization, Social Integration and Community Services*. Baltimore, Maryland: University Park Press.
Wolfensberger, W. and Glenn, L. (1975) PASS 3 – Programme Analysis of Service Systems. Toronto: National Institute of Mental Retardation.
Woodcock, A. and Davis, M. (1978) *Catastrophe Theory*. Harmondsworth: Penguin.
Zerbin-Rüdin, E. (1967) Endogene Psychosen. In P. Becker (ed.) *Humangenetick ein Kurzes Handbuch* vol. 2. Stuttgart: Thieme.

# Name index

Ahmed, S. 196
Anthony, E. J. 198
Anton-Stephens, D. 61
Argyle, M. 199, 215
Ashurst, P. 100
Ayllon, T. 211, 238
Azrin, N. H. 211, 238

Baker, A. A. 81
Bales, R. 202
Bandura, A. 86, 212
Bank-Mikkelson, N. 109
Barlow, D. 239
Barton, R. 5
Barton, W. E. 120, 140
Bellack, D. 231
Bender, M. 90, 135
Bennett, D. 130, 136
Beresford, P. 105
Bertcher, H. 205
Biestek, F. 192
Bion, W. 198
Birch, A. 156
Birch, H. G. 93–5
Birley, J. L. T. 80, 99
Bloom, M. 204
Bluglass, R. 39

Brandon, D. 136, 165, 195
Breuning, S. E. 110
Brewer, C. 86
Brill, N. 169, 173
Briscoe, M. E. 180
Brown, G. W. 5, 79–81, 99
Bryant, B. 215
Burt, Sir C. 93
Butler, A. 40

Caplan, G. 220
Carkhuff, R. 192
Carlyle, T. 79
Carstairs, G. M. 79, 81
Carter, J. 130–32, 136
Cartwright, D. 199
Castle, B. 14
Cath, S. 221
Chaadayev, P. J. 89
Cheadle, J. 125
Chess, S. 93–5
Chien, C. P. 140
Clare, A. 90
Clarke, J. 15
Clarke, R. V. G. 128
Cohen, L. 82
Cole, J. O. 140

Conolly, J. 87
Cooke, G. 217
Cormican, J. 191
Corney, R. H. 180
Cowie, V. 97
Crine, A. 225–26
Cunningham, C. 106
Curran, D. 76

Darley, P. J. 142
Davis, A. benefits 155; community care 3,
    14, 138, 149; day care 129; examinations
    241–43, 253–55; professionals in mental
    health 177; residential care 119–21;
    volunteers and self-help 158, 161
Davis, A. 161
Davis, M. 98
Day, K. A. 116
Dunne, D. 16, 41
Durkheim, E. 83

Early, D. 81
Etherington, S. 155
Evans, R. 169
Eysenck, H. J. 93, 95, 99, 212

Fairweather, G. W. 140–41
Felce, D. 106
Firth, H. 116
Fischer, J. 192
Fisher, M. 40, 77–8, 83
Folkard, S. 82
Foulkes, S. H. 198
Freudenberg, R. K. 81
Friedman, I. 140

Garber, H. 108
George III 87
Giddens, R. G. T. 81
Glasser, P. 199, 204
Glenn, L. 109
Goertzel, V. 140–41
Goffman, E. 5
Gold, M. 111
Goldberg, D. 150, 152–53
Goldstein, H. 188
Gordon, G. C. 140
Gordon, J. 208
Gostin, L. 20, 39, 45
Gunzburg, H. C. 115

Haley, J. 195
Handy, C. 172
Hanrahan, P. 210
Harnes, C. 120
Harris, T. 81
Hawley, T. T. 140
Hayton, C. 155
Heber, F. R. 108

Heine, R. W. 91
Hersen, M. 231, 239
Hewitt, S. E. K. 112
Hey, A. 170
Hinko, E. N. 140
Hinshelwood, R. 124
Hobdell, M. 171
Holden, A. 7
Hollis, J. H. 115
Holme, A. 159
Homme, L. E. 214
Hooyman, G. 171
Houtts, P. S. 111
Hudson, B. 39, 83, 178–79, 210
Huxley, P. 150, 152–53

Irvine, B. 222–23
Ivey, A. E. 193

Jackson, G. 15
Jansen, E. 124
Jenkins, P. 103
Johnstone, E. C. 89
Jones, K. 7
Jones, M. 198
Jones, M. C. 115
Jowell, T. 136

Kadushin, A. 195–96
Kamin, L. 93
Kaplan, D. 221, 224
Kaufman, M. D. 85
Kazdin, A. E. 210
Keith-Lucas, A. 196
Kendell, R. E. 91
Kenny, W. J. 142
Keskiner, A. 140, 142
King, R. D. 119
Klein, D. 220, 223
Krasner, L. 91

Lait, J. 86
Lakatos, L. 240
Lamb, H. R. 140–41
Langsley, D. 224–25
Leff, J. P. 80–1, 99, 214, 229
Leigh, D. 76
Lindemann, E. 220
Lippitt, A. 160

McCormack, M. 127
McGuire, J. 195
McLeish, J. 95
Macrea, J. 86
Maizels, J. 159
Mandelbrote, B. M. 82
Manning, N. 124
Manthei, R. J. 196
Maple, F. 205
Marks, I. M. 217

Marks, J. 76
Mason, E. 221
Matson, J. L. 110
Mayer, J. E. 191, 218, 229
Maynard, H. 140–41
Meacher, M. 39
Medvedev, Z. 18
Meichenbaum, D. 212
Meyers, C. E. 115
Milne, A. A. 176
Minahan, A. 172, 188
Monck, E. M. 79, 82
Morgan, R. 125
Morris, P. 5
Muir, L. groupwork 198; interviewing 189;
    residential care 124; teamwork 168, 177;
    volunteers and self-help 158, 160
Mulick, J. A. 110
Munro, E. A. 196

Nelson, B. 206
Newton, C. 77
Nihira, K. 115
Nirje, B. 109
Northen, H. 201

Obcarskas, S. 76
O'Connor, N. 81
Oliver, J. 234
Olsen, M. R. approved social workers,
    duties of 41, 123; crisis service 122, 219;
    examinations 48–58, 251; family care 80,
    99, 138–39 143; Mental Health Act (1983)
    20, 38–40, 193; residential care 126; social
    perspectives of mental disorder 77; social
    work problems 78; social worker training
    41, 187
Oswin, M. 120

Parad, H. 220–25
Pare, C. M. B. 76
Partridge, M. 76
Patmore, C. 135
Pavlov, I. P. 211
Payne, M. 169, 171
Peace, S. 136
Penfold, M. 106
Pettus, L. 92
Pincus, A. 172, 188
Pinel, P. 87
Poling, A. D. 110
Popper, K. 230, 240
Powell, E. 4
Prait, M. 126–27
Priestley, P. 195
Pritchard, C. 40

Quale, D. 92

Race, D. G. and Race, D. M. 122
Rachman, S. J. 100, 210
Rawnsley, K. 81
Raynes, N. V. 119, 126–27
Rees, S. 218, 229
Reid, W. J. 210
Reiner, B. S. 85
Rose, S. 205
Ross, A. 220, 223
Rush, B. 88
Ryan, J. 120
Ryland, G. 206

Sainsbury, E. 77
Sandall, H. 140
Sanders, D. H. 140–41
Sandifer, M. G. 92
Sarri, R. 199, 204
Satir, V. 190
Schindler-Rainman, E. 160
Scott, R. E. 111
Shearer, A. 106
Sheldon, B. behavioural approach 40, 209,
    211, 213, 218; evaluation of outcome of
    intervention 111, 228; examinations 244–
    46, 259–60; medical model of psychiatry 84
Shields, J. 97
Shoultz, B. 106
Sim, M. 76
Sinclair, I. 128
Skinner, B. F. 211
Slater, E. 97
Slater, H. 143
Small, J. J. 196
Smith, G. 142–43
Smith, J. 106
Solzhenitsyn, A. 18, 88
Stern, R. 211
Storey, P. 76
Stringham, J. A. 82
Stuart, R. B. 211
Szasz, T. 18, 87–8

Temerlin, M. K. 91
Tendresse, J. E. 81
Tharp, R. G. 211
Thomas, A. 93–5
Thomas, D. 101
Thomas, F. 120
Thorndike, E. L. 211
Timms, N. 191, 218, 229
Tizard, J. 119, 128
Topping, G. 79
Towell, D. 120, 161
Townsend, P. 104–05
Trick, K. L. K. 76
Trower, P. 215
Truax, C. 192
Tsuang, M. 93, 97–8

Tuckman, B. W. 200
Tuckwell, P. 105
Tyne, A. 126

Ullman, L. P. 91
Utting, B. 15

Valentine, M. 76
Vandermey, R. 93, 97–8
Vaughn, C. E. 80–1, 99, 214, 229
Vinter, R. 199, 204
Von Mering, O. 140

Walker, M. 114
Wallace, A. 218, 229
Walton, H. 198
Ward, D. 100

Ward, L. 121
Webb, A. 171
Wetzel, R. J. 211
White, T. 7
Whiteley, J. S. 208
Wigglesworth, S. 206
Williams, P. 106
Wilson, G. 206
Wilson, G. T. 100, 210
Wing, J. K. 5, 40, 79–81, 88, 99
Winokur, G. 99
Wittkower, E. D. 81
Wolfensberger, W. 109–10
Woodcock, A. 98

Zander, A. 199
Zerbin-Rüdin, E. 97

# Subject index

accommodation in teamwork 174
ACE *see* Advisory Centre for Education
addictive drugs 75
addresses of voluntary organizations 252–53
admission *see* hospital
adoption studies 93, 96–7
ADSS *see* Association of Directors etc.
Adult Training Centres 102, 105, 107, 131–32, 134
advantages of teams 171–72
advice agencies 154–55
Advisory Centre for Education 105
affective psychosis 68–70
after-care, duty to provide 44
age and guardianship 26
ageing 63–5, 154, 221
agency preparation, volunteers 165–66
aggression 113
agoraphobia 215, 235
Alcoholics Anonymous 75, 252
alcoholism 63, 65, 74–5, 99
All Wales Working Party 106
allowances *see* social security
alternatives to hospital care 117–46; boarding-out 138–46; day care 129–37; residential care 119–28
amnesia, hysterical 72
anxiety states 70–1
apathy 64

appearance of mentally handicapped 108
appointment of approved social workers 42–3
approved social workers 3, 42–3; boarding-out and 145; crisis service and 226; duties of 45–9, 112–15; examinations for 50–8, 241–43, 244–46, 254–60; and local services development 149–57; mental handicap and 101–15; and 1983 Act 25–7; and relatives and guardianship 27; and residential care 119–28; roles and duties 41–58; and teamwork 169–76; working with other professions 178–84
arrested development 61, 113
assessment: compulsory 23–4; goal-setting and evaluation 228–31
Association of Directors of Social Services 15
assumptions about origins of mental illness 89
ASWs *see* approved social workers
attendance allowance 104
audio-visual aids 38, 232
authority in group 200
Aves Report (1969) 159
Avro Students Council 106

baseline data, goal-setting and evaluation 233
baseline designs, multiple 239

BASW *see* British Association of Social Workers

behavioural approaches 209–18; behaviour modification 213–14; modelling procedure 214–15; phobia 215–17; principles, general 211–13

behavioural loss in dementia 64

'behavioural profiles' 94

Belgium, boarding-out 139, 142, 144

Better Services for Mentally Handicapped (1971) 5–8, 102, 104–05

Better Services for Mentally Ill (1975) 5–7, 14, 130, 178

Birmingham: LODAS 182; volunteers 160, 162, 164

boarding-out and substitute family care 138–46; examples of 142–44

breakdown *see* crisis

Brecknock Community Mental Health project 136

Brighton, boarding-out 141

British Association of Social Workers 16, 41–2, 159, 180, 253

British Sign Language 111

Brixton, volunteers 160

Butler Committee 28


Cambridge, education 106

Campaign for Mental Handicap 105, 252

*Care in the Community* 8

'care-sharing' approach 127

causation and symptoms 85

CCETSW *see* Central Council etc.

Central Council for Education and Training in Social Work 16–17, 42–3, 48, 104

cerebral palsy 108

Certificate of Qualification in Social Work 16–17

characteristics, mental handicap 107–09

charisma 200

Cheshire Mental Health Training Programme 17

children 221–23, 236

chronicity, circumventing, in boarding-out 141–42

church 88

circular reasoning 86

class differences 81, 107, 191

'client weaknesses' 161

clinical management of neuroses 72–3

clinical perspectives of mental disorder 61–76; alcoholism 63, 65, 74–5; drugs 63, 65, 75–6; neuroses 70–3; psychopathy 62, 73–4; psychoses 62–70; terminology and classifications 61–2

clinical picture: delirium 65; dementia 63–4

clinical subdivisions, schizophrenia 66

CMH *see* Campaign for Mental Handicap

communication 190–92, 201–02

community: -based social work 178–84; care 14, 102–04, 151, 156; settlement in 161–62; work in team 175–76

compulsion 71

compulsory hospital admission 23–7

conditioning 211, 216

confidentiality 192

conflict in teams 172–73

consent to treatment 31–3

conversion systems, hysterical 72

conveyance to hospital 47

core conditions, interviewing 192–93

correcting applications 47–8

correspondence 38

courts 28–31, 250

Coventry Crisis Service 122–23

CQSW *see* Certificate of Qualification etc.

criminal proceedings 28–31

crisis in psychiatric emergency, management of 182, 219–27; centres 225–26; precipitation of 80; residential care 121–27; treatment 88

criticism of social work 78

'cycle of deprivation' 96


data collection, goal-setting and evaluation 231–33

day care 129–37, 198, 208; approaches to 133–36; mentally handicapped 131–33; mentally ill 129–31

definitions: group 199–202; mental disorder 22–3

delirium 63, 65

delusions 65–7, 213–14, 229–30, 237

dementia 63–5

depression 68–9, 81, 206

'Depressives Associated' 162

'deprivation cycle' 96

Derbyshire, education 106

desensitization 217

designs, single-case experimental 234–39

developmental: approach 110–11; delay 107; research 93–5

Devon, volunteers 160

diagnosis 85, 91–2

differential reinforcement 213

direct observation 231

disadvantage: social 96, 107; of teams 171–72

disagreement in teams 172–73

discharge: hospital 79–80, 103–04; from Mental Health Review Tribunal 34–5

disease concept 88, 91–2

disorientation 64

dissociation 72

dissolution, team 174

doctors *see* medical practitioners

'double blind' 97

Down's syndrome 108

dreams 71
drugs: abuse of 63, 65, 75–6; therapeutic 32, 69–70, 73, 90, 110, 247–48
Duly Authorized Officer 17
duties: hospital managers 37–8; social workers and departments 41–58, 112–15

ECT see electroconvulsive therapy
education: day care, 132–35; differences and communication 191; mentally handicapped 103–08; see also training
Education Act (1981) 103, 105
effects of medical model 85–90
elderly see ageing
electroconvulsive therapy 32, 69, 89
Ely public enquiry 5
emergency see crisis
emotions: communication and 191; high expressed 79–81, 99; loss in dementia 64
empathy 192
employment 81–2, 134–35, 155–56; see also unemployment
encouragement 193
endogenous depression 69
Enlightenment 87
environmental factors 94–6, 98–100, 211
epilepsy 108, 110
Equal Opportunities Commission 9
ESN categories 103
ethnic minorities 175
evaluating goals, group 204
evaluation of outcome to intervention 228–40; examinations for 244–46; goal-setting 228–33; qualitative approaches 239–40; single-case experimental design 231–39
Eve Vale Psychiatric Hospital 141, 143
examination papers 50–8, 241–43, 244–46; answers 254–60
examples of behavioural approach 213–17
exposure to fear 217
extinction 213

failure of social work 77–8
falsification 240
family: advice for 102; emotional 79–81; studies 95–6; see also boarding-out; relatives
Family Service Units 158
Farleigh public enquiry 5
fatigue 191
feedback 192
feeding aids 111
feelings see emotions
financial help 104
formal system 151
foundations of social policy 4–5
'free-floating' anxiety 70
'fugue-states' 71

general agencies in local services 153–56
general practitioners see medical practitioners
generic teams 175
genetic factors 95–9, 211
genuineness 192–93
Glasgow Mental Health Commission 36, 249
goal-planning and mental handicap 111
goal-setting and evaluation in psychiatric social work 211, 228–33; assessment stages 228–31; baseline data, interpretation of 233; data collection, approaches to 231–33
'Good Practices in Mental Health' project 163
government departments 249
grief 220, 223
group homes 102, 107, 122, 161, 198
groupwork practice 197–207; definition of group 199–202; starting 203–07
guardianship: age and 26; boarding-out and 144–46; compulsory 23–7; hospital and 30–1; mental handicap and 115; rehabilitation and 125; relatives and 27; social services department and 44

hallucinations 65, 67–8, 75
health see National Health Service
hearing impairment 111
history of lunacy 87–8
home teaching 106
Homeless Persons Act 155
hormone transplants 32
hospital: admissions 21–7, 45–7, 107–08, 112; boarding-out alternative 144–46; conveyance to 47; discharge 79–80, 103–04; guardianship and 30–1; interim orders 29–30; managers 37–8; readmission 79, 143; remand in 28–9; welfare in 43–4; see also alternatives to hospital care; residential care
Hospital Advisory Service 5
Hospital Plan for England and Wales 5, 140
hostels 102, 105, 122
housing 155
hypothesis 240
hysterical states 72

IDC see Independent Development Council
'immunization effect' 93
inadequate recruitment and training 16–17
inattentiveness 191
income 154–55
incontinence 64
Independent Development Council for People with Mental Handicap 41, 106, 150
indicators 231
Industrial Therapy Organization 81
influence, group 200
informal patients already in hospital 26

information: control 200; sharing 183–84
institutionalization 136, 211
institution-oriented service 119–20
instrumental conditioning 211
integration of mentally handicapped 109–10
intellectual loss in dementia 63–4
intelligence 93, 107, 114
interaction 110
Inter-departmental Committee on Mental
   Health Act 13
interim orders 29–30
interpretation 110, 194
intervention: evaluation of outcome to
   228–53; rejected 17–19; strategies, group
   206–07; see also crisis
interviewing 46, 189–97; communication
   process 190–92; core conditions 192–93;
   medical practitioners 194–95; mentally
   handicapped 112–13; problems 196; skills
   193–94; stages of 194–96
introvert-extravert personality 95

Jay Report (1979) 104, 115, 126, 150
'Joint Finance Arrangements' 7–8
joint working 181–82
jolt treatment 88

King's Fund 105–06, 252

lability, emotional 64
language 191
Law Society and Legal Aid offices 33, 250–51;
   see also courts
learning of behaviour 211
Leeds 106
legislation and policy 1–58; 102–06, 155, 224;
   social policy, mentally disordered 3–12;
   social services departments 41–58; see also
   Mental Health Act (1959); Mental Health
   Act (1983)
life events 80
listening skills 191, 193–94
Lithium 69–70
living group, effect of 79–80; see also family;
   relatives
local authorities: functions 43–5;
   reorganization 6–8, 104; Secretary of State
   and 36–8
Local Authority Act (1970) 6
local services, developing 149–57, key
   elements of 151–57; principles of 150–51
LODAS see Lozells etc.
London: boarding-out 141; 'care-sharing'
   approach 127; day care 129, 134, 136;
   education 106; Mental Health Act
   Commission 36, 249
long-term residential care 126–27
'low profile' support 164

Lozells Open Door Advisory Service 182
lunacy 87–8, 139

Makaton 111
male: alcoholics 99; schizophrenics 79–80, 82
management: of crisis 219–27; of dementia
   64–5; of neuroses 72–3; of problems 100; of
   property of patients 35–6
Manchester, teaching approaches 106
mania 68–9
manic-depression 68, 70
Marriage Guidance Councils 158
mechanical observation 231
mediators 209
medical model in psychiatry, critical
   appraisal of 84–100; environmental
   variables 99–100; genetic factors 92–5;
   genetic research 95–9; implication for
   social work 100; origins and effects 85–90;
   patterns of disease 91–2
medical practitioners: crisis units and 123;
   day care and 131; hospital admission and
   24–6, 31–2; interviewing 194–95; local
   services and 154; mentally handicapped
   and 112; psychiatrist and 17; working
   with 180, 182
medication see drugs
memory loss 63–4
Mental Deficiency Act (1913) 131
mental disorder and handicap 59–115;
   clinical perspectives 61–76; medical model
   in psychiatry 86–100; mental handicap,
   perspectives of 101–15; social perspectives
   of 77–83; see also mental handicap;
   mentally disordered
mental handicap, perspectives of 101–15;
   day care 131–33; developing policy context
   102–06; mental impairment 111–15;
   principles and practice 106–11
mental health see social work and mental
   health
Mental Health Act (1959): amendment of
   13–19, 41–2; boarding-out 139–40;
   community care 102; day care 131;
   guardianship 115; Inter-departmental
   Committee on 13; mentally handicapped
   102, 115
Mental Health Act (1983) 3, 9, 20–40;
   application of 22–3; compulsory
   admission to hospital 23–7; consent to
   treatment 31–3; criminal proceedings and
   patients 28–31; guardianship 23–7, 139;
   local authorities 36–8, 149; mentally
   handicapped and 102, 112–15; Mental
   Health Review Tribunals 31, 33–5; and
   1959 Act 20, 22–5, 35; property and affairs
   of patients, management of 35–6;
   psychopathy definition 73; reading and

listening lists 38–40; removal and return of patients in UK 35; Secretary of State and 36–8; social services departments and 41–58
Mental Health Act Commission 36–7, 249
Mental Health (Amendment) Act (1982) 20
Mental Health Review Tribunals 31–5, 250
Mental Health (Scotland) Act (1960) 44
Mental Health Training Programme 17
mental impairment 22, 111–15
mentally disordered, contemporary social policy 3–12, 22; better services, towards 5–8; day care 129–31; foundations of policy 4–5; in 1980s 8–9; worksheet 10–12; see also clinical perspectives; social perspectives
mentally ill see mentally disordered
Mental Welfare Officers 16–17, 20, 43
MHRT see Mental Health Review Tribunals
MIND see National Association for Mental Health
mobility allowance 104, 111
model: of genetic and environmental interaction 98–9; group 208
modelling 212, 214–15
modification of behaviour 213–14
mood disorders 99
multi-disciplinary care 152, 178; see also teamwork
multiple baseline decisions 239
'multiple personality' 72
MWO see Mental Welfare Officers

Napsbury Hospital Crisis Service 225–26
National Association of Mental Health 252; conference 4; and day care 129; and local services development 150–51; Mental Health Act (1983) and 20, 101; volunteers 158, 160
National Association of Youth Clubs 160
National Development Group and Team 103, 131–33
National Health Service 6–8, 103–04, 152–54
NCIP see non-contributory invalidity pension
NDG see National Development Group
negotiation in teamwork 174
neoplasms 63
network and team, distinction between 170
neuroses 62, 70–3, 99
Nodder Report (1978) 7
non-contributory invalidity pension 104
non-intervention 218
non-possessive warmth 192
non-verbal communication 192, 202
'normalization' principle 109–10
norms, group 199
Northumberland, family support 106
Norway, boarding-out 139, 144
nurses 26

observation 23–4, 212, 231
obsessional states 71–2, 234
occupational therapy 81
open-ended questions 193
operant conditioning 209
operation in teamwork 174
'Ordinary Life, An' 105–06
organic psychosis 62–5
Organisational and Management Problems of Mental Illness 7
orientation in teamwork 173
origins of medical model 85–90
outcome to intervention see evaluation
overlearning 111
over-stimulation 214
Oxford, education 106

paranoid psychosis 66–8
paraphrenia 68
parents 222–23
participant observation 231
PASS see Programme Analysis of Service Systems
pensions 104, 111
persecution delusion 67, 213–14, 229–30
persistence of psychiatric disorder 22–3
personality 95; disorder 62, 64–6, 75
phenothiazine drugs 66, 90
phobia 71, 215–17, 220, 235
physical: handicap 108, 111; injury 63–5; manifestations of disorders 69, 71–2; origins of mental disorders 85
physiotherapy 111
placebo effect 89
policy see legislation and policy
Poor Law Act (1845) 139
positive discrimination 107
potential, residential care 119–22
premature birth 221–22
pre-recruitment of volunteers 165
prevention of psychosis 100
primary psychoses 62, 65–6
principles: developing comprehensive local services 150–51; and practice, dichotomy between 14
problems: interviewing 196; residential care 119–22
professional expertise 85
professions, other, working with 177–87; examination paper specimen 241–43; joint working, establishing 181–82; referral, inappropriate 179–81; sharing information 183–84
Programme Analysis of Service Systems 109
property and affairs of patients, management of 35–6
prosthetic approach to mental handicap 110–11
psychiatric emergency see crisis

psychiatric intervention *see* intervention
psychological: developmental research 93–5; manifestations of anxiety states 70–1
psychopathy 22, 62, 73–4
psychoses 62–70, 100
public enquiries 5

qualitative approach to evaluation of outcome 239–40

readmission to hospital 79, 143
receptors in brain 90
recreation in day care 134–35
recruitment: of social workers 16–17; of volunteers 166
recurring work 182
referral 123, 131; inappropriate 179–81
*Reform of Mental Health Legislation* 21
regression 64
rehabilitation 125
relationships and groups 200
relatives 120–21; admission rights 45; guardianship and 27; local services development 151, 156; obligation to inform 47; schizophrenia and 97; *see also* family
reliability: checks 232; of classifications of disease 91
relocalizing in miniature institutions in boarding-out 137–38
remand to hospital 28–9
remedial group 208
removal and return of patients within UK 35
reports 28–9, 44
residential care 119–28; approaches to 122–27; combining approaches 127–28; problems and potential 119–22
resident-oriented service 120
resources: cut-back 172; knowledge of 149; lack of 15
response-control techniques 210
restriction order 31
retraining 134–35
reward and group influence 200
Richmond Fellowship 124, 252
roles: in groups 202, 205–06; of social services departments 41–58; of teams 170
Royal Commission on Law relating to Mental Illness and Mental Handicap (1957) 4, 14, 131
rules, group 199

Salisbury 141–43
Samaritans 158, 253
SCED *see* single-case experimental design
schizophrenia 65–6: associations 252; discharge and relapse 79–80, 82; employment and 82; over-stimulation of 214; paranoid 68; relatives contracting 97

school phobia 220
'Schools for All' 105
Scotland, boarding-out 139
second opinion 31–2
secondary psychoses 62–5
Secretary of State 36–8
Seebohm Report (1968) 6, 159
segregation of mentally handicapped 108–09
Select Committee on Mental Health Act 20, 31
selection of volunteers 166
self-actualizing model of group 208
self-concept, strong 192
self-expression 194
self-help groups 160–64
self-observation 232
separation 223
services, delivery of 147–87; local services, developing 149–57; other professions 177–87; teamwork 168–76; volunteers and self-help groups 158–67
Settlements 158
sex drive, reduced 32
sharing information 183–84
shock treatment 88
sickness concept 85, 105
single-case experimental design 234–39; AB designs 234–36; ABA designs 236; ABAB designs 236–38; BAB designs 238–39; multiple baseline across settings 239; multiple baseline design 239
situational anxiety 71
size of group 205
Skillmill 17
skills: crisis management 225–27; interviewing 193–94; of teams 170
social confidence 235
Social Education Centre 133
social perspectives of mental disorder 77–82; breakdown, precipitation of 80; depression, origins of 81; families with high expressed emotion 79–81; living group 79–80; social work, question of 78; unemployment and 81–2
social reports 44
social security benefits 104, 111, 154
social services departments and approved social workers' roles and duties 41–58
social work and mental health: alternatives to hospital care 117–46; legislation and policy 1–58; mental disorder and handicap 59–115; services, delivery of 147–87
social work, method and process 185–240; behavioural approaches 209–18; crisis management 219–27; groupwork practice 198–208; interviewing 189–97; outcome evaluation 132–47
social workers *see* approved social workers
Somerset, family support 106, 141

somnambulism 71
Southend, groupwork 106
'special educational needs' 107
special schools 102, 105, 107
specialist contribution 152–53, 156
speech therapy 111
stages: of group development 200–01; of
    interviewing 194–96
starting a group 203–07
status in groups 200
stimulus-control techniques 209
structure, group 200–01
symptoms and causation 85

tasks of teams 170
tautology in medical model 86
taxonomy of teams 170–71
teamwork 168–76
techniques of crisis management 225–27
technology, state of and favoured treatments
    89–90
temperament and environment 94–5
tension 80
terror treatment 88
theoretical considerations of crisis
    management 219–22
therapeutic: communities 123–25; groups
    198, 208
time sampling 232
token economy system 238–39
training: and BASW 41–2; centres 102, 105,
    107, 131–32, 134; day care 134; and IDC 41;
    inadequate 16–17; mental handicap and
    104; requirement of social services
    departments 43; volunteers 166–67; see

also education
treatment 24–5, 29; consent to 31–3; day care
    134; history of 87–9; see also drugs;
    hospital
twin studies 93, 96

unemployment 135, 154
unitary model 187
United States 92, 140, 220, 224
urgent treatment 32–3
USSR 88–9, 95

validity of disease classification 91
value-free diagnosis 85
violent treatment 88
visual impairment 111
'Vocational Service' 106
voluntary care 14, 158–60, 198; guidelines for
    using 165–67
vulnerability factors, depressed women 81

Wales 106, 140–41, 143
Warnock Report (1978) 103, 107
welfare see social security
White Papers see Better Services etc.
Whittingham public enquiry 5
Wolverhampton, education 106
women: carers 8–9; depression 81, 206;
    premature birth 221–22
work see employment
worksheet on social policies and local
    priorities 10–12
World Health Organisation 226

Young Men's Christian Association 158